Readings in Environmental Psychology

Landscape Perception

Readings in Environmental Psychology
Series Editor
David Canter
University of Liverpool, U.K.

The Child's Environment
Editor: Christopher Spencer

Urban Cognition
Editor: Tommy Gärling

Giving Places Meaning
Editor: Linda Groat

Landscape Perception
Editor: Amita Sinha

Perceiving Environmental Risks
Editor: Tim O'Riordan

Readings in Environmental Psychology
Series Editor
David Canter

Landscape Perception

Edited by
Amita Sinha
Department of Landscape Architecture, University of Illinois at Urbana-Champaign, U.S.A.

ACADEMIC PRESS
Harcourt Brace & Company, Publishers
London   San Diego   New York   Boston   Sydney   Tokyo   Toronto

ACADEMIC PRESS LIMITED
24–28 Oval Road
London NW1 7DX

United States Edition published by
ACADEMIC PRESS INC.
San Diego, CA 92101

Copyright © 1995 by
ACADEMIC PRESS LIMITED

All rights reserved
No part of this book may be reproduced in any form, by photostat,
microfilm, or by any other means, without permission from
the publishers

This book is printed on acid-free paper

A catalogue record for this book is available from the British Library

ISBN 0-12-646840-0

Typeset by Galliard (Printers) Ltd, Great Yarmouth, Norfolk
Printed and bound in Great Britain by Hartnolls Ltd, Bodmin, Cornwall

CONTENTS

Preface — vii
D. Canter

Introduction: Varieties of Nature Viewing — 1
A. Sinha

Children's landscape preferences: from rejection to attraction — 11
F. G. Bernáldez, D. Gallardo and R. P. Abelló

Context effects in perceived environmental quality assessment: scene selection and landscape quality ratings — 19
T. C. Brown and T. C. Daniel

Toward a phenomenology of recreation place — 37
L. Fishwick and J. Vining

A cognitive analysis of preference for waterscapes — 47
T. R. Herzog

A cognitive analysis of preference for urban nature — 65
T. R. Herzog

Cross-cultural comparison of landscape scenic beauty evaluations: a case study in Bali — 83
R. B. Hull IV and G. R. B. Revell

The prediction of scenic beauty from landscape content and composition — 99
M. R. Patsfall, N. R. Feimer, G. J. Buhyoff and J. D. Wellman

Preferences and meaning of arboretum landscapes: combining quantitative and qualitative data — 119
H. W. Schroeder

Perspectives on wilderness: re-examining the value of extended wilderness experiences — 137
J. F. Talbot and S. Kaplan

Stress recovery during exposure to natural and urban environments — 149
R. S. Ulrich, R. F. Simons, B. D. Losito, E. Fiorito, M. A. Miles and M. Zelson

A lifespan developmental study of landscape assessment — 179
E. H. Zube, D. G. Pitt and G. W. Evans

Index — 193

PREFACE

It was architects and building engineers who first approached psychologists for advice on the impact that their designs might have on their users. Out of these requests environmental psychology evolved as a distinct discipline in its own right. The early issues of the *Journal of Environmental Psychology*, over ten years ago, showed the dominance of this orientation towards the psychological consequences of aspects of the design and use of buildings. But in subsequent years there has been a growing stream of submissions to JEP that have looked out to the natural landscape. Bringing them together in the present volume serves to demonstrate how far those studies have developed our understanding as well as indicating how very much more there is to explore.

This collection of JEP papers therefore provides a convenient, first hand account of the studies that environmental psychologists have conducted in clearing the ground for explorations of the experience of landscapes. It encapsulates the actual studies that form the basis of this rapidly growing area of environmental psychology, thus providing new students and experienced researchers with direct examples of the actual studies that have been conducted. All too often review articles and textbook summaries obscure the subtleties and hide the excitement of the original journal publications on which most academic fields are based. The present volume redresses the balance by providing a collection of original papers.

In her challenging introduction Amita Sinha shows that there are a number of very different ways of thinking about nature. She argues that these underlie the various psychological studies of landscape, but that research to date has tended to give emphasis to a very limited range of views about nature. Her introduction, in combination with the papers in this volume, therefore provides the outlines for a research agenda that could keep a generation of students busy exploring the psychology of the landscape.

For psychologists schooled in laboratory research the natural landscape may seem to be the last frontier that still has to be conquered. But many other disciplines have been at home in these wilder regions for a number of years. Those geographers, landscape architects, biological ecologists and others will find the present volume a helpful introduction to the opening stages of psychological forays into areas that they may possibly consider their own inviolable domain. The initial papers in a new area of study are often crucial to the development of that field. By bringing the original papers together in one volume it is possible to gain a detailed awareness of the contributions these studies are making to our understanding of the human significance of nature.

As environmental psychology becomes more 'green', reflecting the increasing momentum of the broader cross-national, cross-disciplinary environmental movement, so the study of the natural environment and its significance for people will increase. The planet-saving significance of the environmental movement is in little doubt. It faces a task of such proportions that no discipline should shirk from making a contribution. The present volume illustrates some of the contributions that environmental psychology can make to these important issues.

David Canter, Managing Editor
University of Liverpool

INTRODUCTION: VARIETIES OF NATURE VIEWING

AMITA SINHA
University of Ilinois at Urbana-Champaign, U.S.A.

At the dawn of the 21st first century, when it is apparent that uses of technology have driven nature into vestigial pockets in our physical life worlds, continuing research into the hold that nature has over our state of well-being is very necessary. This age of eco-politics and increasing hysteria about despoilation of natural surroundings further necessitates research into the psychology of nature. Nature affinity has been the province of the mytho-poetic realm of thought. This volume brings the spotlight of scientific scrutiny upon these feelings. There are 11 papers in this volume, covering a range—cognitive, physiological, developmental and cross-cultural aspects of responses to nature. These articles, which are on the cutting edge of research in environmental psychology, will appeal to a broader audience of ecologists, landscape architects and those in the health and recreational professions.

The article by Talbot and Kaplan, on perspectives on wilderness, captures the feelings of awe and wonder which wilderness evokes and the sense of 'oneness' with the natural environment, akin to a spiritual experience. The two papers by Herzog, on the preference for urban nature and waterscapes from a cognitive framework, test a number of qualities such as mystery, spaciousness, complexity and legibility. The liking for mountain streams with rushing water and large expansive water bodies over swampy areas and stagnant creeks points to the sensory delight in sounds and the power that the sense of infinity holds for us. Vegetation in the urban environment was preferred because it introduced an element of mystery and coherence. Whether vegetation is in the fore-, middle-, or background as one is travelling along the famed Blue Ridge parkway in the United States, influences the aesthetic appreciation of its scenic beauty as the study by Patsfall *et al.* demonstrates. The above qualities acting as predictors of preference aid in cognitive processing of the environment in a positive way. They have been formulated by the Kaplans (1989) as qualities responsible for information seeking and retrieval from the environment, so crucial for survival in earlier times.

The paper by Schroeder on the meaning of arboretum landscapes goes beyond in that it combines qualitative data on what experiences with nature refuges can mean in the context of people's lives. Natural landscapes like the woods, where signs of human design were least apparent, were consistently preferred. These experiences were described in terms of serenity and happy feelings also evoked by water and sunshine. A vocabulary of feelings associated with natural elements begins to emerge in these qualitative descriptions.

The paper by Ulrich *et al.* introduces the use of physiological measures in testing the emotional states that accompany stress recovery. This experimental study exposed the subjects to stressors like work-related accidents followed by videotapes of outdoor settings. The results showed that stress measures such as electrocardiogram, pulse transit time, skin conductance and muscle tension, all indicated the recuperative influences of nature. This study is in the long line of research projects that Ulrich has done over the past decade documenting the therapeutic effects of nature. He explains his results from a psycho-evolutionary point of view in which the parasympathetic nervous system is involved in rapid attenuation of stress responses and restoration of energy on exposure to natural settings. These reactions are biologically based, having been learned during evolution when certain natural settings were preferred because of high food potential and low risk. Both physical and mental responses survive to this day in human beings and underlie their continued affinity with nature. The physiological reactions have their psychological counterpart in positive emotions.

Since the majority of papers follow a research methodology based on an experimental tradition, Brown and Daniel's investigation of context effects on evaluation of secenic beauty is very pertinent. It exposes the perceptual and judgement shifts that occur when the subject is asked to evaluate a series of slides in a laboratory situation.

Pristine nature as retreat or escape from human habitation and contact is not an idyll universally preferred. Fishwick and Vining's sample included those who preferred to be in the vicinity of signs of human activity in natural surroundings. This group had far fewer experiences of wilderness than those for whom nature was a true haven, which raises a question regarding the influence of personality on landscape preferences.

The developmental study of landscape assessment over the life span by Zube *et al.* raises some very interesting questions about the psycho-evolutionary framework within which most researchers design their experiments and interpret their results. The strong preference for natural landscapes, documented in scores of studies, could be an age-related phenomenon. Young children do not respond in the same way as adults do, raising the issue of enculturation into the prevailing cultural values in which unspoilt nature is held in high esteem.

Another study on children's landscape preferences by Bernáldez *et al.* shows yet another developmental aspect to appreciation of nature. What has been called 'sublime' revealing nature in its fearsome, mysterious, and even macabre form is enjoyed only after a certain age. Does this mean that the experiential qualities of mystery and fascination held by the Kaplans as explanatory variables for the all-encompassing category of preference are learned rather than being innately given?

Research by Hull and Revell on the cultural differences between tourists and natives in assessments of the scenic value of Balinese rural landscapes throws another wrench into the psycho-evolutionary theory. The Balinese have integrated nature into culture with a thick web of religious associations that is reflected in participant photography. Interestingly enough, the same proclivities were exhibited by the tourists, although for different reasons, perhaps fitting into their notion of the picturesque.

Taken together, these research papers point to many different future directions, showing that only the tip of the iceberg has been revealed when it comes to exploration of the psychology of landscape perception. The archetypal, primordial attraction towards natural elements is brought forth in all the studies. But to what extent this innate preference has been modified by culture, and in what ways, remains to be further investigated empirically. While age has been shown to be a factor, gender has not yet been studied. The different societal roles that men and women have fulfilled in the evolutionary life span of humankind should surface in the way they relate to the natural landscape.

The influences of culture, prior experiences and personality type form overlays over pre-existing genetic biases but four of the papers in this volume have treated them as forces acting separately and independently. Underlying the scientific paradigm guiding these studies is an implicit view of nature which directs the kinds of questions asked and the methods chosen to investigate them. This view could be labelled the evolutionary perspective. The following is a brief description of what this perspective encompasses.

Evolutionary View

Nature is seen through the lens of mankind's struggle to survive in this view. The evolutionary approach, however, stresses only those aspects of nature which have aided in human survival. In this rather deterministic view, natural elements and their configurations serve as archetypes, still eliciting preferences, even though they have lost their primary function. Archetype is to be understood here as a vestige of an image lodged in the psyche, determining aesthetic preference for those habitats which had allowed hunting and foraging and helped in evolution.

The most frequently discussed environment is the parkland or lawn—its universal attractiveness traced to the savannah, man's earliest habitat. The seashore with its plentiful source of food, capable of supporting population densities far in excess of those inland, had been the common habitat in the middle and lower Palaeolithic period. It still exercises a pull with its health and recreational features being the draw. The fertile river valley, which also allowed transportation along long distances and were the cradles of the earliest urban civilizations, determine the power of concavity and convexity in the built environment.

Certain environmental configurations are believed to be universal predictors of preference. Spatial arrangements of the natural environment which allow simultaneously an opportunity to see and hide are pleasing and are labelled as prospect and refuge symbols by Jay Appleton (1975). In the past they had enabled visual access to prey and a retreat to safety. Their remnants may be seen in children's play of hide and seek. Ideally occurring in combination, prospect (mountain, sea) and refuge (cave, forest) symbolized individually, still have a drawing power. Their presence in landscape paintings and their continued use as design elements in landscape architecture testify to their archetypal power. They are symbolized in architecture in the form of towers and the like. Various types of prospects have shaped an entire aesthetic vocabulary of vistas and panoramas.

This paradigm has also shaped much of the empirical research on environmental preferences in psychology. The wide preference for natural environments over built ones in numerous studies is explained in biological and evolutionary terms. The studies use simulations (slides or photographs) of environments showing different elements of nature with or without built structures. The consistent liking for nature is explained by the Kaplans in information-processing terms. Nature allows fascination, i.e. involuntary attention to occur, and thereby performs the role of stress reduction from all the directed attention required in daily life. The fascinating aspect of nature is explained in terms of long aeons of familiarity and nurturance in the natural world. Ulrich's studies with hospital patients show how a natural view in a hospital helps in physical recovery. Other studies in prisons, offices and public housing with views or gardens reveal them to be of importance in reducing stress, bringing about a sense of well-being, and adding to the quality of life. This has encouraged professionals to utilize restorative and therapeutic aspects of gardening in hospitals, geriatric centres, correctional institutions, drug rehabilitation centres, and schools for the developmentally disabled.

Perceptual categories indicating preference are determined by those natural configurations which have aided in the interpretation of opportunities and constraints afforded by the environment. Two important ones are exploration and legibility which have aided human functioning in the past. They still do to a certain extent (though they may not be crucial for survival) but are now responsible for aesthetic perception. A perceptually rich and complex environment which also holds promise of further information (mystery) will be preferred over that which has neither. Thus winding paths and secondary vistas are innately attractive. An environment which is too complex (lacking coherence) or too bland (for example flat open ground with no perceptual cues for finding one's way about) are not legible environments and will provoke dislike, even fear.

This 20th century view of nature held by social scientists such as geographers and psychologists downgrades nature to an atavistic tendency, lodged in the unconscious as a result of millennia of struggle for survival in a natural world. The optimal conditions which had aided sustenance become hard-wired in the brain and exposure to them elicits positive psychological and physiological reactions. This forms the underlying assumption, the hypothesis, and the results of study after study in environmental psychology. Those social scientists, not working in an experimental paradigm, use visual sources like paintings, picture postcards, designed landscapes to prove their point.

An evolutionary perspective, dominant in science, is only one of the manifold views of nature held by different cultures across time. A brief discussion of other views, though by no means exhaustive, can point to broader directions so that environmental psychology research in landscape perception is not confined to a narrow, sectarian field. These four other perspectives—utilitarian, idealist–romantic, transcendalist and ecological—are a very broad classification of the tremendous variety in cultures' ways of coming to terms with nature. They encompass both dichotomous views of nature versus culture and integrative views emphasizing harmony between the two. In the utilitarian perspective, nature is seen apart from God and humankind and can therefore be subjugated and/or exploited for human benefit. The idealist–romantic view is a reflection of the *zeitgeist* of a period in which metaphors are based upon rationality or intuition. The transcendalist sees nature as symbolic of the divine and/or worships her for her own powers. The ecological view is the emerging paradigm of the 20th century stressing the interdependence of human and natural systems. The dominant view of nature shapes preferences and values which are reflected in art, architecture and landscape.

Utilitarian View

What underlies this view is a certain attitude towards nature, fostered by the Judaeo-Christian tradition. The rise of industrial capitalism, as well as dialectical materialism in Marxist thought, transformed it into an exploitative attitude for which nature became a commodity. Progress meant continued growth to ensure which the market constantly supplied a constant demand. In this scenario, human needs take precedence over the rest of the world. Bountiful nature exists to fulfil whatever demands societies make of it in order to ensure their continued progress.

In Christian thought the cleavage between human and the natural world takes the form of a hierarchy in which man, created in the image of God, is superior to his fellow beings. In the creation myths of Genesis and in other writings, the idea of the dominant role of man is clearly expressed. While creation is evidence of existence of God, it is man who is the centre of creation, at the apex of the hierarchy. Nature, rather than embodying any transcendental force, exists as itself.

Man's position as a steward or caretaker of nature implies that nature can be improved upon, modified, and controlled. It is man's fall that caused disorder in nature and a decline in its powers. Natural catastrophes were God's way of punishing mankind for its collective sins. The Garden of Eden myth idealized a Mediterranean type of environment and writings of the Old and New Testament described the landscape in the language of the peasant and shepherd. Nature is to be found in the highland pasture and the grain field, the orchard and the olive grove.

This pastoral version of nature, benign, bountiful and tamed became the foundation for Western landscape tradition in literature and art. It became the aesthetic ideal in garden design. The word 'villa', of Latin origin, passed into Italian and was absorbed into English, designating a country estate where house, garden and countryside were interconnected. Pompeian and Renaissance gardens with their emphasis on axial planning and views into the agricultural landscape became precursors of the French classic garden, the ultimate signature of man's dominion over nature.

The pastoral was also an urban dweller's view of nature, bucolic and benign. It described a 'middle landscape' mediating the extremes of civilization and wilderness, combining their best and avoiding their evils. Jefferson's pastoral vision for America with its icon of the gentleman farmer, typified by the southern plantation, evolved into carefully tended lawns of suburbia and the bucolic images of the corporate landscape in the 20th century. Underlying this image is the concept of land as utility and commodity, available in abundance in the New World, for colonization and conquest.

In the language of this paradigm, 'nature' came to be used synonymously with 'scenery', a prospect seen from a specific standpoint. Landscaped gardens with their contrived stage scenes contributed to this version of nature, to be consumed and appropriated by vision alone. The Renaissance discovery of the rules of perspective in the 16th and the invention of photography in the 19th century helped in the propagation of the picturesque landscape images and their widespread appreciation culminating in the mass scale tourism of today.

No doubt many ills can be blamed on a cultural tradition that emphasizes schism between man and nature. Environmental degradation is the result of the pursuit of material wealth without regard for means and absence of an ideology that provides checks and balances to unbridled greed. Consumptive attitudes towards land as a source of wealth extend to recreation—its demands satisfied by picturesque scenery.

Idealist–Romantic View

This view has shaped the philosophy of art and the Western culture's coming to terms with nature in its different modes of self-expression. It involves a dialectic between two opposing ways of understanding the relationship between 'inner' and 'outer' nature. The idealistic mode of thought sees human nature determined by reason, in pursuit of a universal ideal exemplified by order, symmetry, equilibrium, proportion and harmony. The classicist searches for this ideal in nature as well and imposes upon it an aesthetics derived from this ideal. The romantic view of human nature is governed by feeling and intuition. External nature is seen as a source and inspiration for emotions. This aesthetic ideal allows for vagaries of form and associated meaning.

The tension between the rational and intuitive modes of thought resolves itself in favour of one or the other forming the *zeitgeist* of that age. In a quest to restore equilibrium from the perceived excesses wrought by overemphasis on one mode of thinking, the pendulum of thought swings to the other extreme. Thus antiquity, Renaissance, Enlightenment, and modern periods are interspersed with Gothic, Mannerist and romantic movement in the arts.

The differing interpretations of human nature and the natural order give rise to different meanings of beauty. The classicist believes in the universal ideal of beauty which is absolute, unchanging and embedded in the form itself. The elevation of the general over the particular in the service of unity, simplicity, and clarity constitute order. Transient reality can only be a faulty image of an ideal perfection which reason rather than emotion can fathom.

Aesthetic rules are to be based upon the laws of nature which are orderly and predictable. The Platonic forms, the numeric and spatial ratios underlying the musical harmonies, the golden section behind the Fibonacci series which forms the growth spiral in nature, show the aesthetic ideal explainable in mathematical language which underlies natural forms and processes. The perception of beauty in different sensory modalities is ruled by laws which govern other natural phenomena as well.

For the Greek and Renaissance artists, landscape was not the major theme of art. The French classic garden sought to express that order of the universe visible in harmonic proportions in the visual arts and in music. The neoplatonic shapes of circle and square governed the composition with the natural topography dematerialized to a two-dimensional drawing. The great baroque diagonals, breaking out of the circle and square, extended the authority of the powerful noble over the land. Cartesian philosophy aided in the interpretation of the natural in terms of universal laws of geometry.

Romanticism does not seek a universal aesthetic ideal. Instead of resolution, ambiguity, surprise, mystery are valued in the quest for the ethereal and the intangible. Natural surroundings are meant to evoke inference and resonate with emotional states rather than present a unified order. British empiricism with its belief that knowledge comes from reflection upon sensation provided justification for romantic inclinations. Imagination and empathy were more important rather than reason for glimpsing the undetermined truth, visible in the particular rather than in the universal.

The variety inherent in nature forms a contrast to the perfect uniformity intolerable to the human mind. The natural forms gave rise to different associations—its angularity to hardness, strength and durability; curvilinear forms on the contrary connote softness and smoothness. Nature's cycles of birth, maturity and decay are a dynamic life-force which should be embraced to combat the artificial rigidity and static order of abstraction. Burke's notion of the sublime which acknowledged the majesty, magnitude and grandeur of nature's power called forth the strongest and highest possible emotion.

The English landscape garden, with its sinuous walks and streams, gothic temples and follies, was designed in recognition of the power of associative imagery. Landscape painting, poetry and design derived inspiration from each other in a rare congruence among art forms. While the earlier gardens were filled with emblematic devices, the later ones were more expressive, relying upon the scenery to stimulate the viewer's feelings and imagination. The invocation of variety, surprise and mystery in the constantly shifting scenes of an irregular layout was in direct contrast to the uniformity of the French classic garden. The neoclassic buildings set in a soft, arcadian landscape sought to integrate the classical idiom into a romantic one.

The symbolism of nature as an organic metaphor extends to activities appropriate in a garden. Birth, marriages, love-making, orgies, festivals, celebrate the libidinous and life-affirming connotations of nature. The garden of Eden as a setting for blissful paradise as well as ignominious fall in the Biblical tradition has served as an archetypal image—nature as bountiful innocence and as temptation for sin.

Rousseau's brand of romantic primitivism in which nature was all innocence as was the noble savage found renewed favour during the Industrial Age. It inspired philosophers and poets alike for whom nature came to stand for wisdom, moral goodness, and spiritual comfort. It culminated in the 20th century idea of wilderness experience as psychic renewal and as a refuge from the ills of human civilization.

Transcendentalist View

This view characterizes experience that can be labelled as nature veneration. The sacred concept of nature is not confined to prehistoric societies though they show the most evidence of it in their animistic religious systems. Other more complex religions of highly stratified societies are also localized or place bound with nature and landscape being symbolic of and a setting for the divine. The religious view entails a different mode of vision of the natural world. Nature expresses *numen* or religious power, a subjective awareness of the holy. This *numinous* feeling can be understood further in terms of *mysterium, tremendum* and *fascinas*—modalities of consciousness that lie behind religious experience. A sense of spiritual amazement, overpowering majesty of the divine, and attraction mixed with repulsion characterize these experiences.

Cosmogonies and cosmologies are signalled and determined by natural cycles and topography which are incorporated in mythology. The rhythms of nature are celebrated in the rituals of agricultural societies. In this worldview, where time is cyclical, meaningful history is mythology, enacted by gods of nature personified. Real space is the sacred zone which becomes the centre of the world, delimited from profane space by means of ritual boundary. Landscape is thus transformed through a thick web of symbolic associations with the mode of perception being determined by the religious experience.

Nature is a prime setting for hierophany or revelation of *numen*. Vegetation, water, earth, mountain, even stones are manifestation of the sacred for the believer. Charged with the supernatural, they awaken feelings of adoration and dread. Mountains form *axis mundi*, linking the heavens and the terrestrial world. Mountain is the place where sky and earth meet. It can thus form the world's axis, a centre pregnant with sacred power. Mount Meru is the centre of the world in Hindu mythology. Shrines to Zeus are located on top of Mount Olympus. In the Balinese belief, the navel of the world is Mt Agung, the highest mountain in the island. Important events in Judaism, Christianity and Islam occurred on mountain tops. Architectural elements such as ziggurats, pillars and temple spires duplicate this natural form, their vertical direction symbolic of transcendence. Mountains are also sites of religious monasteries and are pilgrim destinations.

The cosmic tree penetrating the three zones of heaven, earth and the netherworld is an archetypal image appearing in the myths of many religions. Its trunk is the vertical axis, marking the centre while its changing foliage reflects the endless regeneration of cosmos. The Banyan tree in Hindu mythology with its aerial roots provides the image for the universe conceived in the form of an inverted tree. In the folk beliefs of Ireland, it is considered a serious offence to injure or destroy a tree which marked the spiritual powers of a place.

Water holds the potential for all forms and is the eternal regenerator and purifier par excellence. Formless itself, it can be the flood of cataclysm, reabsorbing all within itself that has been created. In Christianity it is a cleanser, symbolic of rededication and rebirth, removing the blemishes of birth. In the Islamic culture, which matured in the desert, water took on a supreme significance, appearing in the centre of the courtyard of the mosque. The tradition of bathing for ritual purification is very old in India and a large number of Hindu pilgrim complexes are on the banks of sacred rivers, lakes and ponds. Water can also have curative power, for example the sacred spring of Acapulo in the Philippines is visited for its healing power.

The earth energy is worshipped in mother goddess figurines or landscape forms. Springs, hills, rocks and caves are places where the spirit of the mother earth is manifested. These are also sites of therapeutic and oracular powers. Artificial mounds (for example, the Neolithic Silbury Hill) celebrate the fertility aspects of nature. It is believed that the megalithic structures of Britain represent sites of earth power where stones bring to the surface the energy of the converging ley lines. The circular and spiral forms of the earth energy can also be detected by dowsing; it is also claimed.

In the worldview dominated by this paradigm, the landscape is imprinted with religion. Buildings may enhance and commemorate the sacredness of the land. In Greek sacred architecture, the temple deity was a natural force with the built structure becoming its sculptural embodiment. The temple and the landscape were thus related to one another, forming a complementary whole.

Geomancy, based on the principle of placing human habitats and activities in harmony with the spirits of the natural world, is practised in China even today. The opposite but complementary principles of *yin* and *yang* are manifested in the way earth current (*ch'i*) shapes the landscape. *Feng-shui* seeks a balance of *yin–yang* forces for a propitious location of houses and graves in harmony with earth, in keeping with Taoist philosophy that human beings are an integral part of the natural world. The landscape takes on a metaphorical quality associated with other elements of the cosmos (metal, animals, colour, etc.).

Nature as a spiritual force to be venerated is a view in which all its aspects, from fearsome to benign, are acknowledged and celebrated. It is believed to have magic–cosmic power over human destiny and well-being. As a setting for hierophany, it is expressive of a higher transcendental power (for example *Brahman*, or universal consciousness in Hinduism). This attitude, found in whichever culture and society, has implied interdependence and harmony between the human and the natural world. It has resulted in a rich mine of prehistoric environmental art and iconography of natural symbols.

Ecological View

This view, on its way to catching the popular imagination, is the 20th century's attempt to fuse together elements from science and religion which had till now occupied strictly segregated compartments of thought. Based on scientific research, this paradigm supports values which involve environmental caring and concern for equitable distribution of its resources. Ethics and science are thus in mutual service of each other.

Based on a biocentric rather than an anthropocentric view, human societies are only one element in the vast, interdependent, mutually regulating system called *Gaia* after the Greek goddess of earth. The earth is a living, breathing whole and all its entities are connected through the web of life. Destruction in one sphere reverberates in others, causing disorder in the system as a whole. Ozone depletion, global warming, destruction of biodiversity etc., caused by human action, affect in a negative sense, human welfare. It is a holistic view of nature, reflecting a shift from atomistic and deterministic thinking in science as well. Biology provides a model to physics in which organisms are self-determining and engage in purposive co-operative behaviour based on genetic make up and choices afforded by the environment.

Ecological thinking is bound to have wide ramifications upon the lie of the land. Marking a shift from a resource consumptive economic set-up to a more diverse, sustainable, localized economy, it can reverse the trend towards the global homogenization of landscapes. The parks and open space networks in densely built-up areas can be more than verdant settings and have the potential of becoming productive and educative landscapes. Nature need no longer remain a mere visual amenity.

What kind of an aesthetic will the ecological view of nature promote? Whatever its final shape, it will be dynamic, based upon natural processes, in contrast to the static picturesque. It will celebrate change and a certain amount of disorder. It will pay heed to the *genius loci*, honouring the local spirits, as the ancients had done.

A Research Agenda for the Future

Each perspective dictates its own research agenda though all of them fall under the rubric of environmental psychology. Research into preferences for explorable and legible landscapes, attractions of prospect–refuge configurations, therapeutic benefits of exposure to nature and gardening, will continue to be based upon the evolutionary premise until refuted. Perception studies should find a way to uncover prevailing cultural attitudes based upon utilitarian, romantic or transcendental views. These open up new areas of psychological research into religious experience constituted by numinous feelings of awe, fascination, sense of tremendous majesty etc. Empirical research into the notions of beautiful, picturesque and the sublime will reveal the power of landscape settings and symbols in terms of emotions evoked. The ecological paradigm could lead to a changing perception of what is visually acceptable and therefore aesthetically pleasing. Psychological research can monitor these attitudinal shifts in order to buttress the argument for sustainable landscapes, and preservation, conservation and restoration of native habitats.

For a broad agenda such as this, studies of an experimental or quasi-experimental nature have to be supplemented by surveys, and qualitative studies of, for example, religious valorization of nature. Literature and art are a rich mine of cultural attitudes towards nature which could become the subject matter for psychological studies. The narrow confines of laboratory settings must be broken for research in this arena to have any validity at all. Nature is largely a cultural construct and only now are its biological underpinnings beginning to be glimpsed. Environmental psychology, an inclusive discipline, should study both the foundations and the superstructure.

Bibliography

Appleton, J. (1975). *The Experience of Landscape*. London: John Wiley.
Bate, W. J. (1946). *From Classic to Romantic*. New York: Harper & Brothers.
Birch, C. (1992). The Postmodern challenge to biology. In Jencks, C. Ed., *The Postmodern Reader*. New York: St Martin's Press.
Clark, K. (1966). *Landscape Into Art*. London: John Murray.
Condon, P. (1991). Radical romanticism. *Landscape Journal*, Spring.
Francis, M. & Hester, R. (Eds.). (1991). *The Meaning of Gardens*. Cambridge, Mass.: MIT Press.
Glacken, C. (1967). *Traces on the Rhodian Shore*. Berkeley: University of California Press.
Hiss, T. (1990). *The Experience of Place*. New York: Alfred Knopf.
Hunt, J. D. (1976). *The Figure in Landscape: Poetry, Painting, and Gardening during the Eighteeth Century*. Baltimore: The Johns Hopkins University Press.
Hunt, J. D. & Willis, P. (Eds.). (1975). *The Genius of the Place—The English Landscape Garden 1620–1820*. New York: Harper & Row.
Kaplan, R. & Kaplan, S. (1989). *The Experience of Nature—A Psychological Perspective*. Cambridge: Cambridge University Press.
Marx, L. (1964). *The Machine in the Garden—Technology and the Pastoral Ideal in America*. New York: Oxford University Press.
Otto, R. (1970). *The Idea of the Holy*. New York: Oxford University Press.
Scully, V. (1991). *Architecture—The Natural and the Manmade*. New York: St Martin's Press.
Shephard, P. (1991). *Man in the Landscape*, 2nd edition. College Station, Texas: Texas A & M Press.
Tuan, Y. (1974). *Topophilia—A Study of Environmental Perception, Attitudes and Values*. Engelwood Cliffs, NJ: Prentice-Hall.
Turner, F. (1991). *Beauty—The Value of Values*. Charlottesville: University Press of Virginia.
Wilson, C. R. (1991). A Conversation with Leo Marx. In *Modulus 20: Stewardship of the Land, University of Virginia Architectural Review*. Princeton Architectural Press.

CHILDREN'S LANDSCAPE PREFERENCES: FROM REJECTION TO ATTRACTION

FERNANDO G. BERNÁLDEZ*, DOLORES GALLARDO**, and ROSA P. ABELLÓ*

Departamento de Ecología, Universidad Autónoma, Madrid and Facultad de Bellas Artes. Universidad de La Laguna, Tenerife***

Abstract

Multivariate analysis of the preference responses of 483 children to landscape photographs allowed the identification of three independent preference dimensions: the 1st and 3rd dimensions (illuminated vs shadowed; rough, harsh vs bland, smooth texture or relief) were considered as forms of a more general 'risk, uncertainty factor' often influencing landscape preference. Younger children (11 years old) showed less preference for both shadowed, less illuminated scenes (1st dimension) and harsh, rough scenes with aggressive forms (3rd dimension) than older children (16 years old). There were no significant differences for the 2nd dimension (landscape diversity).

Introduction

Despite its importance in environmental design and education (Bernáldez, Benayas and De Lucio, 1987) the study of children's landscape preferences is a relatively unexplored subject. Zube, Pitt and Evans (1983) highlight the scarcity of research in this topic and report on the importance of water as a scenic component for children's preferences and the differences between children's, and adults' preferences regarding the naturalistic character and physical complexity of the scene. Bernáldez et al. (1987) describe changes in landscape preference following participation in environmental education activities and confirm a preference for water, while Bernáldez, Ruiz and Ruiz (1984) agreed with Zube et al. on the fact that children tend to prefer less naturalistic, less complex landscapes than adults. In a different context Francès (1968, 1979) identified differences in aesthetic evaluation of themes of varying complexity and congruence according to age and cultural level of children and young adults.

The aim of the study was to analyse the differences in landscape appraisal by children of different ages trying to detect consistent trends in landscape desirability related to age. Former work by Appleton (1978), Bernáldez et al. (1984), Abelló and Bernáldez (1986) and Abelló, Bernáldez and Galiano (1986) on insecurity versus security-giving characteristics in natural landscape has been used to elaborate the experiment's hypothesis.

According to the results of these studies the risk and uncertainty connotations of some natural settings are important ingredients of natural landscape preferences. Moreover, the 'alarming, deterring' or 'stimulating, exciting' character of certain landscape features depends on personal capacity for accepting risk or challenge. These are related to sex, age, familiarity with the subject and personality. Specifically, this study addresses the following hypothesis:

1. Some directions of variation in the patterns of landscape preference are related to visual characteristics with both 'deterring, frightening' and 'challenging, stimulating, exciting' effects.
2. The effect of these characteristics on preference can change with age. Younger children perceive them as frightening and tend to reject scenes exhibiting these features while older children can perceive them as stimulating thus evaluating them positively.

Method

The subjects were children from Gran Canaria and Tenerife (Canary Island) interviewed in their schools. They belonged to two age-groups: 191 were 11 years old and 292 were 16 years old.

Pairwise comparison was employed as described by Rodenas, Sancho Royo and González Bernáldez (1975), Bernáldez and Parra (1979) and Bernáldez, Parra and Quintas (1981). Characteristic landscapes of Tenerife were systematically photographed (coasts, mountains, rocks, woodlands, thickets and croplands) to form a collection of representative slides. These were grouped into classes (strata) with comparable themes (rocks compared to rocks, woodlands to woodlands etc.), similar camera distances and framing, then randomly paired within groups. Fifty pairs were obtained and projected by using two coupled slide-projectors to the 483 subjects in sessions of approximately 70 children.

Subjects were asked to mark on a sheet which photo (left or right) they preferred of each pair. These data can be analyzed by various multivariate techniques (Sancho Royo, 1974; Ruiz, 1985). On the ground of previous experience (see for instance Ruiz, 1985) the following methods were used: (1) correspondence analysis, often called reciprocal averaging (Benzecri, 1973); and (2) detrended correspondence analysis (DCA) an improved eigenvector ordination technique based on reciprocal averaging (Hill, 1979).

The dimensions or independent trends of variation obtained could be interpreted by observing the common characteristics within the series of photo pairs with the highest loadings on a given dimension and simultaneously the consistent differences with their counterparts in each pair. During this inspection the pairs are reversed if the sign of the loading is negative. (Rodenas et al. 1975; Bernáldez and Parra, 1979; Bernáldez et al. 1981). As the interpretations were clear-cut, more sophisticated methods (Abelló et al. 1986) were not deemed necessary.

The correct notation with these methods is 0 for preference of one side (right for instance) and 2 for the other side (n and $n + 2$ or $n, n + 1$ and $n + 2$ if $n + 1$ represent ties or indecisions). In this way the response vector is symmetric and centered, allowing a correct relation between preferences for the right or left side of the pairs (Ruiz, 1985). This notation is equivalent to the more straightforward $+1$, 0, -1 but avoids the use of negative values incompatible with correspondence analysis programmes.

Results

Interpretation of the analysis dimensions

Detrended correspondence analysis of the 483 respondents multiplied by 50 photo-pairs matrix provided three readily interpretable dimensions or axes. The most

FIGURE 1. Examples of picture-pairs with the largest contributions to the three first dimensions obtained in the analysis of landscape preference data. Top, 1st axis, interpreted as an opposition of contrasting landscapes: clear, illuminated scenes rich in detail vs darker, shadowed, scenes with less detail definition. Middle, 2nd axis: diverse, contrasted, varied vs more monotonous landscapes. Bottom, 3rd axis: harshness: rough, rasping, with edges and aggressive forms bland, smooth surfaces.

important photopairs for each of the dimensions are shown in Figure 1. Inspection of the pairs of pictures with loadings higher than 0·30 in absolute value (a convenient threshold chosen after former experimenting with DCA analysis) on the first dimension revealed that this trend of variation consisted in the opposition between clear, well-illuminated scenes rich in detail, with high definition and darker scenes with shadows or with gloomy areas that made the perception of detail more difficult. These pairs consistently possessed high negative loadings when the illuminated pictures were at the right side of the pair and high positive loadings when they were at the left side.

The 10 pairs exhibiting loadings higher than 0·30 in absolute value showed these differences with no exception, making the interpretation very clear-cut. In eight cases the corresponding picture was darker in all its surface and in two cases large but partial shadows and less contrast in the illuminated part diminished the definition of details. In one instance mist added to the shadow which concealed the details.

The second dimension can easily be interpreted as a diversity factor, as the six pairs with loadings higher than 0·30 consistently exhibited this characteristic in the right side picture of the pairs with positive loadings (and vice versa) contrasting with the more monotonous character or their counterparts. 'Diversity' was used to describe the more heterogeneous character of the scene: more balanced proportions of sky, forest, rock, water and grass surfaces, versus much greater dominance of one of these components (for instance, plenty of grass-covered surface with no rock and a tiny portion of sky and forest). The diversity-endowed series of photographs showed, in most cases, more contrasting colours, more marked shadow patterns or were more obviously structured than their 'monotonous' counterparts. This diversity factor is identical to the one found by Sancho Royo (1974) with very different picture material and subject populations.

The third dimension was interpreted as a 'harshness' factor as the corresponding pictures of the eight pairs with loadings higher than 0·3 exhibited a rougher texture containing edges and points, often with a broken contour in the horizon line or in mountain slopes forming sharp, acute or pointed features like teeth. These pictures give a general impression of harshness, evoking concepts of rasping or pricking. Their counterparts (in this case at the right side of the pairs with positive loadings and vice versa) were characterized by consistently exhibiting a relatively smooth surface and an absence or relative scarcity of edges, points or sharp forms. The general impression is one of softer, blander and smoother texture or relief.

Similar 'harshness' factors have already been discovered in factor analysis of landscapes used as stimuli. Aggressive forms in plants, pointed leaves, dead branches, etc. are also responsible for this kind of factor (Abelló and Bernáldez, 1986).

Reciprocal averaging (correspondence analysis) yielded very similar results, the correlation between the three dimensions obtained by both methods was 0·999, 0·900 and 0·968 respectively. The interpretation of the three first dimensions is identical, the only noticeable differences being slight changes in the rank of some photopairs when ordered according to their loadings. In the case of the first dimension these changes seem to reinforce the 'definition of prominent details in dark areas' aspect, at the expense of the 'general cast of shadow' aspect but this does not affect the general interpretation. No meaning could be attributed to the small changes in the other axis.

Relation of preference to age
The coordinates on the first three axes of the 11- and 16-year-old subject populations were compared and significant differences detected for the 1st and the 3rd dimensions by means of a Student's t-test (Figure 2).

The 11-year-old children significantly differ from the 16-year-olds ($t = 4·09$, $P < 0·01$) in their tendency to dislike the darker scenes with less detail characterizing the 1st dimensions of the analysis. The same age group significantly differ from their older counterports ($t = 2·92$, $P < 0·01$) in a tendency to dislike the scenes endowed with characteristics giving rise to the 3rd axis of the analysis: harshness, roughness, abruptness, presence of edges, rasping and pricking features. There is no significant difference in the case of the diversity factor represented by the 2nd dimension.

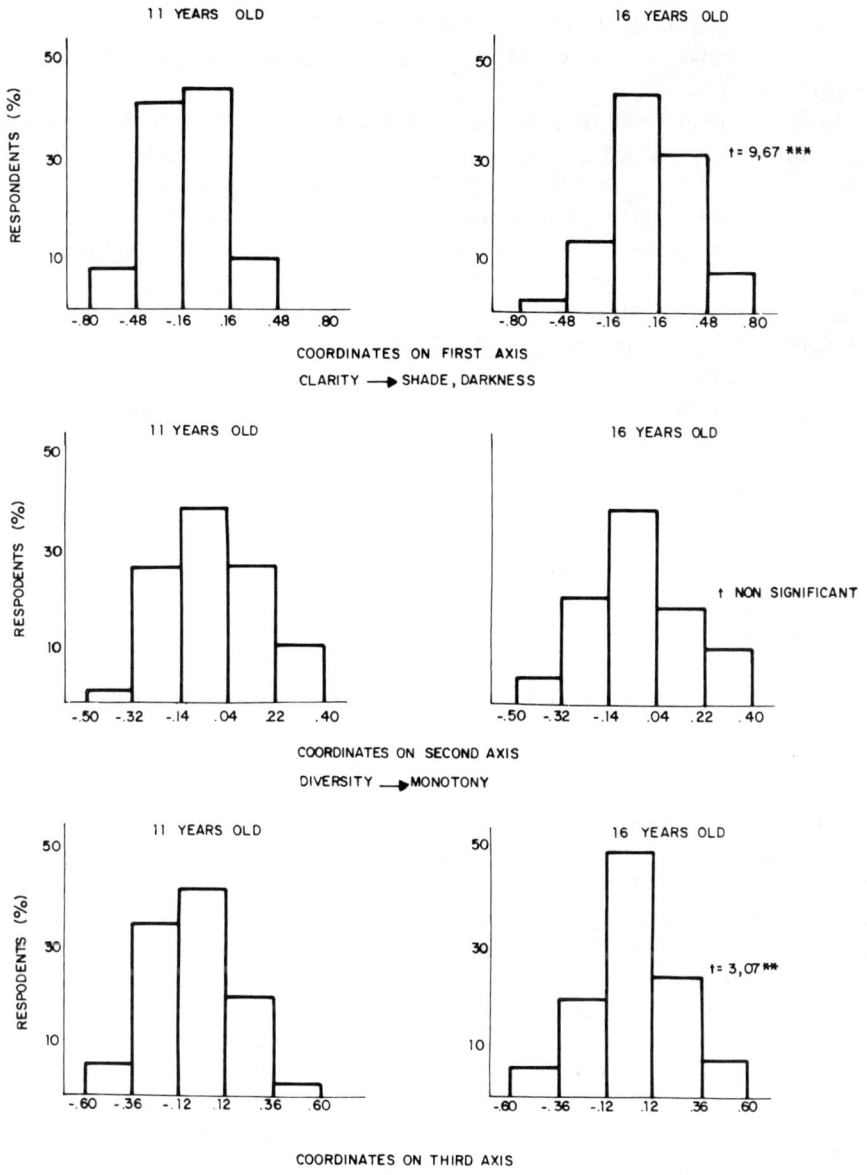

FIGURE 2. Comparison of the position of the 11- and 16-year-old subject populations on the three axes obtained in the analysis of landscape preference data. The 11-year-old children show significantly less preference for both darker, less illuminated scenes (1st axis) and harsh, rough scenes with aggressive forms (3rd axis). There are no significant differences for the 2nd axis (landscape diversity).

Discussion

The 1st and 3rd dimensions (illuminated vs shadowed and harsh, rough vs bland, smooth) relationship to age may be considered as forms of a more general 'risk, uncertainty factor' playing an important role in landscape preference analysis

(Bernáldez and Parra, 1979; Abelló and Bernáldez, 1986). Fear and insecurity have been already considered very important ingredients of landscape aesthetics by Appleton (1978).

The rocky, arid and mountainous landscapes common in the Canary Islands with its lava formations are rich in stirring-up alarming or risk-evoking features but they are by no means unique in this respect. Examples of European landscapes like the pictures from Spain and Germany used by Sancho Royo (1974) contained many features apparently perceived as hostile or risk-evoking by the subjects. For instance, the relief of many alpine and rocky areas and some plant forms were perceived as hostile or aggressive. Moreover, winter landscape with cold signs (snow, mud, defoliated trees, etc.) that rated high as hostile environments are lacking in the Canary collections.

The opposition between illuminated scenes, rich in detail and darker, shadowed scenes with less detail definition is reminiscent of the concepts of both *mystery* and *legibility* of Kaplan and Kaplan (1982). But mystery, as originally defined, implies the consideration of a third dimension, as the observer feels that more information could be obtained if walking deeper into the scene. Legibility as defined by Kaplan and Kaplan (1982) is more closely related to the possibility of the subject finding his/her way easily and making sense of the environment as one wandered farther and farther into the scene.

Darkness and deep shadow, like 'mystery', conceal a part of the scene's information but have a strong risk and uncertainty connotation, related to fears typical of children. Darkness and shadow, like Kaplan and Kaplan's 'mystery', can also stimulate the curiosity of some observers. These circumstances may explain the change from negative influences on preference when the characteristics are perceived as frightening, to positive effect on preference when they are perceived as exciting and stimulating.

After reviewing the effects of challenging characteristic of landscape on preference, Abelló and Bernáldez (1986) concluded that the same visual features may act positively or negatively on preference depending on the subject's personal strategy and his/her capacity to accept challenge. The transition from an alarm or insecurity factor (for younger children) to a stimulating role or ingredient of artistic quality seems to be reflected here. Fear of darkness has often been described as one of the most frequently confirmed phobias related to age, whilst shade, light and shade effects, silhouettes, etc. are some of the most frequently employed resources in paintings, drawings and photography to achieve 'artistic' or 'dramatic' effects.

The change of appraisal with age of the characteristics represented in the 3rd dimension: 'Harshness: rough, rasping; with edges, points and aggressive forms vs bland, smooth, blunt' is very similar. These visual characteristics have challenging connotations that can both alarm and cause anxiety, resulting in a negative influence on the preference of younger children and young adults.

The detection of risk-evoking, hostile characteristics associated with wild, untamed disordered landscapes as factors influencing preference is not new. In some cases they have been reported as influencing appraisal differently depending on age and sociocultural peculiarities (Bernáldez and Parra, 1979). Other work on arousal-eliciting environments are also of interest in this connection. Francès (1979) noted a relationship between a scene's complexity and incongruence and the degree of preference, depending on age and education. Zube et al. (1983) found that higher relative relief strongly enhances scenic quality for young adults, has a moderate effect for the elderly, but is irrelevant as a beautifying factor for young children. They comment that developmental work suggests that optimal arousal levels in children in comparison to adults are elicited by less physically complex stimuli (Wohlwill, 1974). Both Zube et al. (1983) and Bernáldez, et al. (1984) noticed the different preference response to naturalistic landscape of children and the elderly as compared to young and middle-aged adults. In that study it was concluded that the disordered, complex, 'wild' environment was less appreciated by both those under 15 and over 35.

The common factor of these experiments is the risk and/or a factor of uncertainty revealed in the information content (complexity, disorder), mystery or incongruence, which produces rejection (by children or the elderly) or stimulation (youth or adults).

Gender has also been related to the preference for wild, spontaneous, disordered landscapes preferred by male university students vs more ordered humanized landscapes preferred by female students (Bernáldez and Parra, 1979).

The change from the role in preference (from rejection to attraction) of challenging or stimulating may be compared with the observations of Baldwin and Baldwin (1981) in non-human primates. Maturing males increasingly accept environmental challenge and develop an explorative, 'centrifugal' behaviour, tending to explore more remote areas and 'risky' places within the territory hunted by the group. These areas, which are usually avoided by females and younger males, can be accurately mapped (like very dense thickets, wasp nest areas, etc).

References

Abelló, R. P. and Bernáldez, F. G. (1986). Landscape preference and personality. *Landscape and Urban Planning*, **13**, 19–28.
Abello, R. P., Bernáldez, F. G. and Galiano, E. F. (1986). Consensus and contrast in landscape preference. *Environment and Behavior*, **18**, 155–178.
Appleton, J. (1978). *The Experience of Landscape*. J. Wiley & Sons: London.
Baldwin, J. D. and Baldwin, J. I. (1981). *Beyond Sociobiology*. Elsevier: New York.
Benzecri, J. P. (1973). *L'analyse de données*. Vol. I and II. Dumond: Paris.
Bernáldez, F. G. and Parra, F. (1979). Dimensions of landscape preferences from pairwise comparisons. *National Conference on Applied Techniques for Analysis of the Visual Resources*. USDA. Nevada.
Bernáldez, F. G., Benayas, J. and De Lucio, J. V. (1987). Changes in environmental attitudes as revealed by activity preferences and landscape tastes. *The Environmentalist*, **7**, (1), 21–30.
Bernáldez, F. G., Ruiz, J. P. and Ruiz, M. (1984). Landscape perception and appraisal: ethics, aesthetics and utility. *8th International Conference on Environment and Human Action*. Berlin. IAPS 8.
Bernáldez, F. G., Parra, F. and Quintas, G. M. (1981). Environmental preferences in outdoor recreation areas in Madrid (Spain) *J Environmental Management* **13**, 13–26.
Francès, R. (1968). *Psychologie de l'esthétique*. PUF: Paris.
Francès, R. (1979). *Psychologie de l'art et de l'esthétique*. PUF: Paris.
Hill, M. O. (1979). *DECORANA- A FORTRAN Program for Detrended Correspondance Analysis and Reciprocal Averaging*. Ithaca, N.Y: Cornell University.
Kaplan, S. and Kaplan, R. (1982). *Cognition and environment*. Praeger: New York.
Rodenas, M., Sancho Royo, F. and González Bernáldez, F. (1975). Structure of landscape preferences: a study based on large dams viewed in their landscape setting. *Landscape Planning* **2**, 159–178.

Ruiz, J. P. (1985). *Percepción y Gestión del Ecosistema Pastoral de los Ganaderos de la Sierra de Madrid.* Doctoral Thesis. Universidad Autónoma, Madrid.

Sancho Royo, F. (1974). *Actitudes ante el Paisaje Experimental.* Publicaciones de la Universidad de Sevilla: Sevilla.

Wohlwill, J. F. (1974). Human response to levels of environmental stimulation. *Human Ecology,* **2,** 127–147.

Zube, E. H., Pitt, D. G. and Evans, G. W. (1983). A lifespan developmental study of landscape assessment. *Journal of Environmental Psychology,* **3,** 115–128.

CONTEXT EFFECTS IN PERCEIVED ENVIRONMENTAL QUALITY ASSESSMENT: SCENE SELECTION AND LANDSCAPE QUALITY RATINGS

THOMAS C. BROWN* and TERRY C. DANIEL

Rocky Mountain Forest and Range Experiment Station, 3825 East Mulberry, Fort Collins, CO 80524, U.S.A. and the University of Arizona, Tucson AZ, U.S.A.

Abstract

Observer groups rated the scenic beauty of forest scenes represented by color slides presented in the context of different scene mixes. The proportion of scenes from recently harvested, low scenic beauty forests compared with those from unharvested, high scenic beauty forests had a significant effect on judgments of scenes common to both sets. The effects of different scene contexts on scenic beauty judgments can result from changes in observers' perception of the scenes and from shifts in their criteria for assigning ratings. A psychophysical scaling analysis is suggested as a means for dealing with criterion shifts. Because perceptual shifts may also occur, procedures used to assess scenic beauty should be designed to reflect accurately the context to which the assessment applies, and care should be exercised in comparing experimental results obtained in different contexts.

Introduction

Perception of environmental quality has been a major area of study for environmental psychologists, geographers, and other researchers in the environment and behavior field. A considerable battery of methods for gathering and analyzing public response to environmental change has been developed for research and increasingly for application in environmental assessment, planning and management. Methods range from traditional verbal survey instruments, to a variety of perceptual comparisons, rankings or ratings, to several economic techniques, including bidding and trade-off games. The goal of all of these methods is to obtain a reliable and valid assessment of public preferences for alternative environmental conditions. Areas to which these methods have been applied include assessments of the scenic quality of various recreation experiences, visual and aesthetic effects of air pollution in parks and in cities, perceived safety in urban parks, and perceived risk from natural or technological hazards.

Each of these methods requires that assessments be obtained in a survey or experimental situation which typically differs in several respects from the 'real world' situation to which the assessment is intended to be applied. These research situations include an array of information, some of which is presented directly (e.g., in verbal instructions) and some of which is only implied (e.g., by where and by whom the assessment is being conducted). These features of the situation establish a *context* within which the respondent makes and reports his or her perceptions, judgments or choices. Because contextual factors can exert considerable influence on the respondent (Helson, 1964; White, 1975; Fischhoff, Slovic, and Lichtenstein, 1980; Einhorn

---

* To whom correspondence and requests for reprints should be addressed.

and Hogarth, 1981), the relationship between the assessment context and the intended 'real world' context is critical. The issue is one of *external validity*; do the perceptions, judgments, and choices obtained in the assessment context generalize accurately to the real world context?

Context effects are ubiquitous in human judgment-based assessment situations. For example, Wohlwill and Kohn (1973) found that migrants from rural areas judge their city as noisier and more polluted than do migrants from urban areas. And Rowe, d'Arge, and Brookshire (1980) found that people's stated willingness to pay for environmental amenities was affected by the information they were given on what others had bid. Similarly, Lichtenstein and Slovic (1971) found that people apparently use different criteria to assess gambles depending on whether they are put in a rating or a monetary response mode. Among pairs of bets, where one had a higher probability of winning and the other offered more to win, subjects tended to choose the former, but bid more to play the latter.

In landscape quality assessment, studies have investigated several contextual effects. Four components that have been found to have little effect on study results are: the sample of participants/observers used to represent a definable population of observers (Boster and Daniel, 1972; Daniel and Boster, 1976; Shuttleworth, 1980; Kellomaki and Savolainen, 1984; Brown and Daniel, 1984); the landscape representation medium, whether slides, prints, or on-site views (Boster and Daniel 1972; Daniel and Boster, 1976; Jackson and Hudman, 1978; Shuttleworth, 1980; Kellomaki and Savolainen, 1984); the observers' response format, whether paired comparisons, rankings, or ratings, when properly scaled (Buhyoff, Leuschner, and Arndt, 1980; Buhyoff, Wellman, and Daniel 1982); and the time respondents took to view the scenes (Wade, 1982).

Two potentially significant aspects of experimental context in landscape assessment are the season when photographs are presented for judgments and the labels attached to the scenes. Buhyoff and Wellman (1979) found a significant interaction between the season in which photographs were taken and the season in which they were evaluated. For example, preference for fall foliage was greater in the late summer than spring, while preference for green foliage was greater in spring than late summer. Anderson (1981) found that labels such as 'wilderness area' consistently elevated an area's scenic quality ratings, while labels such as 'commercial timber stand' consistently reduced ratings for the same area.

Another potential influence on observer judgments is the range and relative mixture of environmental conditions presented. In landscape assessments, the set of scenes previously viewed determines, in part, the context for any subsequent scene (Russell and Lanius, 1984). If the particular set of scenes presented in an experiment significantly affects the perception and/or judgment of individual scenes, this may limit comparability of experiments, and their generalizability to 'real world' experience.

Studies of human judgment and decision making have found that early questions affect responses to later ones (e.g., Turner and Krauss, 1978; Fischoff *et al.*, 1978). However, there is little, and conflicting, evidence regarding the effects of previously viewed scenes on judgments of forest scenic beauty. Daniel and Boster (1976) reported that values for four of six assessed pine forest areas remained unchanged when slides of a strip cut and a clearcut area were replaced by a burned area and a park-like pine stand. Still, they acknowledged that there were limits (untested) to the context stability of scenic beauty measurements. Brown and Daniel (1984) found indications that ratings of forest scenes differed depending upon the mixture of recently harvested and 'natural' scenes shown in a rating session. However, they did not test for the significance of that effect.

The experiments presented below investigated the effects of previously rated forest landscape scenes on observers' ratings of the scenic beauty of subsequent scenes. Context was manipulated in three experiments by varying the proportion and distribution of forest scenes that showed obvious evidence of recent harvesting activities. The effect of this context manipulation was assessed by observing changes in the ratings of other forest scenes common to all presentations. In the first experiment a strong context manipulation was implemented. The second and third experiments introduced progressively weaker manipulations of scene context, but ones more typical of most actual forest viewing situations.

Experiment I

The approach of this experiment was to establish a strong contextual dichotomy by preceding a common set of forest scenes by one of two very different scene sets. The *low* scenic beauty scene set, rated by one panel, contained color slides that all exhibited obvious evidence of recent harvesting activities and that had generally been rated very low in scenic beauty in previous assessment studies. Scenes in the *high* scenic beauty set, rated by a separate panel, showed no obvious evidence of management activity and had generally been rated high in scenic beauty in previous studies. Scenes of the *common* set, rated by both panels, showed no obvious evidence of management activity, and had been rated from low to high in scenic beauty in previous studies, with an average approximately midway between the high and low sets. The common scenes were presented in the same order to both panels.

Method

Two separate panels of 26 observers were shown a total of 130 photographs (color slides) of forest landscape scenes. All observers were undergraduates at the University of Arizona who had responded to an announcement and each received credit toward a class research participation requirement. The first 80 slides differed between observer panels and were used to establish different contexts for a subsequent common set of 50 scenes that were presented to both panels.

The 80 slides that established the low scenic beauty (SB) context were selected from a pool of approximately 600 slides taken in a large heterogeneous area of ponderosa pine forest in northern Arizona. Slides were taken in the summers of 1980 and 1981, immediately after a selective-cut timber harvest that removed approximately 40% of the overstory trees (see Brown and Daniel, 1984). The low SB context slides were selected to show obvious evidence of recent harvest activities, such as cut limbs, stumps, and disturbed ground, and were required to be in the lowest range of scenic beauty, as determined by previous assessments of the entire pool of slides.

The 80 slides that established the high SB context were selected from a pool of 1,500 slides taken in the same area in the summer of 1979, prior to any harvest activity. These slides were selected from the highest range of the previously established scenic beauty distribution.

The 50 common slides were taken in the same general forest area as the previously shown 'context' slides. Common slides were selected to represent the full range of preharvest forest conditions, and their individual scenic beauty values ranged from low to high.

Instructions to each observer panel were identical and referred to the fact that public perception of scenic beauty is one of many important considerations in the management of the national forests. They were told that their participation in the experiment would help to extend our understanding of public perceptions and preferences for scenic beauty in forest landscapes. The 10-point scenic beauty rating scale was described, ranging from 'very low scenic beauty' (1) to 'very high scenic beauty' (10), and observers were instructed to assign one rating to each scene and to try to use the full range of the rating scale.

Prior to rating the scenes, a sample of 15 of the 80 context scenes appropriate to the panel was shown briefly (3 seconds each) to indicate 'the type of scenes' they would be rating. Observers were told to view the scenes and to think about how they would use the 10-point scenic beauty scale to rate them.

Immediately following the preview, the scenes were shown one at a time for 5 seconds each. Each observer independently rated each slide as it was presented. After the appropriate set of 80 experimental condition slides had been rated, the 50 common slides were presented with no interruption in the procedure. Both low and high SB context panels saw the common slides in the same order. Observers recorded their ratings of all slides on a specially designed sense-mark form which was subsequently optically scanned to enter the ratings into a computer data file.

Results

The reliability of the ratings assigned by the low and high SB context panels was assessed separately by the intra-class correlation coefficient (Ebel, 1951). This measure indicates the expected mean correlation between panels for panels of the same number of observers sampled from the same population. The reliability coefficients were 0·91 for the high SB context panel and 0·89 for the low SB context panel.

Ratings of the slides used to establish the contexts confirmed the basis for their selection for this study; the low SB context slides were rated considerably lower in scenic beauty than the high SB context slides, as shown in Table 1. On the one hand, this seems an expected result. However, if observers had followed instructions fully there would have been little difference in the mean ratings of the two groups. Both panels were told to 'use the full range of the rating scale' in responding to the set of slides they were shown, and that only 'relative differences' were of concern. The fact that there was a substantial difference in the average ratings assigned by the panels indicates that each was applying, to some extent, an extra-experimental or 'absolute' standard in rating the scenes.

The principal focus of this experiment was on the ratings of the common slide set. As shown in Figure 1, the preceding slides had rather strong effects on ratings of the common slides. The common slides were rated higher after the low scenic beauty slides than after the high scenic beauty slides. This effect proved highly significant in an ANOVA, the main effect of context (averaged over the 50 common slides) yielding $F(1, 50) = 10·96$, $P = 0·002$. Closer inspection of Figure 1 reveals that the context established by the first 80 slides declined steadily over the 50 slides of the common set. The difference between ratings by the low and high panels averaged 2·26 rating points over the first ten common slides and declined to 0·92 over the last

TABLE 1
Mean ratings of context and common slides

	Context		
	High SB (Pre-harvest)	Mixed SB	Low SB (Post-harvest)
Experiment I			
Context slides	6·05		4·83
Common slides *	4·85		6·20
Experiment II			
Context slides	5·80	5.64 ‡	5·24
Common slides A †	4·39	5·41	6·59
Common slides B *	4·55	5·20	5·99
Experiment III §			
Context slides	5·57		4·85
Common slides †	4·89		5·36

* Presented in a block at end of session
† Presented mixed in with context slides
‡ High and low SB context slides received mean ratings of 7·00 and 4·27, respectively
§ Averaged from two replications

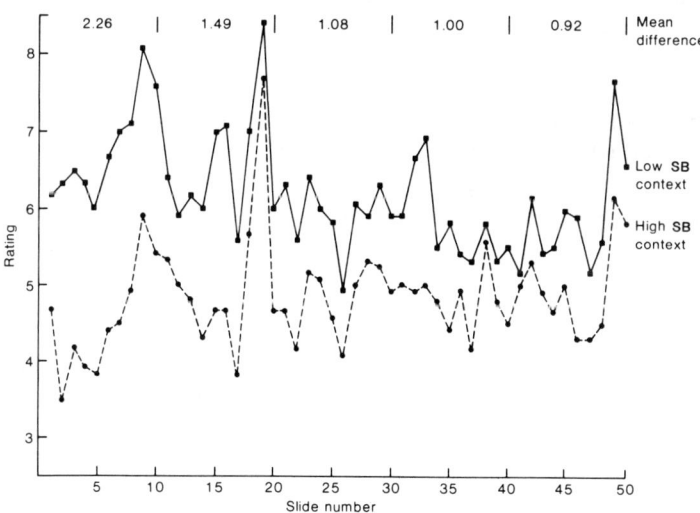

FIGURE 1. Mean ratings of common slides rated in the context of high and low scenic beauty slides.

ten slides. The context-by-slide position interaction proved significant in the ANOVA, $F(49, 2450) = 3·16$, $P < 0·0001$.

While the effect of the context established by the 80 context slides declined over the common slide set, it is important to note that there was still a substantial effect on the ratings of the last 10 slides. Presumably the context effect would eventually dissipate or, more correctly, be replaced by the context established by the current slide set.

The Pearson correlation coefficient of ratings of the common slides, across the two contexts, was 0·59 (Table 2), substantially lower than the intra-class correlation coefficients of the individual panels, which were 0·89 and 0·91, as reported above. The considerable difference between the two measures suggests that the relative ratings of the individual slides differed across the two contexts.

TABLE 2

Intra-class correlation coefficients for high and low SB context panels compared with Pearson correlation coefficients across panels

	Intra-class correlation coefficients		Pearson correlation coefficients*
	High SB Context	Low SB Context	
Experiment I	0·91	0·89	0·59
Experiment II	0·89	0·85	0·67
Experiment III			
Replication 1	0·93	0·89	0·85
Replication 2	0·90	0·85	0·85

* Correlation of mean (across observers) ratings of 50 common slides from the high SB context panel with corresponding ratings from the low SB context panel

Presenting all of the context scenes first was intended to establish firmly the context before introducing the common slides. Under these conditions, effects on ratings of the common scenes were quite large and, while progressively declining over the 50 slide set, were persistent. The second experiment utilizes very similar methods to inspect further the development and maintenance of the context effect.

Experiment II

This experiment used the same slides as did Experiment I, but here the slides were arranged differently. Twenty-five of the 50 common slides were mixed in with the 80 slides used to establish the contexts. The other 25 common slides were included at the end of the presentation. This arrangement enabled assessment of the context effect on the interspersed common slides under 'continuously reinforced' conditions. It was expected that the effect of the context differences on the interspersed common slides would not decline as it did in Experiment I for the common slides presented at the end. Also, mixing the common slides in with the context scenes might be expected to 'dilute' the context difference, as compared with Experiment I.

A third observer group was shown a mixture of 40 low SB and 40 high SB context scenes along with the 25 interspersed common scenes. Again, the other 25 common scenes were presented at the end. This arrangmeent was expected to produce ratings for the common scenes that fell in between those of the other two groups.

Method

This experiment was identical to Experiment I in terms of stimuli, recruitment of observers, general slide presentation procedure, previous slides, and response scale. The difference was in the order and mixtures in which the slides were presented.

Three separate groups of 27 observers each rated a set of 130 slides of forest scenes. Each group saw 80 'context' slides with 25 of the common slides randomly mixed in, followed by the remaining 25 common slides. The context slides, used to establish the different contexts, were presented as follows: one group saw the 80 *high* scenic beauty (pre-harvest) slides; another group saw the 80 *low* scenic beauty (post-harvest) slides; and the third group saw a *mixture*, a random selection of 40 high scenic beauty and 40 low scenic beauty slides. The 25 of the 50 common slides that were mixed in with the context slides were chosen by selecting every other slide from the set of 50 used in Experiment I. They were randomly positioned among the 80 context slides, but the placement of the common slides was the same in all three presentations.

Results

Reliability was again assessed by the intra-class correlation coefficient. This measure was 0·89, 0·85, and 0·96 for the high, low, and mixed SB context panels, respectively, indicating that other panels from the same population would yield very similar ratings.

Ratings of the context slides again reflected the basis for their selection, with the slides used to establish the low SB context rated lower than those used to establish the high SB context (Table 1). Furthermore, as shown in Figure 2, the three different contexts had strong effects on ratings of the common slides. These effects were similar to those observed in Experiment I; the common slides were rated higher when shown with low scenic beauty slides than when shown with high scenic beauty

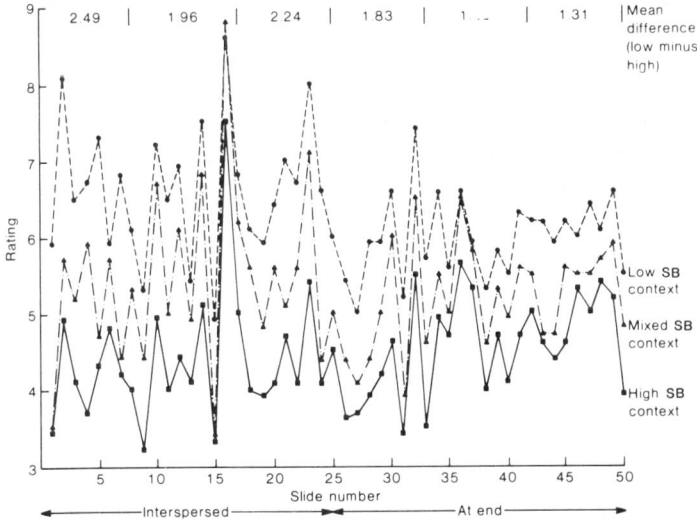

FIGURE 2. Mean ratings of common slides rated in the context of high, low, and mixed scenic beauty slides.

slides. In addition, the ratings of the common slides in the mixed high-low SB context were consistently between the two extremes. Analyses of variance showed that the differences in ratings of the common slides, across the three contexts, were significant, with $F(2, 78) = 25\cdot25$, $P < 0\cdot0001$, for the 25 slides mixed in with the experimental condition slides, and $F(2, 78) = 7\cdot95$, $P = 0\cdot0007$, for the last 25 slides.

As expected, the effect of the context difference on ratings of the interspersed common slides did not dissipate as much as for common scenes presented after the context scenes. Furthermore, the context effect was strong from the beginning of the experiments. Apparently, viewing 15 of the context scenes before beginning to rate scenes and rating the initial context scenes, coupled with the instruction to 'use the full range of the rating scale,' was sufficient to establish a significant context effect. The relative importance of these three aspects of the procedure in establishing the context effect cannot be determined from the data.*

Interspersing common slides with the context slides, at a density of one common to three experimental, appears to have diluted somewhat the context effect on the ratings of the common slides presented at the end. In Experiment I, ratings of the first 25 common slides (all presented after the context scenes) had a mean difference of 1·70 between high and low SB context groups. The average difference for ratings of the common slides that followed the context scenes in Experiment II was 1·44.

The correlations of ratings of the common slides, across pairs of panels, were 0·67 (high versus low SB context), 0·84 (high versus mixed SB context), and 0·76 (low versus mixed SB context). Two of these are considerably lower than the intra-class correlation coefficients (0·85 to 0·96), indicating that the ratings differed across those contexts (Table 2).

Experiment III

The context slides of the first two experiments were selected to establish very distinct differences between the high and low SB contexts. The differences were rather extreme compared with the differences among areas that are typically viewed by visitors to Arizona ponderosa pine forests. The approach in the third experiment was to observe the effects of a substantially more subtle difference in scene context, established by the presentation of two different mixtures of pre-harvest and post-harvest scenes. The slides included in the mixtures were selected without regard to the scenic beauty of the scenes they depicted, and much more closely approximated naturally occurring mixtures than those of the first two experiments. The study design allowed assessment of the effect of these mixtures on a common set of pre-harvest slides.

Method

The methods of this experiment were identical to those of Experiments I and II in terms of recruitment of observers, general slide presentation procedure, and response scale. The slides used in this experiment came from the same slide pools as those of Experiments I and II, but different criteria were used to select the slides.

---

* The instruction requesting that observers use the full range of the rating scale is commonly used where relative differences are of primary interest, and is intended to avoid compression of responses within a narrow range of the rating scale. From experience in previous experiments, we do not expect that the instruction had a major effect on observers' responses. We plan to test for the importance of the instruction and preview procedures in future work.

The original slide pools, from which the slides used in the three experiments were selected, were obtained by taking four slides at each of a large number of randomly selected points in the forest. Some points were photographed before (1979) and again shortly after (1980 and 1981) harvest. The harvest selectively removed about 40% of the trees, but not uniformly, so that some scenes remained essentially unchanged.

In this experiment, for the post-harvest condition, 30 of the sample points inventoried after harvest were randomly selected, with the restriction that at least two of the four slides showed evidence of management activity. For the pre-harvest condition, the same 30 points were used, but of course the slides were taken before harvest. No attempt was made, as it was in the first two experiments, to select scenes of low or high scenic beauty. Some slides in the post-harvest set showed scenes of high scenic beauty, with little or no harvest activity apparent, and some slides of the pre-harvest set showed scenes that were low in scenic beauty. Thus, the pre-harvest condition was represented by 120 slides (four slides at each of 30 points) showing no evidence of harvest activities and the post-harvest condition was represented by 120 slides, with almost 60% of these showing some evidence of harvest activities. Also, 15 preview slides were randomly selected from each group of 120.

In addition to the 120 slides used to establish the pre-harvest and post-harvest contexts, 25 common slides (a subset of the 50 common, pre-harvest slides in Experiments I and II) were interspersed. The same 25 common slides were shown to each panel. Slides were randomly ordered except that a common slide appeared in every fourth position. Thus, each observer viewed 15 preview slides and then viewed and rated 145 slides.

The entire experiment was repeated, with the slide order unchanged, by a different experimenter. Separate observer panels of 20 observers each were used for each condition and each replication of the experiment, requiring a total of four panels.

Results

Two measures of group-to-group reliability were examined. First, the intra class correlation coefficients varied from 0.85 to 0.93 for the four panels. Second, Pearson product moment correlations between replications for pairs of observer groups that saw the same slides were 0.83 and 0.87 for the two pairs of panels.

Ratings of the context slides reflected the relative proportions of slides showing effects of harvest activity. On average, the pre-harvest condition was rated higher than the post-harvest condition (Table 1).

The effect of the context differences on ratings of the common slides was generally similar to the effect obtained in the first two experiments. The ratings of the common slides averaged slightly less when shown with slides of the pr-harvest condition than when shown with slides of the post-harvest condition. As shown in Figure 3, which shows average ratings across both replications, the generally more attractive, pre-harvest condition slides tended to deflate the ratings of the common slides, while the less attractive post-harvest condition slides tended to inflate the ratings of the common slides. The difference in mean ratings of the common set, however, was about three times larger in the first two experiments than in this comparison. Furthermore, analysis of variance showed that the mean difference in common slide ratings was not significant, $F(1, 76) = 3.83$, $P > 0.05$. Thus, for this more subtle, naturally occurring context distinction, changes in the mixture of slides from harvested and

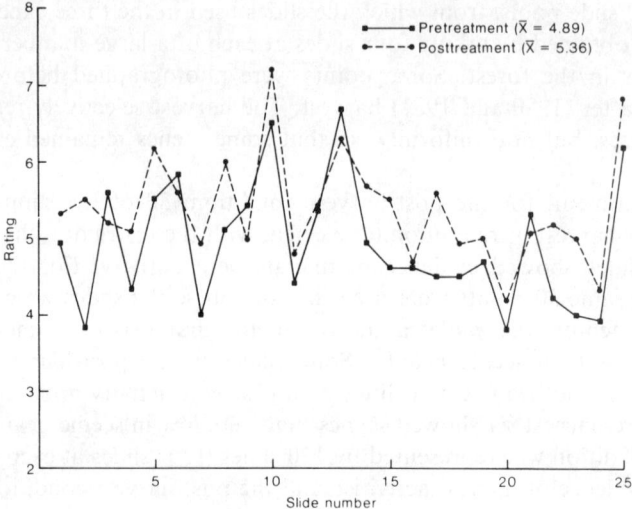

FIGURE 3. Mean ratings of common slides rated in the context of pre-treatment and post-treatment slides.

unharvested areas presented to observers did not significantly affect their mean scenic beauty ratings.

The correlation of ratings of the common slides across the two contexts was 0·85 for each replication. This is similar to the intra-class correlation coefficients (0·85 to 0·93), suggesting that ratings of the individual scenes were not significantly different across contexts (Table 2).

Discussion

Experiments I and II showed that ratings of forest scenes are influenced by the nature of previously viewed and rated scenes. In both experiments, a set of scenes that was common to all context conditions was rated lower in the high SB context than in the low SB context. The slide mixture of Experiment III, where context differences were more subtle, produced similar but non-significant effects on the common scene ratings.

These findings have important implications for comparisons among different environmental assessments, and for the external validity of such assessments. Clearly, when the same forest scenes were assessed in different contexts, scenic beauty ratings were quite different. Which assessment is to be believed? Obviously, neither outcome can be viewed as being 'correct' in an absolute sense; rather, each result has meaning only with respect to the context in which it was obtained. The critical issue is the relationship between the assessment context and the 'real world' context to which the assessment is intended to apply, i.e., the external validity of the assessment.

Context effects can result from changes in observers' *perception* of the assessed environments and/or from shifts in their *criteria* for assigning ratings to the alternative environments. This two-part model, introduced by Daniel and Boster (1976), follows the psychophysical models developed by Thurstone (see Torgerson, 1958;

Nunnally, 1967) and extended by signal detection theory (Green and Swets, 1966), and is only summarized here.

In simplified terms, the model postulates that implicit *perceptual processes* encode the features of the environmental stimulus (e.g., the color slide of a forest scene) and translate them into a subjective impression of the 'attractiveness,' 'aesthetic quality' or, in the present experiments, the 'scenic beauty' of the stimulus. This perceptual process is strongly influenced by the features of the environment in interaction with the sensory and perceptual system of the observer.

Relationships among the characteristics of the set of environments being assessed and the setting in which they are presented can affect the perceptual component by focusing observers' attention upon different features of the environments, leading observers to emphasize certain features and to overlook others. Evidence of such 'perceptual cueing' has been reported by Buhyoff and Leuschner (1978) and Buhyoff and Riesenman (1979). In these studies, information about the cause of apparent damage to trees led observers to be more sensitive to insect damage differences in their ratings of forest scenes. Brown and Daniel (1984) found evidence that the relative proportion of scenes exhibiting different forest management-related features affected the importance of those features in determining observers' ratings of the scenes. Observers may have cued more on the amount of cut tree limbs, tops and stumps when a larger proportion of the scenes being judged represented immediate post-harvest conditions.

To produce an overt response, the perception of the environment must be referenced to a *judgment criterion* scale which, in the present experiments, was a 10-category rating scale. Depending upon the judgment criterion being applied, the observer assigns an overt rating to the forest scene. For example, the perceived scenic beauty of a scene may be sufficient to meet the criterion for the seventh category, but not high enough to reach the eighth category, so the observer would assign a rating of seven to that scene. Criterion scales can vary between observers, or the same observer may change scales from one time to another. As a consequence, responses to the same environment (e.g., ratings of a particular forest scene) can differ even though the perception of the scene is the same. When differences in ratings are due only to criterion shifts, the resulting ratings will be monotonically related, and usually the differences can be resolved by a linear transformation of the rating distributions.*

Context can have substantial effects on the judgment criteria that observers use in expressing their perceptions in the assessment situation. Direct instructions, verbal labels (Hodgson and Thayer, 1980; Anderson, 1981) and more subtle 'social influences' (Simpson *et al.*, 1976) have produced large changes in ratings of scenes that appear better attributed to criterion than to perceptual differences. Differences in the range and proportions of environmental conditions represented in the assessment set could also influence the observer's judgment strategy. For example, the context manipulations in the experiments reported above might tend to require observers to shift their criteria for rating the forest scenes presented; criteria for

---

* Forced-choice (e.g., paired-comparison) and rank-order procedures are generally assumed to by-pass the criterion component. In these procedures the observer's response is only dependent on the relative perceived value of each alternative (Torgerson, 1958; Egan and Clark, 1966; Hull, Buhyoff and Daniel, 1984).

rating the differences among the high SB context scenes would be inappropriate for rating the low SB context scenes.

There is no direct way to observe either the perceptual process or the judgment criterion process; both are implicit psychological constructs that are only indirectly indicated by overt behaviors of observers. How, then, can changes in perception be distinguished from changes in judgment criteria? A number of 'psychophysical scaling' procedures (Torgerson, 1958; Nunnally, 1967) have been developed in an attempt to answer such questions. It is beyond the scope of this paper to discuss these models in detail, but a simplified graphic analysis is presented that captures some of the more important aspects of a psychophysical scaling analysis appropriate to the problem investigated in the experiments described above. This analysis focuses on the differences in mean ratings across panels, as reported in Table 1.

To simplify the illustration, the levels of perceived scenic beauty for the high, low, and common scene sets are treated as fixed values; in typical scaling models the perceived values would be treated as normally distributed variables (Torgerson, 1958; Hull et al., 1984).* Furthermore, as indicated in Figure 4, the perceived scenic beauty values for the high and low SB context scenes are assumed equidistant above and below the values for the common scene set. The equidistant relationship for high and low scenes is largely consistent with the data of Experiments I and II; high scenes were rated an average of 1·27 above, and low scenes 1·21 below, the common scenes.

The rating assigned to a scene is determined by the relationship between the perceived scenic beauty level and the judgment criterion scale being applied by the observer. Two hypothetical criterion scale strategies are shown in Figure 4, an 'absolute' and a 'relative' scale strategy. The 'absolute' strategy assumes that observers come to the assessment situation with pre-established aesthetic criteria that are not affected by the particular assessment context. The 'relative' strategy assumes that observers develop or adjust their judgment criteria to fit the particular assessment context.

As indicated in Figure 4, application of the 'absolute' strategy results in the assignment of the same overt rating for a given level of perceived scenic beauty regardless of context. That is, assuming constant perception, the common scenes would be expected to get the same rating (denoted by 'R_c' in the figure) whether judged in the context of the high or the low scenes. The high and low scenes would be rated correspondingly above and below the common scenes regardless of the context in which they were judged.

In contrast to the 'absolute' strategy, application of the 'relative' strategy results in identical ratings for the high and low scenes in their respective contexts. Observers would shift their judgment criterion scale up or down so that the midpoint of the 10-category criterion scale (6·00) would be centered at the mean of the scenes that they were rating. As a consequence, the common scenes, which are the same in both contexts, would be given very different ratings. As shown in Figure 4, the common

---

* The assumption that the perceived scenic beauty of each scene set remains constant across experimental conditions panels is consistent with the approach used in signal detection theory-based studies. The approach is generally to treat perception as a relatively stable function of stimulus characteristics (the respective scenes are the same across the experiments), and attempt to attribute situational changes in response (ratings) to criterion shifts. Then, if the data shows this assumption to be untenable, a change in perception may be indicated.

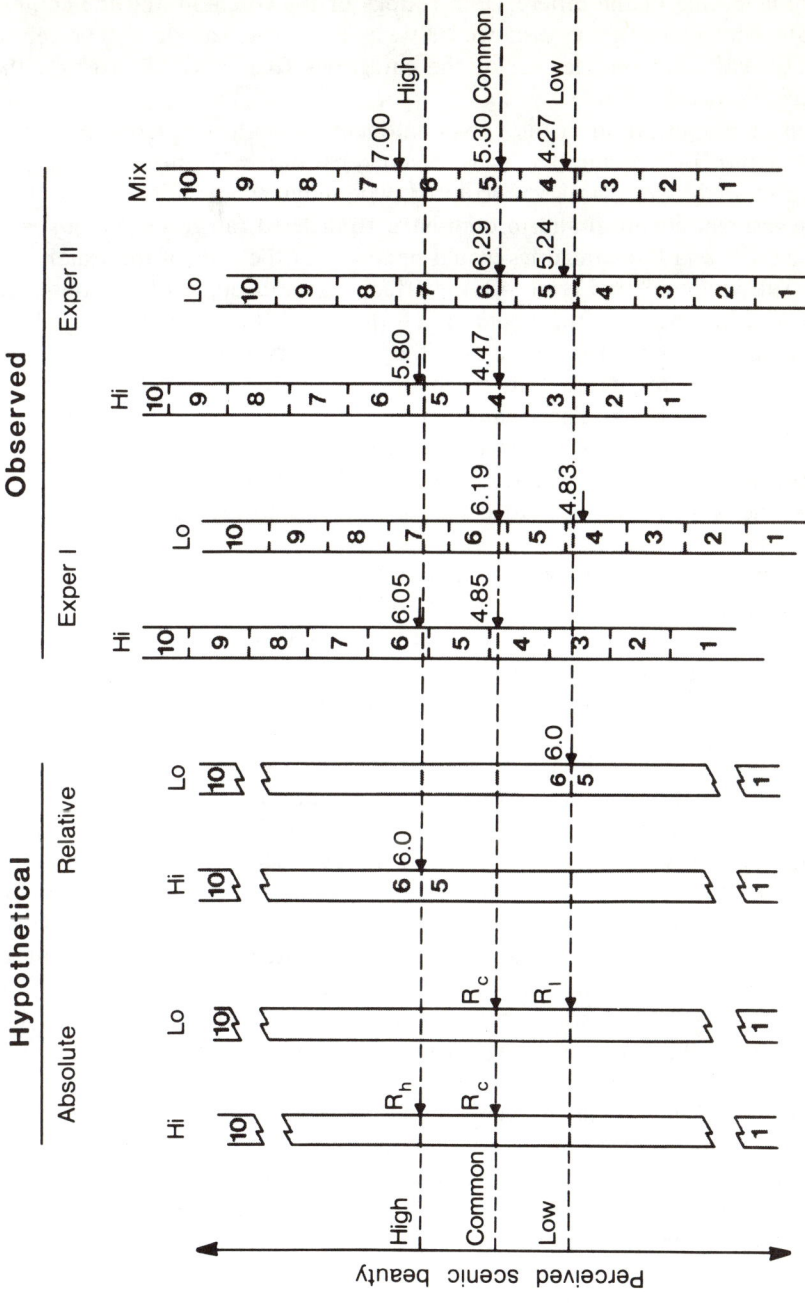

FIGURE 4. Mean ratings of high, low, and common slides according to hypothetical and observed strategies. 'Hi', 'Lo', and 'Mix' indicate the high, low, and mixed SB contexts, respectively, in which the common slides were rated. R_h, R_c, R_l refer to mean ratings of the high, common, and low scenic beauty slides, respectively.

scenes would be expected to have a mean rating less than 6·00 in the high SB context and a mean rating correspondingly more than 6·00 in the low SB context. The actual magnitude of the difference in ratings of the common and the context scenes would depend upon the distance between the scene sets on the perceived scenic beauty scale and on the size of the categories (the 'interval' size) on the judgment criterion scale.

To simplify the application of the two-component model to the actual results of Experiments I and II (Experiment III was excluded because different scene sets were used), an additional assumption was required. The judgment criterion scales of all panels were assumed identical and to each have 10 ordered categories of equal size (although the first and last categories would be 'open' at the ends of the scale). The actual interval size used in Figure 4 was based on the average of the observed differences in ratings between the common and the high SB context scenes, and the common and low SB context scenes, across the five observer panels.

The ratings shown in Figure 4 for each of the panels are the obtained mean ratings reported in Table 1. The location (up or down) of the assumed criterion scales for each panel was determined by the mean rating of the common scenes. That is, the relative position of the scale was shifted up or down as necessary to fit the data for the scenes that were rated by all observers to the assumed perceived scenic beauty of those scenes.

The obtained relationships may be compared to those predicted by the 'absolute' and 'relative' criterion strategies. The results of the two experiments indicate that neither the 'absolute' nor the 'relative' criterion was used exclusively. The very different mean ratings across contexts for the common slides suggests that a 'relative' criterion was used, but differences across contexts for the high and low slides suggests that one cannot rule out some element of an 'absolute' criterion.

Specifically, the results of Experiment I indicate that observers in the high and low SB context conditions did adopt different judgment criteria (Figure 4). For the high SB context, the mean rating of the high scenes was 6·05, very near the midpoint (6·00) value expected for the 'relative' criterion. The average rating for the common scenes was 4·85, considerably below the midpoint value and close to the expected 4·75 (given the criterion scale interval size assumed). The observers in the low SB context, on the other hand, do not appear to have adjusted their judgment criteria sufficiently to fit the low SB context scenes to the 'relative' criterion strategy. The mean rating of 4·83 for the low scenes is well below the 6·00 expected under the 'relative' strategy. The common scene rating of 6·29 is also below the 7·25 that would be expected for the 'relative' strategy.

Results of Experiment II show a very similar pattern. Responses in the high SB context again approximated those expected for the 'relative' criterion strategy. Indeed, the mean rating for the high SB context slides (5·80) suggests a slight 'overshift;' the criterion scale was shifted up about 0·20 units as compared to the hypothetical 'relative' criterion scale. In contrast, the low SB context observers made only modest adjustments in the direction of a relative criterion scale. Their scale was about 0·75 units high as compared to the hypothetical 'relative' scale. The minor differences from Experiment I may, in part, be attributed to the change in procedure; half of the common scenes were mixed in with the context scenes in Experiment II.

The same reluctance to 'compromise aesthetic standards' to accommodate the low SB context scenes is indicated for the mixed presentation group in Experiment

II. A 'balanced' scale, centered at the midpoint of the perceived scenic beauty values assumed in Figure 4, would produce a mean rating of 6·00 for the common scenes. Apparently, however, the criterion scale applied by the mixed group was more like the high relative scale than the low. The common scenes achieved a mean rating of only 5·30. Because the mixed condition data are based on only half of the high and low SB context scenes, some of this shift in ratings may be due to scene sample differences.

As the analysis in Figure 4 indicates, the context effects on mean response per panel observed in the present experiments can, for the most part, be attributed to a simple shift in the location (up or down) of the judgment criterion scale. The assumption of equal interval sizes was largely confirmed, as indicated by the close correspondence of the mean ratings of the high and low SB context scenes to their respective assumed perceived scenic beauty levels. Thus, a relatively simple adjustment, such as expressing ratings in each context condition as a difference from the common scene mean, would eliminate most of the differences between contexts; it does not seem necessary to conclude that the observers on average *perceived* the common scenes differently in the two contexts.

More sophisticated methods for dealing with criterion scale problems include an array of 'standard score' computations, such as 'z scores,' and any of several methods developed by Thurstone (see Torgerson, 1958; Nunnally, 1967). These methods are designed to account for changes in criterion scale interval sizes, as well as the simple 'origin' shifts shown in Figure 4.

The 'Scenic Beauty Estimation' (SBE) method (Daniel and Boster, 1976) is an extension of traditional psychophysical scaling methods to landscape quality assessment (Hull *et al.*, 1984).* The results of applying the SBE scaling to the ratings obtained in Experiments I and II are shown in Figure 5.† The mean ratings differed considerably across the contexts; the common scene averages ranged from a low of 4·47 in the high SB context to a high of 6·29 in the low SB context, with corresponding variations in the ratings for the context scenes. In contrast, the corresponding mean SBE values, which are intended to represent only differences between the scene sets on the perceived scenic beauty scale, are very similar across contexts in both experiments.

One goal of psychophysical scaling methods is to achieve an index that reflects consistent changes in perception regardless of temporary situational (context) changes in judgment criteria. On the basis of the panel means for the above reported experiments, the SBE method would seem to have achieved this goal; the observed SBE values for the scene sets remained quite stable, in spite of substantial shifts in contexts (and ratings). However, the fact that mean SBEs are stable across contexts

---

* As in Figure 4, responses were related to the assumed perceived scenic beauty of the three conditions by computing a common interval size for the response scales. The interval size for the SBE scales of Figure 5 was based on the observed differences between the common and high SB context scenes, and the common and low SB context scenes, across all observer panels.
† The 'by slide' SBE procedure was used to scale the rating responses. Using this procedure, (1) ratings of each observer group were converted to a set of standardized scores, one per slide, based on the frequency distribution of the observers' ratings for a given slide, (2) the mean of the standardized scores for the common slides for each observer group was then subtracted from the standardized scores for each slide the group rated to yield a standardized difference score for each slide, and (3) the difference score was multiplied by 100 to yield SBEs for each slide. Mean SBEs were then computed for the common and context conditions.

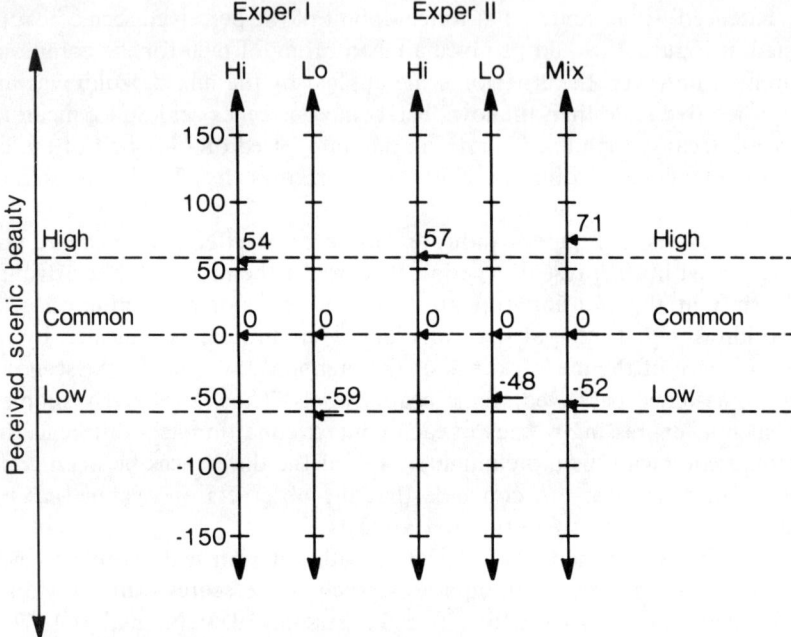

FIGURE 5. SBEs of high, low, and common slides. 'Hi', 'Lo', and 'Mix' indicate the high, low, and mixed SB contexts, respectively, in which the common slides were rated.

does not insure that individual slide values will be comparable. Correlations of common slide SBEs from the high and low SB context conditions were 0·59 and 0·67 in Experiments I and II, respectively, indicating that substantive differences between values for individual common slides remain after the SBE scaling. This pattern of results could indicate context-induced changes in perceptions.

Closer inspection of the data presented in Figures 1 and 2 suggests, however, that a more complex criterion effect may be involved, one that is not accounted for by the SBE or standard z-score adjustments of the ratings. In particular, there is an obvious order effect in Figures 1 and 2; the difference between high and low SB context ratings progressively declines over the 50 common slides. When serial order is included as a covariate in a multiple regression between high and low SB context SBEs for the common slides, multiple correlations improve to 0·77 and 0·82 for Experiments I and II, respectively. These values are still short of the internal reliability coefficients in Table 2, but indicate that most of the difference between contexts can be attributed to shifts in judgment criteria.

It seems clear that observers in the above experiments used different judgment (rating) criteria in the contexts established by the high and low slide sets. This conclusion is supported by the fact that differences in ratings of the common slides can largely be accounted for by relatively simple, monotonic scale adjustments. However, context-induced changes in perception cannot be dismissed entirely; even with the modifying effect of serial order taken into account, there were still differences between common slide ratings in the two contexts. Moreover, the attribution of the observed context effects to the judgment criterion component of the two part model is substantially directed by *a priori* theoretical considerations. Perceived environmental quality is postulated to be a relatively consistent process that is strongly related to the features of the environmental stimuli. Judgment criteria, on the other hand, are assumed to be less stable and more strongly affected by personal, social and situational (context) factors. Of course, these data might also be fitted by a model which assumes that judgmental standards are stable, and that perception is the more volatile of the two components. A choice between these two models cannot be made on empirical grounds.

Conclusion

The context effects demonstrated above have important implications for methods of assessing perceived environmental quality. The comparability of different environmental assessments and the external validity of assessment results (i.e., the extent to which the results may be generalized to the 'real world') may potentially both be compromised by changes in context. Sometimes the context change affects only judgment criteria. Methods that account for criterion effects and provide standardized indices can help to make assessment results more generalizable. However, assessment contexts may have effects that are not addressed by scale manipulations—such as context-specific cueing on different aspects of a multidimensional stimulus. In these cases, the choice of contexts must be based on the goals of the assessment. Because the true nature of a context effect cannot necessarily be determined, the assessment context should, to the extent possible, be made to match the 'real world' context to which the results are to be applied. In any case, further research is needed to determine the impact of the assessment context on judgments and to better understand how and to what extent perceptual cueing occurs.

Acknowledgements

We thank the reviewers, whose thoughtful comments have helped make this a better paper, and Joanne Vining and Sara Kocher for their assistance to this research.

References

Anderson, L. M. (1981). Land use designations affect perception of scenic beauty in forest landscapes. *Forest Science*, **27**, 392–400.

Boster, R. S. and Daniel, T. C. (1972) Measuring public responses to vegetative management. *Proceedings of the Sixteenth Annual Arizona Watershed Symposium*, Arizona Water Commission. Phoenix, Az., pp. 38–43.

Brown, T. C. and Daniel, T. C. (1984). *Modeling forest scenic beauty: concepts and application to ponderosa pine*. (USDA Forest Service Research Paper RM-256), Rocky Mountain Forest and Range Experiment Station, Fort Collins, CO.

Buhyoff, G. J. and Leuschner, W. A. (1978). Estimating psychological disutility from damaged forest stands. *Forest Science*, **24**, 424–432.

Buhyoff, G. J. and Riesenman, M. F. (1979). Manipulation of dimensionality in landscape preference judgments: a quantitative validation. *Leisure Science*, **2**, 221–238.

Buhyoff, G. J. and Wellman, J. D. (1979). Seasonality bias in landscape preference research. *Leisure Sciences*, **2**, 181–190.

Buhyoff, G. J., Leuschner, W. A. and Arndt, L. K. (1980). Replication of a scenic preference function. *Forest Science*, **26**, 227–230.

Buhyoff, G. J., Wellman, J. D. and Daniel, T. C. (1982). Predicting scenic quality for mountain pine beetle and western spruce budworm damaged forest vistas. *Forest Science*, **28**, 827–838.

Daniel, T. C. and Boster, R. S. (1976). *Measuring landscape aesthetics: the scenic beauty method*. (USDA Forest Service Research Paper RM-167), Rocky Mountain Forest and Range Experiment Station, Fort Collins, CO.

Ebel, R. L. (1951). Estimation of the reliability of ratings. *Psychometrika*, **16**, 407–424.

Egan, J. P. and Clark, F. R. (1966). Psychophysics and signal detection. In J. Sidowski (ed), *Experimental Methods and Instrumentation in Psychology*. New York: McGraw-Hill.

Einhorn, H. J. and Hogarth, R. M. (1981). Behavioral decision theory: processes of judgment and choice. *Annual Review of Psychology*, **32**, 53–88.

Fischhoff, B., Slovic, P. and Lichtenstein, S. (1980). Knowing what you want: measuring labile values. In T. S. Wallsten (ed), *Cognitive Processes in Choice Decision Behavior*, Hillsdale, NJ: Erlbaum Associates.

Fischhoff, B., Slovic, P., Lichtenstein, S., Read, S. and Combs, B. (1978). How safe is enough? A psychometric study of attitudes towards technological risks and benefits. *Policy Sciences*, **8**, 127–152.

Green, D. M. and Swets, J. A. (1966). *Signal Detection Theory and Psychophysics*. New York: Wiley.

Helson, H. (1964). *Adaptation Level Theory*. New York: Harper and Row.

Hodgson, R. W. and Thayer, R. L. (1980). Implied human influence reduces landscape beauty. *Landscape Planning*, **7**, 171–179.

Hull, R. B., IV, Buhyoff, B. J. and Daniel, T. C. (1984). Measurement of scenic beauty: the law of comparative judgment and scenic beauty estimation procedures. *Forest Science*, **30**, 1084–1096.

Jackson, R. H. and Hudman, L. E. (1978. Assessment of the environmental impact of high voltage power transmission lines. *Journal of Environmental Management*, **6**, 153–170.

Kellomaki, S. and Savolainen, R. (1984). The scenic value of the forest landscape as assessed in the field and the laboratory. *Landscape Planning*, **11**, 97–107.

Klukas, R. W. and Duncan, D. P. (1967). Vegetational preferences among Itasca Park visitors. *Journal of Forestry*, **65**, 18–21.

Lichtenstein, S. and Slovic, P. (1971). Reversals of preference between bids and choices in gambling decisions. *Journal of Experimental Psychology*, **89**, 46–55.

Nunnally, J. C. (1967). *Psychometric Theory*. New York: McGraw-Hill.

O'Brien, R. M. (1979). The use of Pearson's R with ordinal data. *American Sociological Review*, **44**, 851–857.

Rowe, R. D., d'Arge, R. C. and Brookshire, D. S. (1980). An experiment on the economic value of visibility. *Journal of Environmental Economics and Management*, **7**, 1–19.

Russell, J. A. and Lanius, U. F. (1984). Adaptation level and the affective appraisal of environments. *Journal of Environmental Psychology*, **4**, 119–135.

Shuttleworth, S. (1980). The use of photographs as an environmental presentation medium in landscape studies. *Journal of Environmental Management*, **11**, 61–76.

Simpson, C. J., Rosenthal, T. L., Daniel, T. C. and White, G. M. (1976). Social-influence variations in evaluating managed and unmanaged forest areas. *Journal of Applied Psychology*, **61**, 759–763.

Torgerson, W. S. (1958). *Theory and Methods of Scaling*, New York: Wiley.

Turner, C. F. and Krauss, E. (1978). Fallible indicators of the subjective state of the nation. *American Psychologist*, **33**, 456–470.

Wade, G. (1982). The relationship between landscape preference and looking time: a methodological investigation. *Journal of Leisure Research*, **14**, 217–222.

White, G. M. (1975). Contextual determinants of opinion judgments: field experimental probes of judgmental relativity boundary conditions. *Journal of Personality and Social Psychology*, **32**, 1047–1054.

Wohlwill, J. F. and Kohn, I. (1973). The environment as experienced by the migrant: an adaptation level approach. *Representative Research in Social Psychology*, **4**, 135–164.

TOWARD A PHENOMENOLOGY OF RECREATION PLACE[1]

Lesley Fishwick*[2] and Joanne Vining†

*Department of Environment, Newcastle Polytechnic, Wynne-Jones Centre,
Ellison Place, Newcastle-upon-Tyne NE1 8ST and
†Institute for Environmental Studies, University of Illinois,
1101 West Peabody Drive, Urbana, IL 61801-4723, U.S.A.

Abstract

This study uses a process-tracing methodology to examine qualitative aspects of the person–place relationship. Eighteen participants completed a series of decisions concerning intentions to visit outdoor recreation sites. Each participant 'thought-aloud' during the decision-making process and described thoughts and feelings that influenced their decisions. The resulting verbal transcripts were content analysed and revealed that specific qualities of landscape infuse a site with a sense of place for some individuals. Significantly different life-worlds became apparent as some participants identified with natural pristine places whereas others identified with developed places. Past experience heavily influenced decisions as places were sensed as a combination of setting, landscape, ritual, routine and in the context of other places. Implications for future research and natural recreation site management are discussed.

Introduction

'To be human is to live in a world that is filled with significant places: to be human is to have and know your place' (Relph, 1976).

Relph (1976) argues persuasively that a place is not just the where of something, rather place is a meaningful phenomenon. It follows that landscapes embody meanings. Such meanings vary according to the type of landscape and according to the individual. These dynamics highlight the complex nature of environmental perceptions. However, much of the traditional research has produced simplistic interpretations. Numerical scales to express the degree of liking for particular landscapes reveal little of how individuals react to these landscapes. Researchers have focused in one direction of human–environment interaction, that of individual to place. The relationship of places to individuals has been neglected. As a consequence we have a meager understanding of the constitution of places and the ways in which we experience them (Relph, 1976; Seamon, 1982; Zube, 1984; Pickles, 1985; Schroeder, 1991).

A more qualitative approach offers insight into aspects of human–environment interactions. Specifically the present study explores dynamics of outdoor recreation choices by content analysis of qualitative decision-making transcripts. The following questions were posed to explore experiential dynamics of intentions to visit outdoor recreation sites:

(1) What are the meanings and values associated with preferred outdoor recreation sites?

(2) What qualities of landscape infuse an outdoor recreation setting with a sense of place for individuals?
(3) How important are these landscapes in the contexts of people's lives?

Review of Literature

Much of the research examining how people respond to different types of outdoor environments constructs statistical models for predicting landscape quality (Brown & Daniel, 1984). Similarly studies on recreation choice processes produce classification systems such as the Recreation Opportunity Spectrum (Clark & Stanley, 1979; Manfredo *et al.*, 1983). Both areas of research focus on functional and visual considerations and describe places merely in terms of location and appearance. Critics argue that such quantitative approaches have become increasingly meaningless and divorced from everyday life (Pickles, 1985; Schreyer *et al.*, 1985). At best these empirical studies of landscape preference are rather limited in what they reveal of individual's feelings. To answer questions concerning meaning of places and landscapes to individuals we turn to phenomenological analyses of human–environment interactions. Such analyses have begun to redress the prior neglect of qualitative approaches to studying environmental experiences (Wilson & Slack, 1989).

The literature reviewed focuses on understanding how individuals experienced landscapes and the significance of places in people's lives. As such, this led us to phenomenological approaches to highlight subjective meanings and intuitive descriptions of environmental experiences. Phenomenology explores the things and events of daily experience and emphasizes subjective meanings and intuitive descriptions of the world. Works by Husserl (1911) and Heidigger (1927) were a reaction to a sense that the sciences had lost their relationship to everyday life. Phenomenology as a method attempts to overcome this distance by bringing back subject-matter to original experience. In everyday existence, people are caught up in what the phenomenologists call the 'natural attitude', that is, the unquestioned acceptance of the things and experiences of daily living. The world of the natural attitude is called the 'life-world', the 'taken-for-granted' pattern and context of everyday life. The phenomenologist seeks to make this life-world a focus of attention and to re-examine the nature of this world afresh. Things in Nature, persons and personal communities, social forms and formations, poetic and plastic formations, every kind of cultural work all become headings for phenomenological investigation (Husserl, 1911).

Studies range from documenting the meaning and significance of architecture (Norberg-Schulz, 1979), place (Tuan, 1971, 1977; Violich, 1985), landscape (Chenoweth & Gobster, 1988), and space (Relph, 1981), to discussing the geography of the life-world (Seamon, 1979, 1987). Some of the basic tenets of this work include the notion of people being immersed in their world through a multi-faceted net of intentions. The studies focus on a 'feeling subject' and outline emotional linkages between person and place. Seamon (1979) portrays individuals as having a sense of attachment to certain places. In examining the relationship from the opposite direction, Relph (1976) argues that place is the essence of human intention and a fusion of meaning, act and context. He emphasizes that the identity individuals have with a place is important, in particular whether they experience it as insiders or outsiders. Relph (1976) develops this interpretation of place focussing on this authentic–inauthentic dichotomy. An authentic experience is a direct and genuine experience of a place which comes from a profound identity with it. In contrast, an inauthentic experience is stereotyped, artificial, planned by others and is often expressed through the 'dictatorship of they'.

Seamon (1979, 1982, 1987) described similar dimensions of the person–place relationship when analysing day-to-day experiences of places, spaces and environment. He outlines that an insideness–outsideness dichotomy marks the essential core of place experience. In this analysis the concept of 'at-homeness' captures the sense of possession and control, the renewal of self, the at-easeness and the freedom to be, and the atmosphere of friendliness and warmth generated by a successful home. Similarly, Norberg-Schulz (1979) captures the concept of dwelling in terms of a sense of belonging and feelings of orientation and identification. He suggests the essence of a place is its 'atmosphere' and describes the structure of a place in terms of landscape, settlement, space and character. By anchoring dimensions of the person–place relationship in concepts of meaning and structure Norberg-Schulz (1979) then outlines formal properties of a system of relationships which underlie the 'genius loci' or spirit of a place. In these phenomenological approaches the 'feeling subject' reveals a sense of attachment to places. Places are significant and have meaning to individuals. Concepts such as 'at-homeness' (Seamon, 1979), sense of belonging and identification or genius loci (Norberg-Schulz, 1979) represent dimensions of the person–place interaction. The present study analyses a qualitative data-set on decision choices to visit an outdoor recreation area. The aim is to determine whether meanings and significance exist and thereby suggest the notion of a natural recreation place.

Method

Participants were recruited by placing notices around campus asking for individuals interested in outdoor recreation. To avoid bias due to familiarity with State Parks, participants who had recently moved to the area were selected. Nine male and nine female students participated and received $3·50 per hour for completing the study.

To obtain detailed transcripts concerning outdoor recreation settings we devised a problem-solving activity. Participants made a series of choices concerning sites they would visit. The choices focused on decisions between pairs of site descriptions. We developed a set of ten site descriptions from Illinois State Park brochures. Place names were removed from the descriptions, but most of the original text was preserved. Each description included a map, a photograph of the area and text describing the activities and the physical and cultural characteristics of the site. As shown in Table 1 the site descriptions offered various combinations of natural features such as forests, lakes, gorges, swamps and beaches.

We gave participants two site descriptions and asked them to decide which site they would visit. They were instructed to 'think aloud' into a desktop tape recorder and express all thoughts and feelings that occurred during the decision process. Participants attended ten sessions and each session lasted a maximum of one hour. Tape recordings of the verbal reports (i.e. protocols) provided a record of the information, contingencies, feelings and perceptions the participants experienced during the decision process.

Transcripts from two decision activities and a debrief interview were combined to form the data set for this study. In one activity, ten participants evaluated and

TABLE 1
Features of recreation sites

Environment	Features
1 Beach	Swimming, trails, concessions, fishing, camping
2 Woods	Trails, baseball diamond, picnicking
3 Forest	Trails, hunting, picnicking
4 Forest	Horse and nature trails, hunting, camping
5 Lake	Trails, fishing, boating, camping, concessions
6 Lake/Swamp	Fishing, boating, hunting, picnicking
7 Lake	Fishing, boating, hunting, camping, picnicking
8 Lake/Canyons	Horse trails, fishing, camping, picnicking
9 Lake/Forest	Trails, fishing, hunting, camping, picnicking
10 Lake/Springs	Trails, fishing, boating, camping, picnic, concessions

made choices between all possible pairs of the ten site descriptions. This method produced approximately 50 hours of tape-recorded protocols (Vining & Fishwick, 1988). The second activity involved a set of hierarchical choices in which eight participants were given pairs of site descriptions of increasing similarity (independent coders developed ratings of site similarity). This created increased levels of choice difficulty and yielded 30 hours of tape recorded data (Vining *et al.*, 1989). Finally, all the participants were interviewed at the completion of the sessions. The debrief interview consisted of open-ended questions focussing on their decision-making strategy and asking what influenced their choices.

Data Analysis

The first step of the analysis was to transcribe the tape recordings into verbatim written descriptive accounts of individuals making recreation choice decisions. We reviewed these accounts with the intent of 'seeing through the particulars to discover what is essential' (ideal, typical) elements of recreation places. Next, we reviewed the transcripts to derive the general experiential structures and patterns. These analyses were facilitated by transferring all of the transcripts into a text data base and labelling segments of the text according to the sites, choice pair and the participant number. The data base allowed us to manipulate the transcripts to analyse numerous sets or views of the text to highlight specific patterns that occurred and revealed dimensions of the person–place relationship. For example, all participants making the choice between site 1 and site 4 were analysed within the same view. In this way we searched for the essential elements of specific sites as identified by the participants. Similarly, all choices involving each individual were placed together in the same view to identify the essential elements (e.g. attraction to water) that occurred throughout their decisions.

In the next phase of analysis we attempted to recognize the participants intention towards recreation places by examining how they described and gave meaning to their unfolding decisions. The attempt was to disclose the phenomenon of recreation place by reconstructing the worlds of individuals, their meanings and interpretations and by exploring the underlying behavioural and experiential structures of places which influence individuals' recreation choices.

Results

In making decisions concerning which site to visit the participants described their feelings towards different types of environments. Initially, they described recreation places in terms of activities they would pursue and their decisions were relatively abrupt. In the later transcripts the participants were more reflective during the decision process. They probed aspects of recreation choices that they had previously taken-for-granted by outlining in detail the various factors which influenced their decisions. All of the participants were able to articulate their feelings although some had a sense of place in the outdoor settings, others did not.

As individuals began to question exactly what attracted them to specific places an overriding pattern was an attraction to water. In many instances individuals initially attributed the importance of water to the presence of associated activities such as fishing, swimming, and windsurfing. The choice was justified in terms of the greater variety of activities and scenery available at water sites.

> 'You probably have a greater amount of vegetation, and that may be the reason that I go to water because there is more there in that respect'.

> ' I prefer site 10 because it has water ... I'm not any great swimmer or anything but it has more variety'.

However, on further reflection participants suggest that there is more about the presence of water and the surrounding atmosphere. Often they realized the taken-for-grantedness of the calm and soothing effect of water as they choose to visit a water site even though they could not partake in some of the activities.

> '... it is beautiful that they have waterfalls when it rains because I guess in my mind the water is a very natural soothing thing, escape, retreat'.

> 'I want to say because it's nice to look at, too, but I think it is something more than that, and I don't know what it is ... probably just the beauty'.

The attraction to water was the clearest pattern during the content analysis. The next pattern, divided the participants into two distinct groups, those that preferred natural features and those that preferred developed aspects of the parks. The majority of individuals searched for areas of relatively pristine environments. Accordingly the presence of certain facilities such as concession stands irritated them and provoked negative reactions.

> 'I don't personally like the idea of having concessions stands there ... it seems like it doesn't belong there for some reason ... it just doesn't fit the scenery, somehow ... the concession stand just seems wrong, I don't know why and I can't explain it, ... because with a concession stand I picture a ball park or a park you see in the middle of a city ... a concession stand just does not belong out in nature like that .... The commercialisation, and just having things everywhere you go, you can't even really get away from it'.

'... they've got a big power company right there. You can't escape city life if it's right there'.

'I'm not too crazy about having an airstrip right by the camping area ... the noise might take away from the relaxation and the getaway'

The presence of facilities such as picnic areas and lodges reminded these individuals of the types of place they were trying to temporarily escape, namely the city. These thoughts were echoed when participants noticed other developed aspects near the parks. Consistently participants choose parks that offered them a chance to get away from it all. In turn, factors such as the size of the park, presence of walk-in camp-sites and the shape of the lake became important in their decisions as this influenced their opportunity to avoid crowds of people.

'Number 10 looks more attractive ... you can get to more places in a boat ... seems like a lot better hiking trails ... gets you away from the city environment'.

'... what I like best about number 10 is that it does have the option of walking into a camp site ... you're gonna separate the people who are out there with the intentions of bringing all the conveniences of the city into the woods and people that want to get away from it all'.

These participants indicated that they would do their utmost to find remote areas of the park in an attempt to be surrounded by an undeveloped, natural environment. For several individuals the possibility of being able to get away from people and be by themselves was linked to past experience of finding special places:

'I know if I'm going to a place ... with 5000 acres ... I could find something to do ... even if it ends up being an hour hike by myself ... I've found lots of neat things ... I'll go there and I'll find a cave or something that's not marked there, or I'll find a pretty waterfall, or something that's just there. No trails or anything like that, and those places tend to be kind of special. I mean you remember where they are, and sometimes you don't tell anybody about them'.

'I guess I like the idea of being able to get lost. Just be out in nature'.

As previously mentioned, however, this desire to get away from signs of civilization was not the same for all the participants. A minority of individuals searched for developed aspects of the parks because they wanted to be reassured that they were not 'out in the wilderness'.

'... it has a concession stand ... which would be nice you wouldn't feel as if you were in a primitive place with nothing to do'.

'... camping can be fun but it is nice to have the restaurant ... where you can leave your campground and get back to society once in a while'.

These quotes indicate how the same attributes of an environment produce very different reactions from individuals. The differing reactions are in part explained by individual's past experience of outdoor recreation settings. In reviewing the transcripts of the individuals who preferred the more developed aspects of the sites it became clear that they had limited previous experience of outdoor recreation settings. Throughout their decisions the only references to similar environments was in the context of picnics and short walks.

'Particularly the ones with picnic areas that's the main thing that I would think about past experience because I've had lots of family reunions and things'.

They often evaluated the parks and especially the more developed features in terms of how it suited all groups or in terms of what they themselves may do, even though they had not participated in the activity before. Furthermore, they read the text verbatim, rarely requested additional information and made few if any inferences from the text.

> 'I think it is really nice that you can land there. I've always wanted to fly'.

> 'Trap shooting I've never done which I'd like to try'.

> 'Modern camping and primitive camping and a lodge ... that's really nice ... it should be open to the largest scope of people that it can be'.

In stark contrast, the more experienced participants made many inferences from the text and site descriptions and requested more information on specific aspects. Additionally, they continually referred to previous outings in similar environments. These individuals often identified with specific places with comments such as 'I am a water person' or 'I am a fishing person'. These experienced participants indicated that they feel 'comfortable' in the outdoors. In these transcripts the voice of the wilderness lovers came through often linked to 'the change of mind' that this environment evokes and the feeling of 'escape'.

> '... usually I'm not going to stay for a couple of hours, I'd like to stay overnight ... I don't get much out of an outdoor recreation experience until I've been in it for a while. You sort of have to adjust your way of thinking when you are out in the woods'.

> 'For me going to the park is getting away from everything ... it's just like retreating ... when I go walking through a park I like to think of things in my mind ...'.

> 'I usually go by myself, it's sort of a Rousseau kind of idea ... a romantic sort of thing. I like to go by myself and just getting away from things, and just have basic thoughts ... a lot of times ... I'll bring my fishing stuff but not use it'.

For experienced and less experienced participants a unifying theme in their decisions was the sense that a recreation place meant doing something different from the 'life-as-usual'. In deciding which parks to visit they searched for uniqueness combined with activities they like to pursue. Commenting on his hardest decision between a park that has fishing which he enjoys and another park which has rocks and caves one individual indicated that the search for uniqueness overrode his intention to fish:

> '... that was the hardest decision ... I choose the one with the caves even though the fishing may not be as good, you can do it anytime. Most anywhere. But going to a cave, there aren't many of them around, so that's a lot more unique than the fishing would be'.

The majority of participants searched for something different about the environment noting that this meant that it was a change from life-as-usual. Similarly, they rejected sites that did not offer anything new and often described such sites in as 'back yard' type of environment.

> '... canyons, there's all different kinds of things it is neat because you get to see things that you don't get to see in everyday life'.

> '... the photograph looks like out of my bedroom window back home, and I couldn't get excited about that'.

> '... the waterway is nice, the trees are nice more full, more undergrowth thicker than in 2 where everything seems to be developed and cleared out to look pretty. I don't know it's like camping in your living room'.

In summary, at first glance participants assess outdoor recreation places in terms of activities. However, a more in-depth analysis reveals that recreation places are sensed as a combination of setting, landscape, ritual, routine, people, personal experiences and in the context of other places. A crucial dimension is past experience in certain types of environment which may in turn lead to a sense of belonging to that place. Individuals who expressed 'feeling at-home' in the natural environment strived to escape elements of the city and searched for areas where they could get away from all development. In contrast, the less experienced users noted thay they felt lost in the outdoor sites and seemed alienated from the natural environment. They felt comfort in being surrounded by human-built structures such as lodges and concession stands.

Discussion

The results of the study indicate that the decision-making activity induced the participants to reveal feelings and intentions concerning specific environments. The complex nature of the person–place relationship became evident as the same environment prompted very different reactions from different individuals. The content analysis illuminated very different life-worlds and captured several dimensions of environmental perceptions.

The meanings and values associated with preferred recreation sites were heavily influenced by past experience. For experienced outdoor individuals an ability to be by oneself in a natural environment guided many of their decisions. They captured a sense of belonging and a sense of being-at-one with nature. The setting, landscape, ritual, routine and personal experiences linked together to produce a solid environmental image as suggested by Lynch (1960). These individuals were able to give vivid descriptions of environmental features such as types of trees and shapes of lakes and then make inferences from the text as to what they would be able to do at specific sites. When they believed that they would be totally surrounded by nature, their responses reflected Heidegger's (1971) notion that dwelling means to be at peace in a protected place. To be at peace and relax were the most often cited reasons for choosing such a site. This encompasses Norberg-Schulz (1985) notion of specific places as retreats and concurs with Wilson and Slack's (1989) findings of tranquillity and protection from external pressures as basic qualities identified by waterfront users.

In contrast, the less experienced users lack of personal experience and lack of ritual and routine at recreational sites combined to make environmental image making difficult during the decision making process. These individuals expressed concern and a feeling of being unprotected away from civilization. To overcome this they sought the availability of developed human-built structures in the park. Relph (1976) noted a similar phenomenon with motorized campers and individuals who had little sense of places they visited and who preferred to take with them part of their 'home' which insulated them against the strangeness of new and different places.

Qualities of landscape that infuse an outdoor recreation setting with a sense of place differ across individuals. Accordingly, the notion of recreation place may be misleading. The sense of place was not always in terms of recreation but varied from a place of solitude and retreat to a place to picnic and walk. The sense of place in turn influenced the expectations that the participants held regarding the sites. Some searched for natural aspects while others searched for developed aspects. This has implications for managers who are attempting to respond to the needs and wishes of users of natural areas. In larger parks it is possible to set aside areas which could please both the individuals seeking solitude and pristine nature as well as those who prefer social interaction in more developed area. It may be impossible to provide both areas in a small acreage. Managers may then decide to compromise between the two extremes (thereby probably pleasing no one) or decide which type of park to create. Additional research should address the plausibility of these policy options.

The strong differences in perceptions and requirements of experienced and less experienced users also has implications for future research. To further investigate the qualitative dimensions of the influence of past experience on environmental perceptions is a fruitful avenue of research. Our study gathered responses of a small group of individuals on a set of hypothetical choice problems. The decision-making activity could incorporate more realistic contexts and settings and include a more in-depth assessment of their past experience.

Notes

(1) Support for this research was provided by the USDA Forest Service North Central Forest Experiment Station.
(2) Correspondence should be addressed to the first author.

References

Brown, T. C. & Daniel, T. C. (1984). Modelling forest scenic beauty: concepts and application to ponderosa pine. *USDA Forest Service Research Paper RM-256*. Rocky Mountain Forest and Range Experiment Station, Fort Collins, CO, 35 pp.
Chenoweth, R. E. & Gobster, P. H. (1988). The nature and ecology of aesthetic experience. Unpublished paper Department of Landscape Architecture, University of Wisconsin-Madison.
Clark, R. N. & Stanley, G. H. (1979). The recreation opportunity spectrum: a framework for planning management and research. *General Technical Report PNW-98*. Portland: OR: USDA Forest Service, Pacific Northwest Forest and Range Experiment Station.
Heidegger, M. (1927). *Being and Time*. Translated by Macquarrie, J. & Robinson, E. New York: Harper and Row, 1962.
Heidegger, M. (1971). *In Poetry, Language and Thought*. New York: Harper and Row.
Husserl, E. (1911). *Philosophy as a Rigorous Science*. Translated by Lauer, Q. New York: Harper Torchbooks, 1965.
Lynch, K. (1960). *The Image of the City*. Cambridge, MA: MIT Press.
Manfredo, M., Driver, B. & Brown, P. (1983). A test of concepts inherent in experience based setting management for outdoor recreation areas. *Journal of Leisure Research*, 3(3), 263–283.
Norberg-Schulz, C. (1979). *Genius Loci: Towards a Phenomenology of Architecture*. New York: Rizzoli.
Norberg-Schulz, C. (1985). *The Concept of Dwelling: On the Way to Figurative Architecture*. New York: Rizzoli.
Pickles, J. (1985). *Phenomenology, Science and Geography: Spatiality and the Human Sciences*. Cambridge: Cambridge University Press.
Relph, E. (1976). *Place and Placeness*. London: Pion.
Relph, E. (1981). *Rational Landscapes and Humanistic Geography*. London: Croom Helm.
Schreyer, R., Knopf, R. C. & Williams, D. R. (1985). Reconceptualising the motive/

environment link in recreation choice behaviour. In G. H. Stanley & S. F. McCool, Eds., *Proceedings on Symposium of Recreation Choice Behaviour.* Ogden, UT.

Schroeder, H. (1991). Preference and meaning of Arboretum landscapes: combining quantitative and qualitative data. *Journal of Environmental Psychology*, **11**, 231–248.

Seamon, D. (1979). *A Geography of the Life-world.* London: Crook and Helm.

Seamon, D. (1982). The phenomenological contribution to environmental psychology. *Journal of Environmental Psychology*, **2**, 119–140.

Seamon, D. (1987). Phenomenology and environment-behavior research. In E. Zube & G. Moore, Eds., *Advances in Environment, Behavior and Design.* New York: Plenum Publishing.

Tuan, Y. F. (1971). Geography, phenomenology and the study of human nature. *Canadian Geographer*, **2**, 181–192.

Tuan, Y. (1977). *Space and Place: the Perspective of Experience.* Minneapolis: University of Minnesota Press.

Violich, F. (1985). Toward revealing the sense of place. In D. Seamon & R. Mugeraeur, Eds., *Dwelling, Place and Environment.* Dordrecht: Nijhoff.

Vining, J. & Fishwick, L. (1988). A process tracing approach to recreation choice problems. *Final Report, Cooperative Agreement No. 23-86-07.* Chicago: USDA Forest Service, North Central Forest Experiment Station, 19 pp.

Vining, J., Walker, M., Meistrell, M. & Fishwick, L. (1989). An extension of the process tracing methodology to recreation and resource management problems. *Final Report, Cooperative Agreement No. 23-87-10.* Chicago: USDA Forest Service, North Central Forest Experiment Station, 90 pp.

Wilson, D. & Slack, A. (1989). Toward an applied phenomenology: the case of abandoned pier use in Hoboken, New Jersey, USA. *Environmental Management*, **13**(1), 117–123.

Zube, E. H. (1984). Themes in landscape assessment theory. *Landscape Journal*, **3**(2), 104–110.

A COGNITIVE ANALYSIS OF PREFERENCE FOR WATERSCAPES

THOMAS R. HERZOG

Department of Psychology, Grand Valley State College, Allendale, Michigan 49401, U.S.A.

Abstract

Preferences for waterscapes were studied as a function of content categories, viewing time and six predictor variables: spaciousness, texture, coherence, complexity, mystery, and identifiability. A non-metric factor analysis of the preference ratings for the longest viewing-time condition yielded four dimensions: (1) Mountain Waterscapes, (2) Swampy Areas, (3) Rivers, Lakes, and Ponds, and (4) Large Bodies of Water. Mountain Waterscapes was the most preferred category and Swampy Areas by far the least preferred. The Mountain Waterscapes category was characterized by rough surface textures, while within the category spaciousness, coherence, and mystery were positive predictors of preference. The Swampy Areas category was low in spaciousness; within the category, coherence was a positive predictor of preference. With longer viewing times, Mountain Waterscapes were liked better but Swampy Areas were liked less. The results indicate that type of waterscape, viewing time and the predictor variables all play a role in determining preference. Some broad implications of these findings for environmental planners were suggested.

Introduction

Water has long fascinated human beings. The list of activities that humans enjoy on, in, under, or near waterways is extensive: swimming, skiing, diving, fishing, throwing stones, building homes, sketching, photography, frog watching, meditating, etc. R. Kaplan (1977) suggests that even those who are far from any waterway derive enjoyment from knowing that water is 'there' and available. Small wonder, then, that environmental decision makers of all sorts have taken a keen interest in this valuable natural resource.

Several excellent reviews of approaches for studying landscape perception have appeared recently (Arthur *et al.*, 1977; Zube *et al.*, 1982; Daniel and Vining, 1983), including one specifically oriented toward waterscapes (Levin, 1976). The more recent reviews seem to be converging on a classification of landscape perception paradigms into four categories. Following Zube *et al.*, these are the expert, psychophysical, cognitive and experiential paradigms. The expert approach involves evaluation of landscape quality by skilled and trained observers. Daniel and Vining (1983) distinguish two variants of this approach based on whether the expert observers emphasize ecological or formal aesthetic landscape variables. The remaining approaches typically assess reactions of nonexperts. The psychophysical approach seeks relationships between physical features of the environment and judgments of preference or aesthetic value. The cognitive approach attempts to relate landscape value judgments to cognitive variables deriving from the information afforded by the environment. The experiential (or phenomenological) approach seeks an in-depth understanding of the total experience of individuals when they interact with landscapes. Applying traditional criteria of reliability, sensitivity, validity and utility, Daniel and Vining (1983) concluded that a merger of the psychophysical and cognitive approaches currently provides the best avenue to an adequate landscape assessment system.

The research reported here attempted to test the general usefulness of an approach from within the cognitive category in accounting for waterscape preferences. This 'informational' approach has been described in detail by the Kaplans (Kaplan and Kaplan, 1978, 1982). Its key tenet is that humans evolved in environments wherein the processing of spatial information was crucial to survival. Hence, the analysis of preference should concentrate on the types of environments and the kinds of cognitive processes that would be especially important in such a scenario. Recent studies of natural environments containing water that have used this approach include Levin (1976), Lee (1979) and Ellsworth (1982). Ellsworth, in fact, compared the informational approach and the expert approach empirically and found the former to be superior.

The informational approach stresses both content and process in accounting for environmental preference. Content refers to both specific features of the environment and more general features. Specific contents include trees, water, fire and animals. In the present context, one might ask whether there are specific subcategories within the superordinate category of water. The literature provides some hints. Rivers and marshes proved to be a useful distinction for Ellsworth (1982), with rivers easily more preferred. Likewise, Calvin *et al.* (1972), found that their raters did not care for their single scene depicting an algae bloom. On the other hand, scenes of rushing water received high preference ratings. R. Kaplan (1984) recently reported that participants in a wilderness outing program rated photographs of swampy regions relatively low in preference and gave even lower ratings to such scenes after their wilderness experience than before. Hence, it might be expected that three important categories within the domain of water environments would be rushing water (probably including waterfalls) rivers and streams, and swampy areas.

General contents refer to what Gibson (1979) has called affordances. The issue here is the kind of features that determine what one can do in an environment. Locomotion is an environmental affordance, and it will depend on such general features as how finely textured the ground surface is. Safety is another affordance, and it will depend on the extent to which the environment contains configurations that could serve as hiding places. Appleton (1975) refers to this property as refuge. A third affordance, derived from Appleton, is prospect. It refers to the opportunity an environment provides for unhindered seeing into the distance, and it should depend on how spacious the environment seems. The role of such general contents can be assessed by asking participants to rate them. In the present study, two of these variables were investigated, spaciousness and texture. Neither has been formally investigated for environments containing water although, informally, Levin (1976) found spaciousness to be a useful dimension for distinguishing among her riverscape categories.

Two important cognitive processes are proposed in the informational approach, making sense and involvement (Kaplan and Kaplan, 1978, 1982). Making sense refers to the process of organizing an environment so that it is possible to find one's way around in it. Involvement refers to the process of engaging and sustaining one's interest in an environment. Both processes were presumably crucial to evolving humans, and therefore environments that permit both to function successfully should be highly preferred. Environmental features that should aid the making-sense process would include the degree of order present in the immediate environment (coherence) and the extent to which the environment contains features that allow one to build a useful map of the larger environment that cannot be apprehended in a single glance (legibility). Likewise, features that should aid involvement would include the amount of information in the immediate environment (complexity) and the extent to which the environment suggests that one could obtain new information if one were to travel deeper into it (mystery).

Some evidence exists for the utility of most of these variables in accounting for preferences for environments containing water. For example, Ellsworth (1982) found that coherence was negatively correlated, and mystery positively correlated, with preferences for marshes. Complexity was positively correlated with preferences for rivers. R. Kaplan (1977) found that coherence was positively related to preference for her riverscapes. Levin (1976) found that the most preferred river scenes were also highest in mystery. In the present study, participants rated the scenes for three of the process variables: coherence, complexity, and mystery.

A variable that cuts across both the making-sense and involvement processes is the extent to which the current environment resembles a class of environments the observer knows well. This 'sense of familiarity' (as opposed to actual familiarity with the particular environment currently being observed) should aid in making sense of the current environment but might lead to a premature exhaustion of interest in it. Which effect will predominate will depend on a number of factors: the particular type of environment, how well endowed it is with the other making-sense and involvement properties, and how strong the sense of familiarity is. Despite the complexity of its operation, sense of familiarity should play a role in accounting for environmental preference. To distinguish this variable from actual familiarity, it was dubbed 'identifiability' in the present study. It has not previously been investigated as a predictor of preference for environments containing water.

A final variable investigated in this study was viewing time. A great deal of debate recently concerns the rapidity of preference judgments and whether they necessarily involve cognitive processing. Some hold that preference is the outcome of a rapid, automatic, global assessment of an environment and that it requires little or no cognitive processing (Ittelson, 1973; Zajonc, 1980; Ulrich, 1983). Rational, deliberative cognitive analysis follows the preference judgment and may modify it, according to this approach. Standing in lonely opposition is Lazarus (1982) who concedes that preference may indeed be rapid, automatic (that is, largely outside conscious awareness) and based on global environmental features, but it is nonetheless the result of cognitive processing. He chides the opposition for undermining its own position by using such phrases as 'little' or 'minimal' cognitive processing in describing preference judgments. The informational approach sides with Lazarus. Preference is, among other things, based on the cognitive processes of making sense and involvement. Many of the variables involved in these processes, such as coherence and mystery, are based on relatively global environmental features and can be assessed rapidly and automatically. In fact, the informational approach argues that humans are biased by evolution to do just that (S. Kaplan, 1979). Nonetheless, further deliberative analysis may modify the initial preference reaction. Hence, viewing time becomes a relevant concern. To tap the initial preference reaction when no opportunity to return to the stimulus for further consideration is provided, this study used very brief viewing times (20 and 200 ms). For comparison purposes, a viewing time that allows ample opportunity for extended consideration and deliberative analysis was also included (15 s). Two key questions are whether waterscape preferences differ for brief and extended viewing times and whether any such differences are similar for all types of waterscapes.

The major objectives of this study, then, were to investigate both content and process as predictors of preference for environments containing water. The study differed from other studies of waterscapes using the informational approach in three respects. First, this study contained the broadest sample of waterscapes yet attempted. While other studies have sampled only a few types of waterscapes at most, this study sampled as broad a range as possible, including waterfalls, mountain streams, rivers, lakes (large and small), ponds, creeks and swamps. As a corollary, this study contained the largest sample of waterscapes ever investigated (70 waterscapes; only Ellsworth, with 60, comes close). Second, this study assessed more informational variables than any of the others cited. On the other hand, no attempt was made to assess all of the variables implicated by the informational approach. An exhaustive and final test of the approach is both presumptuous and naive. The model evolves and the variables change over time as a better understanding of the processes involved is achieved. Hence, the intent here was to provide a test of the general usefulness of the approach by broadly sampling relevant variables. Third, this study investigated viewing time as a possible determinant of preference. Viewing time for individual waterscapes has not been investigated previously. Ulrich (1981) did find tendencies toward higher *alpha*-amplitude and heart rate during sequences of 60 waterscapes as compared to 60 urban scenes, providing some empirical confirmation of the potential relevance of cumulative viewing effects.

Method

Participants

The sample consisted of 259 introductory psychology students of both sexes at the University of North Carolina. Participation fulfilled a course requirement. Twelve sessions of from 17 to 26 participants were conducted.

Stimuli

The settings consisted of 70 color slides of natural environments containing water. An attempt was made to sample as wide a variety of such settings as possible. As a result, the settings included waterfalls, rushing mountain streams, rivers, lakes (both small and large), ponds, swampy areas and creeks (ranging from crystal clear to stagnant and covered with green slime). No settings contained people, and human influences were minimal. The settings were drawn from the following states: California, Michigan, New York, Utah, Washington and Wyoming.

Procedure

All participants rated each of the 70 scenes for one of seven variables. All ratings used a five-point scale ranging from 1 = 'not at all' to 5 = 'a great deal'. The six predictor variables were identifiability, coherence, spaciousness, complexity, mystery and texture. *Identifiability* was defined as 'how much of a *sense of familiarity* (rather than actual familiarity) you have for this scene. How easy would it be for you to get to know this scene?' *Coherence* was 'how well the scene "hangs together". How easy is it to predict from one portion of the scene to another?' *Spaciousness* dealt with 'the *feeling of spaciousness* that the scene conveys. Ask yourself how much room there is to wander around in.' A *complex* scene was one that 'contains a lot of elements so that it promises further information if only you could have more time to look at it from your present vantage point.' By contrast, *mystery* was present when a scene 'promises further information if you could walk deeper into it.' *Texture* referred to 'how fine-grained the ground surface is', or 'if the ground surface is obscured by objects in the foreground, then rate the scene on how fine-grained the surface of the obstruction is.' These variables are discussed in more detail by S. Kaplan (1975). The criterion variable, preference, was defined as 'how much you *like* the scene, for whatever reason.'

Sessions proceeded as follows. First, nine sample slides were shown which participants rated mentally to help them get used to the task and the five-point rating scale. Then participants provided written ratings for 80 slides, presented in two sets of 40 each, with a brief intermission between sets. Within each set, the first three and the last two slides were always the same and were considered filler slides (data not analysed). The remaining 70 slides from both sets were presented in four different orders to the 12 rating groups.

Six of the groups rated the slides on the predictor variables. Three groups rated for identifiability, coherence and spaciousness; the other three groups rated for complexity, mystery and texture. In these six groups, each participant rated for only one predictor variable, with approximately one third of each group rating each variable. The same three different orders of scene presentation were used for the three groups that rated each set of predictor variables. Viewing time was 15 s for each scene. Final sample sizes were 22 for identifiability and 21 for each of the other five predictor variables.

The other six groups rated the scenes for the criterion variable, preference. The order in which all twelve groups were scheduled was determined randomly. The viewing time was 15 s for four of the preference groups, 20 and 200 ms for the other two preference groups. The brief viewing times were achieved by using an electronic shutter mounted in front of the projector lens. Four different orders of scene presentation were used for the 15-s preference groups, the first three of which were the same as those used for the groups rating the predictor variables. The two brief viewing-time groups had the same presentation order as the first of the 15-s groups. Final sample sizes were 21, 26, and 85 for the 20-ms, 200-ms and 15-s preference conditions, respectively.

Analysis

To evaluate reliability of measurement for each variable, final samples were divided into half samples and mean ratings for each scene were computed based on each half sample. The two sets of 70 mean-per-scene scores were then intercorrelated for each variable and corrected by the Spearman–Brown formula to yield split-half reliability coefficients for each variable.

To discover the categories embodied in the participants' responses, the preference ratings of the 70 scenes in the 15-s condition were analysed via non-metric factor analysis, specifically the Guttman-Lingoes Smallest Space Analysis III (SSA-III) (Lingoes, 1972). SSA-III is a nonmetric version of principal-axes factor analysis with squared multiple correlations in the diagonal of the original input correlation matrix and a varimax rotation of the final solution. The procedure finds a solution of the user-specified dimensionality that best fits the rank order of the original correlation matrix rather than the more stringent linear transformation of the original correlations required by metric factor analysis. Given the less stringent criterion of fit, proponents of nonmetric analysis argue that more stable solutions in fewer dimensions can be found.

Following the SSA-III analysis, category (or factor) scores were computed for each subject who rated for preference. The category score was simply the mean rating for all of the scenes comprising a category. To assess the effects of categories and viewing time on preference, these category scores were subjected to a two-way analysis of variance, with categories as a within-subjects factor and viewing time as a between-subjects factor. Significant effects were further explored by the Tukey-B test for *post hoc* comparisons (Wike, 1971) utilizing Cicchetti's (1972) modification for interaction tables and Kramer's (1956) modification for unequal samples where appropriate.

The predictor variables were analysed following two strategies. Both used mean-per-scene scores as raw data and scenes as the unit of analysis. The first strategy was to check for mean differences in the predictors across categories. This was accomplished by performing a multivariate analysis of variance (MANOVA) with categories as the independent variable and the six predictors as dependent variables. Significant effects were further explored by the Tukey-B test with Kramer's modification, as described above. The second strategy was to examine correlations between the predictor variables and preference, taking into account the intercorrelations among the predictors. This was accomplished economically by using multiple regression analysis with preference as the criterion variable and the other six rating variables as predictors. Such analyses were carried out for the entire set of 70 scenes and also separately for the scenes within each category where possible. Finally, a regression analysis was performed on only the scenes that fell into the SSA-III categories ($N = 57$). Dummy vectors for the category effect were generated so that the relative influence of categories versus rated predictors could be assessed.

Results

Reliability of measurement
Table 1 presents the Spearman–Brown corrected split-half reliability coefficients for each variable in this study. As is evident, reliability was excellent for the criterion variable, preference, and acceptably high for all of the predictor variables.

Categorization of scenes
As described earlier, non-metric factor analyses (the Guttman–Lingoes Smallest Space Analysis III) were performed on the preference ratings on the 70 scenes in the 15-s condition. Solutions in four to seven dimensions were examined. All yielded four interpretable dimensions. The four-dimensional solution is reported here. It yielded communalities for the 70 scenes ranging from 0·17 to 0·56. For descriptive purposes, dimensional composition was determined by including all scenes with a factor loading greater than 0·40 on a given dimension and no loading greater than 0·35 on any other dimension.

TABLE 1
Spearman–Brown corrected split-half reliability coefficients for each rating variable

Variable	No. of raters	Viewing time (s)	Reliability
Spaciousness	21	15	0.92
Texture	21	15	0.92
Coherence	21	15	0.82
Complexity	21	15	0.93
Mystery	21	15	0.84
Identifiability	22	15	0.79
Preference	85	15	0.99
Preference	26	0.2	0.95
Preference	21	0.02	0.91

The dimension with the greatest number of scenes (23) included two types of waterscapes: mountain lakes and rushing water. The rushing water scenes were primarily of two kinds: waterfalls and rushing mountain streams. In the main, the dimension can be characterized as dealing with water in mountain environments although it did include a few scenes of very swiftly moving rivers in settings not obviously mountainous. This dimension was named *Mountain Waterscapes* (Figure 1, top row).

The second dimension, with 18 scenes, consisted of the following types of settings: stagnant creeks covered with scum or green slime, small streams containing dirty brown water, marshlands, and lakes with prominent swamp features (e.g., reeds) near the shoreline. This dimension was named *Swampy Areas* (Figure 1, second row).

The third dimension contained 11 scenes and was an obvious conglomerate. It included rivers, lakes, and ponds with no outstanding features (mountainous setting, marshlike elements) that would place them in another category. This dimension was simply called *Rivers, Lakes, and Ponds* (Figure 1, third row).

The last dimension consisted of only five scenes. Every one of them was a view of a large body of water such as Lake Michigan, Lake Erie, or Lake Ontario. Parts of the shoreline or, in one case, an island were visible in these scenes, but in every case the body of water extended all the way to the horizon. This dimension was named *Large Bodies of Water* (Figure 1, bottom row).

As a check on the validity of the preceding category interpretations, a group of 18 undergraduate students in a psychology research methods course was provided with the above descriptions. They were shown the 57 scenes in a random order for 15 s each and asked to place each scene into one of the four categories by writing a number from 1 to 4 on a response sheet. Their rates of agreement with the above categorization were as follows: 83, 92, 80 and 97% for Mountain Waterscapes, Swampy Areas, Rivers, Lakes and Ponds, and Large Bodies, respectively.

The prediction of preference

Content and viewing time. Table 2 contains means and standard deviations for the preference category scores described in the Analysis section as a function of waterscape category and viewing time. Marginal means for each variable are also included. Table 3 is a source table for the analysis of variance that was performed on the category scores. As is evident, there was a significant main effect of waterscape

FIGURE 1. Top row: two scenes from the Mountain Waterscapes category. Second row: two scenes from the Swampy Areas category. Third row: two scenes from the Rivers, Lakes, and Ponds category. Bottom row: two scenes from the Large Bodies of Water category.

TABLE 2
Means and standard deviations (in parentheses) of preference ratings as a function of waterscape category and viewing time

	Waterscape category				
Viewing time	Mountain Waterscapes	Swampy Areas	Rivers, Lakes and Ponds	Large Bodies of Water	Mean
15 s	3·99 (0·57)	2·13 (0·60)	3·11 (0·64)	3·28 (0·88)	3·13
200 ms	3·92 (0·52)	2·61 (0·49)	3·24 (0·58)	3·42 (0·65)	3·30
20 ms	3·45 (0·44)	2·66 (0·37)	3·23 (0·46)	3·67 (0·66)	3·25
Mean	3·89	2·31	3·16	3·37	3·18

TABLE 3
Analysis of variance source table for ratings as a function of waterscape category and viewing time

Source	Sum of squares	df	Mean square	F	P
Total	397·53	527			
Between Subjects	102·25	131			
Viewing Time (V)	2·71	2	1·35	1·75	>0·05
Error	99·54	129	0·77		
Within Subjects	295·28	396			
Categories (C)	172·31	3	57·44	202·14	<0·001
V × C	13·00	6	2·17	7·63	<0·001
Error	109·97	387	0·28		

category and a significant interaction of waterscape category and viewing time. The Tukey-B test on the main effect of waterscape category showed that each of the four marginal means differed from each of the others ($P<0.05$). The Tukey-B test on the interaction showed that for the Mountain Waterscapes category, only the 20-ms viewing time differed from each of the other two viewing times ($P<0.05$). For the Swampy Areas category, only the 15-s viewing time differed from each of the other two viewing times ($P<0.05$). No pairwise comparisons were significant for the remaining two waterscape categories.

Predictor variables. Table 4 contains means and standard deviations for each of the six predictor variables as a function of waterscape category. Thus, only the 57 scenes that fell into one of the four waterscape categories are included in this analysis. As indicated in the Analysis section, these statistics are based on mean-per-scene scores as raw data and scenes as the unit of analysis. Tables 5 and 6 summarize the MANOVA that was performed on these data. As shown, the multivariate tests were all significant and so were the univariate tests except for the coherence variable. Tukey-B tests were performed for the other five predictor variables. Only effects at $P<0.05$ are reported. For spaciousness, only the means for Swampy Areas and Large Bodies of Water differed significantly. For texture,

TABLE 4
Means and standard deviations (in parentheses) of rating variables as a function of waterscape category

	Waterscape category			
Variable	Mountain Waterscapes	Swampy Areas	Rivers, Lakes and Ponds	Large Bodies of Water
Spaciousness	3·11	2·45	2·95	4·11
	(1·11)	(0·77)	(0·60)	(0·17)
Texture	2·05	2·69	3·20	3·80
	(0·82)	(0·48)	(0·60)	(0·50)
Coherence	3·38	3·07	3·20	3·66
	(0·59)	(0·44)	(0·62)	(0·47)
Complexity	3·39	3·44	2·87	2·08
	(0·73)	(0·49)	(0·63)	(0·93)
Mystery	3·25	3·24	3·23	2·42
	(0·53)	(0·63)	(0·61)	(0·75)
Identifiability	2·43	2·64	3·40	3·22
	(0·51)	(0·38)	(0·37)	(0·34)

TABLE 5
Multivariate analysis of variance for rating variables as a function of waterscape category.

Test name	Value	F (approx.)	df	P
Pillais	1·31	6·45	18, 150·00	<0·001
Hotelling	3·41	8·85	18, 140·00	<0·001
Wilks	0·14	7·78	18, 136·25	<0·001

TABLE 6
Univariate F-tests (3, 53 df) for rating variables as a function of waterscape category

	Sum of squares		Mean square			
Variable	Effect	Error	Effect	Error	F	P
Spaciousness	11·88	40·83	3·96	0·77	5·14	<0·005
Texture	18·27	23·28	6·09	0·44	13·87	<0·001
Coherence	1·81	15·66	0·60	0·30	2·04	>0·05
Complexity	9·27	23·33	3·09	0·44	7·02	<0·001
Mystery	3·09	18·96	1·03	0·36	2·88	<0·05
Identifiability	8·36	10·09	2·79	0·19	14·63	<0·001

Mountain Waterscapes differed from each of the other three categories, and Swampy Areas differed from Large Bodies of Water. For complexity, Large Bodies of Water differed from Mountain Waterscapes and Swampy Areas. For mystery, Large Bodies of Water differed from each of the other three categories. For identifiability, Mountain Waterscapes and Swampy Areas each differed from the remaining two categories but not from each other.

Table 7 presents intercorrelations among the rating variables of this study. These correlations are based on mean-per-scene scores for all 70 scenes. The preference data are for the 15s condition, the same viewing time used for the predictor variable ratings.

TABLE 7
Intercorrelations among the rating variables for all 70 scenes

	Preference	Spaciousness	Texture	Coherence	Complexity	Mystery	Identifiability
Preference							
Spaciousness	0·42**						
Texture	−0·15	0·42**					
Coherence	0·33**	0·27*	0·24*				
Complexity	0·18	−0·08	−0·54**	−0·30*			
Mystery	0·09	−0·40**	−0·32*	−0·28*	0·52**		
Identifiability	−0·11	0·14	0·33**	0·14	−0·29*	−0·20	

* $P < 0·05$.
** $P < 0·01$.

It is evident that spaciousness and coherence were the only significant predictors of preference. However, 11 of the 15 intercorrelations among the predictor variables were significant, and these relationships need to be taken into account when evaluating the prediction of preference. Hence, a multiple regression analysis was performed with preference as the criterion variable and the remaining variables as predictors. The results are summarized in the first three columns of Table 8. The six predictors accounted for almost half of the variance in preference, and the unique contributions of spaciousness, texture, coherence, and mystery were all significant. In general, waterscapes high in spaciousness, coherence and mystery, but low in texture (that is, featuring coarse or uneven ground surface), were preferred to waterscapes with the opposite characteristics. It was possible to do the same regression analysis separately for the scenes within the Mountain Waterscapes and Swampy Areas categories. The results are summarized in the middle six columns of Table 8. For Mountain Waterscapes, the six predictors accounted for 71% of the preference variance, with coherence and mystery as significant positive predictors of preference and spaciousness as a very nearly significant positive predictor. For Swampy Areas, the predictors accounted for 74% of the preference variance. Coherence was the only significant predictor, with texture and complexity approaching significance. All three were positively related to preference. For the two remaining categories, there were not enough scenes to permit a meaningful regression analysis. It may be noted that none of the simple correlations between preference and predictor variables were significant for these two categories.

TABLE 8

Multiple regression analysis summary results for preference: regression weights (B), F-ratios (F), significance levels (P) and squared multiple correlations (r^2)

Variable	All scenes ($N = 70$)			Mountain Waterscapes ($N = 23$)			Swampy Areas ($N = 18$)			All category scenes ($N = 57$)		
	B	F	P	B	F	P	B	F	P	B	F	P
Spaciousness	0.62	29.52	0.00	0.19	4.31	0.05	0.29	2.67	0.13	0.13	2.56	0.12
Texture	−0.43	11.36	0.00	0.02	0.02	0.89	0.46	3.37	0.09	0.09	0.72	0.40
Coherence	0.54	11.18	0.00	0.36	9.72	0.01	0.51	6.06	0.03	0.37	12.21	0.00
Complexity	−0.11	0.46	0.50	−0.13	0.64	0.44	0.53	4.16	0.07	0.36	9.71	0.00
Mystery	0.49	8.01	0.01	0.78	11.19	0.00	0.04	0.04	0.85	0.13	1.40	0.24
Identifiability	−0.10	0.38	0.54	0.21	1.64	0.22	−0.02	0.01	0.93	0.03	0.05	0.82
Category 1[a]										0.57	4.47	0.04
Category 2										−1.17	19.72	0.00
Category 3										−0.18	0.56	0.46
r^2	0.46			0.71			0.74			0.86		
P	<0.00			10.00<			<0.01			<0.001		

[a] Categories 1–3 refer to the dummy vectors generated to test the waterscape category effect.

Two final sets of analyses attempted to assess the relative contributions of the content categories and the rated predictor variables to preference. These analyses included only the 57 scenes that fell into one of the four content categories. Three dummy vectors representing the degrees of freedom for the category effect were generated. Two regressions were performed. In one, the six rated predictors were entered first as a block of variables followed by the three category vectors as a second block. In the other regression, the opposite order of entry was used. The final results of both analyses were necessarily identical and are summarized in the last three columns of Table 8. Categories and rated predictors together accounted for 86% of the preference variance. Among the predictors, only the unique contributions of coherence and complexity were significant. The unique contributions of the category vectors are of no interest since they represent arbitrary comparisons among the categories. More to the point, when the six rated predictors were entered first, they accounted for 53% of the preference variance ($P<0.001$), similar to what was found in the analysis for all 70 scenes. The content categories then accounted for 33% of additional variance ($P<0.001$). However, when the content categories were entered first, they accounted for 73% of the preference variance ($P<0.001$), with the rated predictors then accounting for an additional 13% of preference variance ($P<0.001$). Thus, whether considered in terms of isolated contribution or additional contribution, the content categories are more potent than the rated variables in predicting preference.

Discussion

Content categories

Since the content category names and descriptions were reasonably well confirmed by the validity check reported earlier, these categories deserve to be taken seriously. It is evident that these categories agree fairly well with the category speculations presented in the introduction. As in other studies, scenes of rushing water appear to form a useful category although in this instance the category also included mountain lakes. Likewise, tainted water, whether it be brown, green or scummy, forms a distinct group. Finally, as in the other studies reviewed earlier, what might be called 'ordinary' rivers and lakes also form a separate group. The one new category consists of large bodies of water. It is not especially surprising that such a category should exist, and probably the reason it has not appeared before is that such scenes simply have not been included in earlier studies. Of course, the categories of any given study depend on the specific scenes and people sampled. Nevertheless, waterscape categories of the kind reported here might well turn out to have rather broad generality inasmuch as they stress such basic perceptual qualities as movement (rushing water vs. stagnant streams) and spaciousness (rivers and lakes vs. large bodies of water).

The prediction of preference

Content. The content categories have a strong impact on preference. The final regression analyses show that the content categories are more potent than the rated predictor variables in accounting for preference. Specifically, mountain lakes and rushing water are the people's choice, whereas swampy areas are unlikely ever to attract an enthusiastic following. The latter result parallels R. Kaplan's (1984) finding for similar environments. These category differences presumably coincide with the intuitions of those professionals who decide which natural areas should be used for recreational purposes. Somewhat more unexpected, perhaps, is the finding that large bodies of water are liked better than rivers, lakes and ponds. The preference advantage for large bodies of water may reflect nothing more than a sand-and-surf mentality among our college-age raters. Alternately, it might have something to do with the outstanding feature of these scenes, their spaciousness. This possibility will be discussed further below.

Predictor variables. Except for coherence, the predictor variables differ on the average across categories and thus help to characterize the categories further. The Tukey-B tests reported earlier suggest the following profiles. Mountain Waterscapes are distinguished by low textures. This correctly indicates that these scenes are seen as not easily navigable. The distinguishing feature of Swampy Areas is their low spaciousness. The most notable average feature of the Rivers, Lakes and Ponds is their relatively high identifiability. The Large Bodies of Water have the most distinguishing features. They are high in spaciousness and texture, low in complexity and mystery. The implications of these profiles for individual category preferences will be discussed shortly. The profiles are presented here because they have some bearing on the regression analysis relating preference to the six rated predictor variables for the entire set of 70 scenes.

Four predictor variables had a significant impact on preference for the complete set of 70 scenes. As indicated by the regression analysis, the most preferred waterscapes are high in spaciousness, coherence and mystery, but low in texture. The category differences noted above can account, at least in part, for this pattern. The most spacious categories, Large Bodies and Mountain Waterscapes, are also the most preferred, while Swampy Areas is lowest on both variables. Thus, the categories form clusters of scenes that tend to anchor the low–low and high–high regions of the preference–spaciousness space, creating a positive relationship between the two variables. A similar trend holds for the coherence and preference means although, admittedly, the coherence means do not differ across categories. An additional factor affecting the overall preference–coherence space is that *within* the two largest categories, coherence also has a strong positive relationship to preference (see Table 8). The negative overall influence of texture is probably a result of the anchoring effect of the Mountain Waterscapes category which is highly preferred but very low in texture. There is nothing in the pattern of category means for mystery to suggest any plausible category anchoring effects in the overall preference–mystery space. It should be noted, however, that *within* the Mountain Waterscapes category, mystery has a very strong positive impact on preference (see Table 8), and this must contribute to its impact on preference for the entire set of 70 scenes.

The Mountain Waterscapes category had a low mean rating for texture. Within the category, three variables were positive predictors of preference: mystery, coherence, and spaciousness (see Table 8). The combination of low texture (that is, uneven terrain) and high preference for this category contradicts the general argument that environments affording locomotion should be liked and those impeding locomotion disliked. However, it should be noted that mountains might be expected to be atypical in this regard. One does not normally expect to navigate through mountains. The regression analysis shows that texture has no predictive power within this category. The fascination for mountains lies elsewhere. Its source is probably cognitive rather than physical. Mountain Waterscapes are fascinating to watch, especially from a distance (the positive influence of spaciousness). The best examples are artistic in the sense that the water and its surrounding elements form a well organized pattern (the positive influence of coherence). At the same time, partial concealment draws one into the scene cognitively and is also valued (the positive influence of mystery).

The low-preference Swampy Areas category was generally low in spaciousness. Coherence and, to a lesser extent, complexity and texture were positive predictors of preference within the category. Besides their unlikeable content, these scenes generally afford one little opportunity for the larger view (low spaciousness) and thus little prospect of finding relief anywhere nearby. Increased complexity in these scenes provides some relief since it typically means that there are other more interesting things to look at than the swampy water. The main concern, however, is with making sense of the environment (coherence) and the opportunity to locomote (texture). In these settings, it is apparently desirable to be able to figure out just where you are and how you could leave quickly.

Regression analysis was not possible within the remaining two categories, and none of the simple correlations between rated predictor variables and preference were significant. The category of Rivers, Lakes and Ponds was noteworthy only for its relatively high identifiability. Even so, the means for all predictor variables were within a half point of the middle of the rating scale, and the mean preference for this category was 3.16 (compared to a grand mean preference of 3.18). These, then, are familiar kinds of waterscapes but are not otherwise memorable in any respect assessed in this study.

The Large Water Bodies category had the most striking profile of mean predictors. This was the lowest of all categories in the involvement variables (complexity and mystery) but highest in the affordances of prospect (spaciousness) and locomotion (very smooth surface textures). Although there were no significant category differences in coherence, it may be noted that Large Water Bodies had the highest mean rating on this making-sense variable. On the surface, it all seems to add up to a category of large, smooth, well-ordered, dull settings. Yet preference was moderately high, second only to Mountain Waterscapes. The key to this puzzle may lie in the extremely high spaciousness ratings of these scenes. The sight of water extending to the horizon may evoke a sense of awe in the presence of vastness which is reflected in the preference ratings. However, vastness is not enough; vast barren wastelands are unlikely to be very well liked. With their orderliness and smooth textures, these scenes may well facilitate a feeling of tranquility that encourages relaxation and meditation. If, as the Kaplans (Kaplan and Kaplan, 1982; S. Kaplan, 1983) suggest, one reason people turn to nature is to rest their fatigued voluntary attention mechanism, then what could be more relaxing than a vast smooth watery surface extending to the horizon? Tranquility is thus seen as playing a mediating role between spaciousness and preference. This speculative suggestion is researchable. One need only add to the present study ratings of tranquility and/or physiological measures like *alpha*-amplitude to assess the implied comparisons between large non-turbulent bodies of water and other waterscapes.

Viewing time. Viewing time interacts with content categories in that preference reactions to the most- and least-liked categories are heightened with increased viewing time. In so far as this bears on the preference–inference debate, it seems to suggest that initial rapid preference reactions are either unaltered or simply heightened by further conscious cognitive deliberation. From the informational perspective, this implies that the initial rapid cognitive analysis is the more important (that is, functional) process, since further opportunity to view and consciously analyse a landscape simply reinforces any initial extreme reactions and does not alter initial moderate reactions. The key difference between the two sides in the preference–inference debate is whether cognition is importantly involved in the initial preference reaction. The informational approach predicts such involvement. A meaningful future step in evaluating this prediction would be to find out whether ratings on the predictor variables with brief viewing times tend to be similarly upheld with extended viewing times. Meanwhile, the viewing time trends reported here should suggest to environmental planners the kinds of waterscapes that may bloom or wither psychologically under extended scrutiny.

Implications

This study yielded several useful insights about preferences for waterscapes and some intriguing suggestions for future research. The results confirm the general usefulness of the informational approach in accounting for waterscape preferences. To the extent that it is possible ultimately to discover the specific physical features relevant to the cognitive processes of making sense and involvement, this approach has the potential to be the merger of psychophysical and cognitive approaches that Daniel and Vining (1983) recommend. The results also point to the utility of the methodology of empirically forming preference categories, examining differences across categories, and looking for relationships within the categories. It is a method that can be used with any environmental domain and has been so used successfully (e.g. Herzog *et al.*, 1976, 1982; Herzog, 1984). Thus, environmental decision-makers who want to understand the perceptions and preferences of their clients might find this method very helpful.

More specifically, the results reported here suggest the following guidelines for planners.

(1) Content matters. In waterscapes, it is evident that clarity and freshness, as embodied in mountain lakes and rushing water, are highly valued. The other side of the coin is that swampy areas, especially stagnant creeks, are not liked. Extended viewing does not reverse these reactions; it heightens them. This may not be surprising, but there is value in verifying commonly held intuitions empirically. These results have an obvious application in urban settings. They suggest that the use of waterfall sculptures and other attempts to introduce rushing water into urban environments are based on sound intuitions.

(2) The most preferred waterscapes are at least moderately high in both making-sense and involvement variables. This result appeared both in the overall regression analysis and in the regression analysis of the most preferred category, Mountain Waterscapes. Similar results have been found for other natural environments (Herzog, 1984). As discussed in the introduction, this pattern of results seems very sensible from an evolutionary perspective. For practical purposes, it suggests that in choosing or designing waterscapes for viewing enjoyment, one would do well to insure that the settings in question are sufficient in both making-sense (legibility, coherence) and involvement (complexity, mystery) features.

(3) Certain general affordances possessed by waterscapes seem to play an important role in their preference. In particular, spaciousness has emerged in this study as positively related to waterscape preference in that the most spacious waterscape categories are also the best liked. Thus, all other things equal, the waterscape that provides a long view or is itself at the end of a long view will probably be preferred.

Acknowledgements

This research was supported in part by National Research Service Award No. 1 F32 MH05938-01 from the National Institute of Mental Health. Part of the work was completed while the author was on sabbatical leave at the Thurstone Psychometric Laboratory of the University of North Carolina at Chapel Hill. I thank my sponsor, Forrest Young, and the entire staff of the Thurstone Laboratory. I also thank Stephen and Rachel Kaplan of the University of Michigan for their continuing support and friendship and James Blakey of Grand Valley State College for photographic assistance.

References

Appleton, J. (1975). *The Experience of Landscape*. London: John Wiley.
Arthur, L. M., Daniel, T. C. and Boster, R. S. (1977). Scenic assessment: an overview. *Landscape Planning*, **4**, 109–129.
Calvin, J. S., Dearinger, J. A. and Curtain, M. E. (1972). An attempt at assessing preferences for natural landscapes. *Environment and Behavior*, **4**, 447–470.
Cicchetti, D. V. (1972). Extension of multiple-range tests to interaction tables in the analysis of variance: a rapid approximate solution. *Psychological Bulletin*, **77**, 405–408.
Daniel, T. C. and Vining, J. (1983). Methodological issues in the assessment of landscape quality. In I. Altman and J. F. Wohlwill (eds), *Behavior and the Natural Environment*, Vol. 6. New York: Plenum, pp. 39–83.

Ellsworth, J. C. (1982). Visual assessment of rivers and marshes: an examination of the relationship of visual units, perceptual variables and preference. Master's Thesis, Utah State University.

Gibson, J. J. (1979). *The Ecological Approach to Visual Perception*. Boston: Houghton Mifflin.

Herzog, T. R. (1984). A cognitive analysis of preference for field-and-forest environments. *Landscape Research*, **9**, 10–16.

Herzog, T. R., Kaplan, S. and Kaplan, R. (1976). The prediction of preference for familiar urban places. *Environment and Behavior*, **8**, 627–645.

Herzog, T. R., Kaplan, S. and Kaplan, R. (1982). The prediction of preference for unfamiliar urban places. *Population and Environment: Behavioral and Social Issues*, **5**, 43–59.

Ittelson, W. H. (1973). Environment perception and contemporary perceptual theory. In W. H. Ittelson (ed.), *Environment and Cognition*. New York: Seminar Press, pp. 1–19.

Kaplan, R. (1977). Down by the riverside: informational factors in waterscape preference. In *River Recreation Management and Research Symposium*. USDA Forest Service General Technical Report NC-28, pp. 285–289.

Kaplan, R. (1984). Wilderness perception and psychological benefits: an analysis of a continuing program. *Leisure Sciences*, **6**, 271–290.

Kaplan, S. (1975). An informal model for the prediction of preference. In E. H. Zube, R. O. Brush and J. G. Fabos (eds), *Landscape Assessment: Values, Perceptions, and Resources*. Stroudsburg, Pennsylvania: Dowden, Hutchinson & Ross, pp. 92–101.

Kaplan, S. (1979). Perception and landscape: conceptions and misconceptions. In *Proceedings of Our National Landscape Conference*. USDA Forest Service General Technical Report PSW-35.

Kaplan, S. (1983). A model of person-environment compatibility. *Environment and Behavior*, **15**, 311–332.

Kaplan, S. and Kaplan, R. (eds) (1978). *Humanscape: Environments for People*. Belmont, California: Duxbury (Division of Wadsworth). (Ann Arbor, Michigan: Ulrichs.)

Kaplan, S. and Kaplan, R. (1982). *Cognition and Environment: Functioning in an Uncertain World*. New York: Praeger Publishers.

Kramer, C. Y. (1956). Extension of multiple range tests to group means with unequal numbers of replications. *Biometrics*, **12**, 307–310.

Lazarus, R. S. (1982). Thoughts on the relations between emotion and cognition. *American Psychologist*, **37**, 1019–1024.

Lee, M. S. (1979). Landscape preference assessment of Louisiana river landscapes: a methodological study. In *Proceedings of Our National Landscape Conference*. USDA Forest Service General Technical Report PSW-35, pp. 572–580.

Levin, J. E. (1976). *Riverscape Preference: On-site and Photographic Reactions*. Master's Thesis, University of Michigan.

Lingoes, J. C. (1972). A general survey of the Guttman-Lingoes nonmetric program series. In R. N. Shepard, A. K. Romney and S. B. Nerlove (eds), *Multidimensional Scaling*, Vol. 1. New York: Seminar Press, pp. 52–68.

Ulrich, R. S. (1981). Natural versus urban scenes: some psychophysiological effects. *Environment and Behavior*, **13**, 523–556.

Ulrich, R. S. (1983). Aesthetic and affective response to natural environment. In I. Altman and J. F. Wohlwill (eds), *Behavior and the Natural Environment*, Vol. 6. New York: Plenum, pp. 85–125.

Wike, E. L. (1971). *Data Analysis*. Chicago: Aldine-Atherton.

Zajonc, R. B. (1980). Feeling and thinking: preferences need no inferences. *American Psychologist*, **35**, 151–175.

Zube, E. H., Sell, J. C. and Taylor, J. G. (1982). Landscape perception: research, application, and theory. *Landscape Planning*, **9**, 1–33.

A COGNITIVE ANALYSIS OF PREFERENCE FOR URBAN NATURE

THOMAS R. HERZOG

Grand Valley State University, Allendale, Michigan 49401, U.S.A.

Abstract

Preferences for urban environments containing prominent natural elements were studied as a function of content categories, viewing time, and nine predictor variables: spaciousness, refuge, coherence, legibility, complexity, mystery, typicality, nature, and age. A nonmetric factor analysis of the preference ratings for the longest viewing time yielded four dimensions: Older Buildings, Concealed Foreground, Tended Nature, and Contemporary Buildings. Tended Nature was best liked, Older Building least liked, and there was very little difference in preference ratings with brief and longer viewing times. Regression analyses revealed three variables as independent positive predictors of preference: coherence, mystery, and nature. Practical and theoretical implications of the results were explored. Overall, the results support the usefulness of the Kaplans' informational model of environmental preference.

The research reported in this paper had two goals. The first was to investigate preferences for urban environments containing prominent natural elements in the form of trees, foliage, and other vegetation. The second goal of the study was to test the usefulness of a theoretical approach to environmental preference known informally as the informational approach and described in detail by the Kaplans (Kaplan and Kaplan, 1978, 1982; S. Kaplan, 1987). The approach fits within what Zube, Sell, and Taylor (1982) called the cognitive paradigm, Daniel and Vining (1983) the psychological model, and Zube (1984) the behavioural viewpoint. The approach will be described below.

Although the literature dealing directly with preferences for urban nature is not extensive, it does emphasize the importance of nature in urban settings. R. Kaplan (1983) provides a review of early studies supporting the following conclusions: (a) natural settings in general are strongly preferred over urban settings; (b) among urban settings, those containing nature are most preferred; (c) so-called 'unmanaged' nature is relatively less preferred than landscaped areas; (d) trees are highly-valued components of urban nature. In addition to these general conclusions, the studies reviewed by Kaplan also point to the importance of certain informational variables to be described below. Recent studies highlighting the influence of nature in urban preference judgments include Im (1984), Hudspeth (1986), and Talbot and Kaplan (1986). In addition, there is a line of research suggesting that urban nature has therapeutic effects (Ulrich, 1984; Heerwagen and Orians, 1986; Verderber, 1986). A similar theme emerged from another set of studies reviewed by R. Kaplan (1983) which emphasized the

---

Reprint requests should be sent to Thomas Herzog, Department of Psychology, Grand Valley State University, Allendale, Michigan 49401.

satisfactions derived by urban residents from activities such as gardening or simply from the knowledge that natural areas are available nearby in the urban environment. Schroeder's (in press) review of research on urban forests reiterates many of these same issues and themes.

As noted above, the present study of preferences for urban nature was guided by the informational approach of the Kaplans. This approach asserts that evolving humans found spatial information processing crucial to survival. Therefore, the analysis of environmental preference should focus on the kinds of settings (or contents) and the kinds of cognitive processes that would be important to such an organism. In addition to the references listed earlier, which provide details of this approach, R. Kaplan (1984) has contributed a helpful discussion of the approach as it applies specifically to urban nature.

The informational approach stresses both content and process. Contents are of two types: general and specific. General contents refer to configurations that determine what one can do in an environment. Thus, they are similar to Gibson's (1979) concept of affordances. Appleton (1975, 1984) suggested two very important affordances, refuge and prospect [1]. Refuge refers to potential hiding places in an environment, prospect to vantage points from which one can see unhindered into the distance. Woodcock's (1982) empirical investigation of primary and secondary versions of these affordances showed that primary prospect (the view from a vantage point like that described above) was positively related to preference. The other predictors based on Appleton's theory fared less well; in fact, primary refuge (the view from within a hiding place) was negatively related to preference.

The present study investigated two affordances, refuge and spaciousness. Refuge was defined as how much the setting provides the opportunity for being hidden and thus seems closer to Woodcock's secondary refuge (seeing a potential hiding place) than his primary refuge. Spaciousness was defined as the feeling of depth conveyed by a setting, the feeling that one would have to go a long way to reach its farthest point. Spaciousness thus defined can be seen as a stand-in for primary prospect. Spaciousness plays a dual role in the informational approach since it also depends on how well-organized a setting is in depth. Such organization contributes to the overall understanding of an environment, a process discussed below. In any event, the expectation was that refuge and spaciousness would be positively related to preference.

Specific contents, in contrast, refer to what S. Kaplan (1987) calls 'primary landscape qualities', certain particular contents that seem to have a special effect on preference, perhaps the result of fairly specific evolutionary biases. Candidates include water, foliage, and trees. In the context of urban nature, the general question raised by the possibility of specific salient contents is whether the category can be subdivided meaningfully. This question can be answered by using empirical procedures, described below, to form categories based on preference ratings, and then considering whether the categories make sense, both intuitively and in the further empirical analysis of preference. Past studies of urban preference (Herzog, Kaplan, and Kaplan, 1976, 1982) strongly suggest that one basis for forming urban categories will be the age of built structures in the settings. It is also possible, as S. Kaplan (1979) suggests, that some categories may be based on the spatial configuration of natural elements.

The informational approach proposes that two general cognitive processes are involved in environmental preference, understanding and exploration (S. Kaplan, 1987). Understanding refers to comprehending or making sense of an environment, exploration to having one's interest aroused and held by the environment while being attracted toward sources of additional information. Both processes have survival value, and thus environments that engage both should be preferred. Variables promoting understanding include the degree of order or organization in the immediate setting (coherence) and the apparent ease of wayfinding in the larger environment that includes the immediate setting (legibility). (Spaciousness, as defined above, could be considered one component of legibility, and thus contribute to understanding the environment.) Exploration would be promoted by the richness or diversity of the immediate setting (complexity) and by the promise of new information if one could travel deeper into the environment (mystery). The empirical utility of mystery and coherence has been demonstrated many times (Herzog, 1984, 1985, 1987; Herzog, Kaplan, and Kaplan, 1976, 1982; S. Kaplan, 1987; Herzog and Smith, 1988), but the other two variables have received less consistent empirical support, perhaps because of difficulties in defining them clearly to raters. In the present study, all four variables were investigated.

A variable that cuts across both the understanding and exploration processes is the resemblance of the current setting to environments the observer knows well. This 'sense of familiarity' should aid understanding but, if overdone, may detract from exploration. Under the name 'identifiability', this variable has been a generally positive predictor of preference in several studies (Herzog, Kaplan, and Kaplan, 1982; Herzog, 1984, 1987). Recently, Purcell (1986) found a very similar variable, ratings of 'how good an example of a category' a given setting was, useful in accounting for preferences for churches. In the present study, Purcell's definition was used, and the variable was called typicality.

Two more rated predictor variables were included in the study primarily because past research (Herzog, Kaplan, and Kaplan, 1976, 1982) had emphasized their importance. The first was the amount of foliage or vegetation in a setting (nature). This variable was also included because it qualifies as one of S. Kaplan's (1987) 'primary landscape qualities' and because it could serve as a check on how sensitive participants were to the amount of nature in urban settings. Second, the age of the 'elements' in each setting was assessed (age). If age is a basis for category formation, ratings of age would provide supportive evidence for such an interpretation. In addition, it seemed possible that age might be directly related to preference, regardless of category effects. Finally, inclusion of age in the set of predictor variables should shed light on the circumstances under which age might be related to higher or lower preference reactions. Thus, aside from their theoretical interest, the results for age could have practical implications in guiding strategies for preserving older structures.

A final variable investigated was viewing time. Preference reactions were assessed with a very brief viewing time (100 ms) and an extended viewing time (15 s). There are both empirical and theoretical grounds for expecting an effect of viewing time on preference. Empirically, viewing-time effects have been found repeatedly in past research on environmental preference (R. Kaplan, 1975; Herzog, Kaplan, and Kaplan, 1982; Herzog, 1984, 1985, 1987). Theoretically, such effects make sense if one assumes that with very brief viewing times the quality of the sensory data is sometimes limited, leading to what information-processing theorists call data-limited processing. In such instances, extended viewing time could very well yield a difference in preference. The nature of the difference would depend on which information is successfully processed from the brief glimpse of the scene. For example, if the brief glimpse picks up features suggesting that safety may be an issue, then extended viewing time might yield reassurance and a higher preference rating. On the other hand, if information that would normally evoke safety concerns is missed in the brief glimpse, then extended viewing would probably reveal it and lead to a lower preference rating. Thus, there are theoretical grounds for expecting a variety of viewing-time effects and, in some instances, no effect. Therefore, it is worthwhile to investigate viewing time.

In summary, the major objective of the study was to investigate preferences for urban nature in the context of the Kaplans' informational model of environmental preference. To do so required an assessment of content and process as predictors of preference. A methodological issue should be noted. Colour slides were used as surrogates for actual environments. Although some researchers seem dogmatically opposed to this approach, a thorough review of landscape simulation research by Zube, Simcox, and Law (1987) gave it a strong endorsement on grounds of reliability and validity.

Method

Participants
The sample consisted of 354 undergraduate students, 236 females and 118 males, at Grand Valley State University. The students received extra course credit for participation. Twenty-seven sessions of from 5 to 21 participants were conducted.

Stimuli
The settings consisted of 70 colour slides of urban environments containing prominent natural components. An attempt was made to sample a variety of natural elements (trees, shrubs, flowers, weeds, grass) ranging in condition from well-tended to completely neglected. No settings contained water or other prominent non-vegetation natural elements. No settings contained people since they have been found to be powerful distractors (Herzog, Kaplan, and Kaplan, 1976). Since age of buildings has been shown to affect preference reactions (Herzog, Kaplan, and Kaplan, 1976, 1982), settings contained structures ranging in age from very new to relatively older. All settings were drawn from the western half of Michigan's lower peninsula, the vast majority from the city of Grand Rapids and its suburbs.

Procedure
Participants rated each of the 70 settings on one of ten variables. All ratings used a 5-point scale ranging from 1 = 'not at all' to 5 = 'a great deal'. There were nine predictor variables. *Spaciousness* was defined as 'the feeling of spaciousness or depth the scene conveys, how much room there is to wander into it. To what extent does the structure of the scene suggest that one would have to go a long way to each its farthest point?' *Refuge* was 'the opportunity for being hidden, the chance to see without being seen'. *Coherence* was 'how well the scene "hangs together". How easy is it to organize and structure the scene?' *Legibility* was 'how easy it would be to find your way around in the environment depicted ... to figure out where you are at any given moment or to find your way back to any given point in the environment'. *Complexity* was 'how much is going on in the scene, how much there is to look at', how much 'the scene contains a lot of elements of different kinds'. *Mystery* was present when a setting 'promises more to be seen if you could walk deeper into it'. *Typicality* referred to the 'extent the scene seems

to be a representative example of its class. How good an example is the scene of whatever category it belongs to?' *Nature* was 'how much foliage or vegetation there is in the scene'. *Age* was 'how old the elements in the scene seem to be'. The criterion variable was *preference*, defined as 'how much you like the scene, for whatever reason'.

Sessions proceeded as follows. First, five sample slides were rated to help participants get used to the task and the rating scale. Then participants rated 80 slides, presented in two sets of 40 each, with a brief intermission between sets. In both sets, the first three and the last two slides were considered filler slides. The remaining 70 slides from both sets yielded the data for analysis. These 70 slides were presented in three different orders, with each order used for nine of the twenty-seven sessions. Each order of slide presentation was used in one-third of the sessions in which each variable was rated. One of the orders of slide presentation was generated randomly. The second presentation order was the reverse of the first order, and the third presentation order was devised by interchanging the halves of the first order.

Eighteen of the sessions were devoted to the predictor variables. In such sessions, three predictor variables were rated simultaneously, with each participant rating for only one variable and approximately one-third of the group rating each variable. For each order of slide presentation, three sets of three predictors were chosen randomly without replacement from the pool of nine predictor variables. Each such set of three predictors was used in two sessions with its designated order of slide presentation. Viewing time was 15 s for each slide. Final sample sizes were 29 each for spaciousness, mystery, and age, 28 for nature, 27 each for complexity and typicality, and 25 each for refuge, coherence, and legibility.

Nine sessions were devoted solely to the criterion variable, preference. Viewing time was 15 s for six of these sessions and 100 ms for the other three. One-third of the sessions for each viewing time used each order of slide presentation. The brief viewing time was achieved by using an electronic shutter mounted in front of the projector lens. Final sample sizes were 76 and 34 for the 15-s and 100-ms viewing times, respectively. The larger sample for the 15-s viewing time was necessary as a basis for the factor analysis described below.

Analysis

To evaluate reliability of measurement for each variable, final samples were divided into half samples, and mean ratings for each setting were computed based on each half sample. The two sets of 70 mean-per-setting scores were then intercorrelated for each variable. The resultant correlations were corrected by the Spearman-Brown formula to yield split-half reliability coefficients for each variable.

To discover the content categories embodied in the participants' preference reactions, the preference ratings from the 15-s condition were analysed by nonmetric factor analysis, specifically the Guttman-Lingoes Smallest Space Analysis III (SSA–III) (Lingoes, 1972). SSA–III is a nonmetric version of principal-axes factor analysis. It uses squared multiple correlations in the diagonal of the input correlation matrix and a varimax rotation of the final solution. The procedure finds a solution of the user-specified dimensionality that best fits the rank order of the original correlation matrix rather than the more stringent linear transformation of the original correlations required by metric factor analysis. Proponents of nonmetric analysis argue that more stable solutions in fewer dimensions can be found. For descriptive purposes, dimensional composition was determined by including all settings with a factor loading greater than |0·40| on one dimension only. With this criterion, for each dimension containing enough settings to provide a basis for interpretation, all factor loadings for included settings had the same sign. Hence, such dimensions may be treated as clusters or categories of similar settings.

To evaluate the effects of content categories and viewing time, two types of scores were computed as raw data for analysis. The first, a category score, was simply the mean rating for all settings comprising a category. Thus, for each rating variable, every participant had a category score for each of the environmental categories resulting from the nonmetric factor analysis. The second type of score was a setting score, the mean for each setting based on all participants who rated each variable. Thus, for each rating variable, every setting had a setting score. Two analyses of variance were carried out for each ratings variable. The first used category scores as the dependent variable, and the second used setting scores. The first analysis allows conclusions to be generalized to the population of participants, the second analysis to the population of settings. For both analyses, the independent variable was environmental category. For preference ratings only, a second independent variable was viewing time. Significant effects were explored further by the Tukey-B test (Wike, 1971), with Cicchetti's (1972) modification for interaction tables and Kramer's (1956) modification for unequal samples where appropriate. For all tests of inference, only effects with $P < 0.05$ in both category-score and setting-score analyses were considered statistically significant. In addition, for setting scores, a multivariate analysis of variance was performed on all nine predictor variables as a set. The multivariate test statistics provide further protection against Type I errors. Such an analysis was not possible for category scores.

Two kinds of additional analyses were carried out on the setting scores. First, to understand better how the variables of the study worked together, two multiple regression analyses were performed with preference (15-s viewing time) as the criterion variable. The first analysis included all 70 settings, and the other nine rated variables served as predictors. A second stepwise multiple regression included only the 37 settings in the environmental categories. The nine rated predictors were entered first as a block of variables followed by a set of dummy vectors representing the degrees of freedom for environmental categories. Second, prediction of preference (15-s viewing time) within each of the environmental categories was assessed by examining the simple correlations between the rated predictor variables and preference and also the simple correlations among the rated predictor variables. This approach was necessary because of the limited number of settings per category, which meant that multiple-regression analysis was not feasible within categories.

Results

Reliability of measurement
The Spearman-Brown reliability coefficients for the rating variables ranged from 0·77 for typicality to 0·98 for both preference (15-s viewing time) and nature. All exceeded 0·90 except for complexity (0·88), mystery (0·78), and typicality (0·77). The minimum acceptable reliability for basic research suggested by Guilford (1954) and Nunnally (1967) is 0·50. Thus, reliability of measurement exceeded conventional standards.

Environmental categories
Nonmetric factor analysis (Smallest Space Analysis III) of the 15-s preference ratings yielded four interpretable dimensions. The six-dimensional solution is reported here. It

TABLE 1
Means and standard deviations (in parentheses, for category scores, left, and settings scores, right) as a function of environmental category for each rated predictor variable

Variable	Environmental category			
	Older buildings	Concealed foreground	Tended nature	Contemporary buildings
Spaciousness	2·03	2·45	3·05	2·61
	(0·42, 0·51)	(0·47, 0·49)	(0·48, 0·63)	(0·45, 0·77)
Refuge	3·58	2·97	2·54	2·26
	(0·48, 0·72)	(0·51, 0·58)	(0·51, 0·49)	(0·57, 0·61)
Coherence	1·84	2·82	3·63	3·23
	(0·58, 0·30)	(0·52, 0·53)	(0·42, 0·46)	(0·50, 0·59)
Legibility	1·99	2·64	3·30	3·30
	(0·65, 0·27)	(0·58, 0·50)	(0·49, 0·29)	(0·60, 0·31)
Complexity	2·32	2·66	2·83	3·00
	(0·65, 0·44)	(0·73, 0·49)	(0·59, 0·54)	(0·60, 0·37)
Mystery	2·89	3·40	3·31	2·67
	(0·83, 0·36)	(0·64, 0·24)	(0·61, 0·37)	(0·59, 0·40)
Typicality	3·17	3·01	3·25	3·29
	(0·78, 0·50)	(0·57, 0·49)	(0·55, 0·31)	(0·59, 0·45)
Nature	3·22	3·79	3·74	2·59
	(0·54, 0·60)	(0·47, 0·71)	(0·49, 0·46)	(0·35, 0·51)
Age	4·10	3·21	2·90	2·60
	(0·87, 0·27)	(0·49, 0·74)	(0·49, 0·83)	(0·59, 0·50)

yielded communalities ranging from 0·15 to 0·63. The criterion for dimensional composition was discussed in the Analysis section.

The dimension or category with the greatest number of settings (12) consisted of older buildings and was named *Older Buildings*. A second category (10 settings) was characterized by prominent (though not complete) foreground concealment involving natural elements (trees, hedges, foliage). It was named *Concealed Foreground*. The third category (8 settings) consisted of carefully tended or cultivated natural elements usually accompanied by relatively contemporary buildings. The distinguishing feature of this group was carefully arranged flower plots, well-trimmed hedges, or other noticeably manicured natural elements. The category was named *Tended Nature*. The last category (7 settings) consisted of contemporary buildings accompanied by nature that varied greatly in its perceived degree of care or cultivation. It was named *Contemporary Buildings*.

One way to differentiate the categories empirically is to examine differences across categories in the mean ratings on predictor variables. Table 1 contains means and standard deviations for all nine predictor variables as a function of environmental category. Results for both category and setting scores are included. The means are the same for either type of score. Table 2 presents analysis of variance summaries for the category effect based on both types of scores. As mentioned in the Analysis section, it was possible to perform a multivariate analysis of variance on all of the predictors in the case of setting scores. All of the multivariate test statistics (Pillai, Hotelling, Wilks) for the effect of environmental category were significant at $P < 0.001$. As Table 2 indicates, the univariate tests of the category effect were significant for all of the predictor variables except typicality.

FIGURE 1. Scene from the Older Buildings category.

The following is a brief summary of post-hoc tests, indicating significant ($P < 0.05$) pairwise differences among means for both category and setting scores. Tended Nature was higher in spaciousness than Older Buildings. On the other hand, Older Buildings exceeded both Tended Nature and Contemporary Buildings in refuge. Tended Nature exceeded both Concealed Foreground and Older Buildings in coherence, and Concealed Foreground was higher than Older Buildings. Both Contemporary

FIGURE 2. Scene from the Concealed Foreground category.

FIGURE 3. Scene from the Tended Nature category.

Buildings and Tended Nature exceeded the remaining two categories in legibility, and Concealed Foreground was higher than Older Buildings. Contemporary Buildings exceeded Older Buildings in complexity. Both Concealed Foreground and Tended Nature exceeded the other two categories in mystery, and both exceeded Contemporary Buildings in nature. Finally, Older Buildings exceeded all other categories in age.

FIGURE 4. Scene from the Contemporary Buildings category.

74   T. R. Herzog

TABLE 2
Analysis of variance summaries for each predictor variable as a function of environmental category

	Category scores			Setting scores		
	F	df	p	F	df	p
Spaciousness	76·12	3,84	0·000	5·00	3,33	0·006
Refuge	54·59	3,72	0·000	8·19	3,33	0·000
Coherence	77·16	3,72	0·000	27·67	3,33	0·000
Legibility	48·57	3,72	0·000	30·03	3,33	0·000
Complexity	9·39	3,78	0·000	3·77	3,33	0·020
Mystery	11·30	3,84	0·000	8·83	3,33	0·000
Typicality	1·56	3,78	0·205	0·66	3,33	0·583
Nature	116·76	3,81	0·000	7·08	3,33	0·001
Age	42·37	3,84	0·000	11·36	3,33	0·000

The prediction of preference

Categories and viewing time. Table 3 contains preference means and standard deviations, for both category and setting scores, as a function of environmental category and viewing time. The cell means are the same for either type of score. The table also contains analysis of variance summaries for both types of scores. As is evident, both main effects and the interaction were statistically significant. Post-hoc tests were carried out as described in the Analysis section. For the main effect of environmental category, Tended Nature was rated highest in preference, Older

TABLE 3
Means (top row), standard deviations (for category scores, middle row, and setting scores, bottom row), and analysis of variance summaries for preference scores as a function of environmental category and viewing time

	Environmental category				Mean	
Viewing time	Older buildings	Concealed foreground	Tended nature	Contemporary buildings	Category scores	Setting scores
15 s	1·53 0·46 0·36	2·83 0·64 0·58	3·58 0·54 0·41	2·64 0·57 0·57	2·64	2·53
100 ms	2·05 0·58 0·45	3·23 0·55 0·35	3·46 0·49 0·52	2·86 0·58 0·56	2·90	2·83
Mean: Category scores Setting scores	1·69 1·79	2·95 3·03	3·54 3·52	2·71 2·75		

	Category scores			Setting scores		
	F	df	p	F	df	p
Category (C)	224·23	3,324	0·000	30·34	3,33	0·000
Viewing Time (V)	10·77	1,108	0·001	13·38	1,33	0·001
C × V	8·30	3,324	0·000	4·18	3,33	0·013

Buildings lowest, and Concealed Foreground and Contemporary Buildings did not differ from each other. The significant interaction was characterized by a somewhat different pattern of category differences for brief and extended viewing times. At 15-s viewing time, the pattern of category differences duplicated the pattern for the main effect of environmental category. However, at 100-ms viewing time, only Older Buildings were rated lower than the remaining categories. A different, perhaps clearer, perspective on the interaction can be obtained by examining viewing-time differences within each category. The preference advantage for the 100-ms viewing time held only for Older Buildings and Concealed Foreground.

Predictor variables. Table 4 presents intercorrelations among the rated variables based on setting scores for all 70 settings. All of the predictor variables except typicality were significantly correlated with preference. However, 21 of the 36 intercorrelations among predictor variables were also significant. The results of the multiple regression analyses, which take correlations among predictors into account, are presented in Table 5. In the analysis of all 70 settings (left third of Table 5), the nine rated predictors accounted for 87% of the preference variance, with significant contributions from coherence, mystery, and nature. Settings high in these variables were most preferred. In the analysis of the 37 category settings, summarized in the rest of the table, two points are noteworthy. First, when only the rated predictors were entered into the analysis (middle third of Table 5), the results duplicated those of the preceding analysis. Second, when environmental categories were added as predictors (right third of Table 5), there was virtually no improvement in prediction (increase in preference variance accounted for of 0.01, $P > 0.05$), and the same three rated predictors continued to play the most powerful roles although nature was only marginally significant ($P = 0.06$).

Since there were not enough settings for multiple regression analysis within each environmental category, simple correlations were examined. Only correlations significant at $P < 0.05$ are reported. Coherence was positively correlated with preference in all four environmental categories ($r = 0.59, 0.79, 0.86$, and 0.93 for Older Buildings, Concealed Foreground, Tended Nature, and Contemporary Buildings, respectively). The pattern of positive correlations with preference in all categories also held for mystery and nature, but in each case the correlations were significant only for Concealed Foreground (0.70 and 0.80 for mystery and nature, respectively) and Contemporary Buildings (0.96 and 0.89, respectively). The only other significant

TABLE 4
Intercorrelations among the rating variables for all 70 settings

	Spa	Ref	Coh	Leg	Com	Mys	Typ	Nat	Age
Preference (15 s)	0.46	−0.29	0.83	0.58	0.32	0.49	−0.02	0.49	−0.57
Spaciousness		−0.33	0.55	0.65	0.57	0.19	0.44	0.08	−0.28
Refuge			−0.45	−0.66	−0.28	0.16	−0.03	0.34	0.53
Coherence				0.77	0.40	0.21	0.16	0.19	−0.71
Legibility					0.63	−0.04	0.34	−0.10	−0.63
Complexity						0.13	0.37	−0.18	−0.26
Mystery							−0.18	0.45	−0.04
Typicality								−0.26	0.00
Nature									0.07

Note: Column abbreviations are Spaciousness, Refuge, Coherence, Legibility, Complexity, Mystery, Typicality, Nature, and Age. For $|r| > 0.23$, $P < 0.05$; for $|r| > 0.30$, $P < 0.01$.

TABLE 5
Multiple regression analysis summary results: regression weights (B), partial correlations (r_p), F-ratios (F), significance levels (p), and squared multiple correlations (R^2)

Variable	All settings (N = 70)				All category settings (N = 37)							
	B	r_p	F	p	B	r_p	F	p	B	r_p	F	p
Spac	−0·08	−0·13	1·07	0·30	−0·08	−0·16	0·69	0·41	−0·04	−0·09	0·20	0·66
Refu	−0·09	−0·14	1·27	0·26	−0·07	−0·14	0·54	0·47	−0·01	−0·01	0·00	0·95
Cohe	0·62	0·60	34·39	0·00	0·68	0·75	35·51	0·00	0·56	0·65	17·42	0·00
Legi	0·11	0·09	0·51	0·48	0·29	0·27	2·08	0·16	0·24	0·24	1·41	0·25
Comp	0·10	0·13	1·11	0·30	0·05	0·07	0·13	0·72	0·03	0·05	0·06	0·81
Myst	0·46	0·45	15·34	0·00	0·45	0·51	9·63	0·00	0·40	0·46	6·28	0·02
Typi	−0·02	−0·02	0·03	0·86	−0·17	−0·26	1·91	0·18	−0·16	−0·24	1·52	0·23
Natu	0·39	0·55	25·98	0·00	0·24	0·44	6·64	0·02	0·21	0·38	3·95	0·06
Age	−0·08	−0·14	1·21	0·28	−0·00	−0·00	0·00	0·98	−0·00	−0·01	0·00	0·97
Cat1									−0·25	−0·31	2·47	0·13
Cat2									0·00	0·00	0·00	0·99
Cat3									0·24	0·41	4·95	0·04
R^2		0·87				0·95				0·96		
p		0·00				0·00				0·00		

Note: Variable abbreviations are Spaciousness, Refuge, Coherence, Legibility, Complexity, Mystery, Typicality, Nature, and Age. Cat1–Cat3 refer to the dummy vectors generated to test the Environmental Category effect. The criterion variable is Preference (15 s viewing time).

correlations with preference involved Older Buildings (0·76 with complexity), and Contemporary Buildings (−0·77 with age). These simple correlations with preference should be treated with caution because there were several significant correlations among predictor variables [2].

Discussion

Environmental categories
Two of the categories obtained in this study appear to be based primarily on the age of the buildings depicted (Older Buildings and Contemporary Buildings). In contrast, the other two categories appear to be based primarily on spatial configuration. For Concealed Foreground, the emphasis is on partial concealment in the foreground, which should enhance mystery. Tended Nature focuses on neatness and order in the configuration of natural elements, which should enhance coherence. As characterized, these two categories bear some resemblance to S. Kaplan's (1979) categories of enclosed spaces and open, well-defined spaces, respectively. These may not be the most important distinctions among the categories, but they are the most noticeable. They also correspond fairly closely to the speculations about bases for categories offered in the introduction.

The mean ratings on the predictor variables permit a more empirical approach to the issue of validity of category interpretation. The age-based categories should be at opposite ends of the rank ordering of categories for age. As Table 1 indicates, they were. Likewise, Tended Nature had the highest mean rating for coherence, and Concealed Foreground was relatively high in mystery. These results are consistent with the proposed category interpretations. Finally, note that the categories were not perceived as equal in nature content. The two configurational categories, where natural elements were the primary focus for categorization, were rated highest in nature. The two age-based categories, where the focus was on buildings, were rated lowest in nature.

One problem with the above scenario is that although Concealed Foreground was relatively high in mystery, as demanded by the interpretation offered, so was Tended Nature. Therefore, mystery does not distinguish between the two categories. This problem may be more apparent than real. Mystery has several different components which have been explored empirically (Gimblett, Itami, and Fitzgibbon, 1985). The proposed interpretation for Concealed Foreground focuses on one component of mystery, foreground screening, which should yield fairly high mystery ratings for the category. It does not follow that another category cannot also be fairly high in mystery. In fact, the scenes in Tended Nature have a number of mystery components including screening (but not as prominent as in the Concealed Foreground category), interposition, and visual access via pathways. The point is that foreground screening appears to be the most noticeable characteristic of the Concealed Foreground category, whereas orderliness and tendedness are most noticeable in the Tended Nature scenes. In the final analysis, it is wise to acknowledge that category names are convenient labels for tentative interpretations. The appropriateness of such interpretations is always subject to further empirical testing.

The prediction of preference

Viewing time. There was a slight advantage in preference ratings for the brief viewing time, but it held for only two of the categories, Older Buildings and Concealed Foreground. This may mean that certain details of those settings were missed in the brief glimpse but seen with extended viewing time, and those details depressed preference. For Older Buildings, information about the surrounding neighbourhood might well lead to safety concerns. For Concealed Foreground, extended viewing might lead to a greater awareness of these settings as hiding places for muggers. For Tended Nature and Contemporary Buildings, there is little reason to think that extended viewing would raise safety concerns. This interpretation is highly speculative and should be taken as a proffered hypothesis to be verified by further research.

Categories. It is abundantly clear from the analyses of variance summarized in Table 3 that the categories make a difference in preference reactions. Tended Nature was most preferred, in agreement with R. Kaplan's (1983) review of the literature on urban nature preference. Least liked by far was the category of Older Buildings. It is very important to zero in on the reasons for the dislike of the Older Buildings category. Is it simply a matter of age, or are other factors involved? The answer matters because it would affect the kind of practical advice offered to urban planners and because it bears on theories of environmental preference. It is worth noting that older-building categories have fared differently in past research. The category was among the least liked in Herzog, Kaplan, and Kaplan's first study (1976), but not in their subsequent study (1982). Thus, age alone may not be the determining factor.

Predictor variables. The regression analyses show that (a) among the rated predictors, only coherence, mystery, and nature had power to predict preference independently from all other variables, and (b) the categories added nothing to the predictive power possessed by these three variables. Thus, it is not surprising that the rank order of the categories for mean preference (Table 3) can be predicted by examining the means for just three of the predictor variables: coherence, mystery, and nature (Table 1). Tended Nature, the most-preferred category, has high ratings on all three predictors. Concealed Foreground, next most preferred, has high ratings on two of these predictors, mystery and nature. The third most-preferred category, Contemporary Buildings, has a high rating only on coherence and low ratings on mystery and nature. Older Buildings, least liked, is high in none of these predictors but is relatively low in mystery and very low in coherence. Clearly, these three predictors do a very good job in accounting for preference differences across categories.

Two consequences of these results follow immediately. First, note that age is conspicuously absent from the set of effective preference predictors. It is somewhat paradoxical that the Older Buildings are clearly low in preference (Table 3), their age is clearly noticed (Table 1), and yet age does not predict preference (Table 5). In this study, the reason seems to be that age is strongly correlated (negatively) with coherence (Table 4), and coherence is the dominant predictor. This makes some sense. A problem with many older buildings is that they are unkempt and their grounds are both unkempt and disorderly. As far as preference is concerned, the culprit is not age but upkeep and orderliness. This proposal offers interesting possibilities for further research on preferences for older buildings. Meanwhile, it seems likely that age alone need not be a drawback to preference.

The second consequence of the regression results is theoretical. Note that of the three effective predictors, one is, in the language of the informational model, a primary landscape variable (nature), one is an understanding variable (coherence), and one is an exploration variable (mystery). Thus, several components of the model received empirical support, and the general usefulness of the model is nicely illustrated.

It should be noted that although the categories added nothing to the predictive power already possessed by the three effective predictors, the reverse was not true. Coherence, mystery, and nature predicted preference independently of category differences. In other words, these three predictors were consistently and positively related to preference within categories as well as across categories. The analysis of simple correlations within categories led to the same conclusion. The power of these three predictors within categories lends further support to their importance in accounting for preference.

The fact that the categories did not predict preference apart from the rated predictors in no way diminishes the importance of the categories. The present finding is exceptional. In most past research on preference where this issue has been assessed, categories did predict preference independently of rated predictors (Herzog, 1985, 1987; Herzog and Smith, 1988). More importantly, even when categories do not predict preference, they provide valuable insights into how the environmental settings are perceived and grouped by observers.

What about the six predictor variables that were ineffective in accounting for preference? One, typicality, stands alone. Not only was it uncorrelated with preference in any of the analyses, but it had only moderate correlations with a few of the other predictors (Table 4). Apparently typicality worked for Purcell (1986) because all his settings came from one category explicitly identified by the researcher. When settings come from several unspecified categories, subjects may be overwhelmed by the task of judging how good a category exemplar a specific setting is. It would probably be advisable to revert to the 'sense of familiarity' approach which, as noted in the introduction, has worked well in the past. The other five ineffective predictors appear to be part of a six-variable cluster dominated by coherence [3]. The network of strong correlations among these variables can easily be traced from Table 4. Coherence dominates the cluster in that none of the other variables was able to predict preference independently from coherence. For the informational approach, there is some good news here, but mostly bad news. The good news is that spaciousness was strongly related to legibility, as anticipated. The bad news is that in predicting preference, legibility could not be distinguished from coherence, and neither could complexity. The latter is supposed to be an exploration variable, not part of an understanding cluster. The generality of these findings about relationships among rated predictors is open to question. Still, as noted in the introduction, coherence and mystery have been the most successful predictors of preference in past research. Thus, the informational approach might benefit from improved definitions of its other two predictors, complexity and legibility. Finally, note that the independent status of refuge as an affordance was not confirmed in this study.

Two potential problems with the regression analyses should be mentioned. The first is the strong correlations among some of the rated predictors. In regression analysis, this is known as multicollinearity. When it exists, the replicability of regression coefficients for the predictors involved is called into question. This may be a problem for the cluster of predictors dominated by coherence. On the other hand, the primacy of coherence in this study is compatible with past research, as noted above. A related problem is the ratio of predictor variables to cases. In the last step of the stepwise regression, there were 12 predictors and only 37 cases (or scenes), clearly a less than ideal ratio. Although this problem also suggests caution in reaching conclusions, it is noteworthy that the set of effective predictors remained stable across all regression analyses.

In conclusion, this study has shown that preferences for urban settings with prominent natural components can be studied profitably from the informational perspective. The results have both practical and theoretical implications. Practically, the importance of age as an organizing principle for perception in urban settings has once again been emphasized. In addition, the results provide several suggestions about how to offset negative features of older urban settings. In particular, planners may wish to concentrate their efforts on manipulating three variables: coherence, mystery, and nature. Theoretically, the results point to the importance of primary landscape qualities and the cognitive processes of understanding and exploration in accounting for urban preferences. Many intriguing and researchable questions remain unanswered. Two examples: Does age ever have an effect on urban preference apart from its typically negative relationship with coherence? How can one distinguish empirically between properties of the immediate setting, like coherence, and those of the larger environment that contains the immediate setting, like legibility? Answers to questions like these will deepen our understanding of urban preferences and will contribute to the further development of a comprehensive cognitive theory to explain them.

References

Appleton, J. (1975). *The Experience of Landscape*. London: John Wiley.
Appleton, J. (1984). Prospect and refuge re-visited. *Landscape Journal*, **3**, 91–103.
Cicchetti, D. V. (1972). Extension of multiple-range tests to interaction tables in the analysis of variance: a rapid approximate solution. *Psychological Bulletin*, **77**, 405–408.

Daniel, T. C. and Vining, J. (1983). Methodological issues in the assessment of landscape quality. In I. Altman and J. F. Wohlwill (eds), *Behavior and the Natural Environment*, New York: Plenum, pp. 39–83.

Gibson, J. J. (1979). *The Ecological Approach to Visual Perception*. Boston: Houghton Mifflin.

Gimblett, H. R., Itami, R. M. and Fitzgibbon, J. E. (1985). Mystery in an information processing model of landscape preference. *Landscape Journal*, **4**, 87–95.

Guilford, J. P. (1954). *Psychometric Methods* (2nd ed.). New York: McGraw-Hill.

Heerwagen, J. H. and Orians, G. H. (1986). Adaptations to windowlessness: a study of the use of visual decor in windowed and windowless offices. *Environment and Behavior*, **18**, 623–639.

Herzog, T. R. (1984). A cognitive analysis of preference for field-and-forest environments. *Landscape Research*, **9**, 10–16.

Herzog, T. R. (1985). A cognitive analysis of preference for waterscapes. *Journal of Environmental Psychology*, **5**, 225–241.

Herzog, T. R. (1987). A cognitive analysis of preference for natural environments: Mountains, canyons, deserts. *Landscape Journal*, **6**, 140–152.

Herzog, T. R., Kaplan, S. and Kaplan, R. (1976). The prediction of preference for familiar urban places. *Environment and Behavior*, **8**, 627–645.

Herzog, T. R., Kaplan, S. and Kaplan, R. (1982). The prediction of preference for unfamiliar urban places. *Population and Environment: Behavioural and Social Issues*, **5**, 43–59.

Herzog, T. R. and Smith, G. A. (1988). Danger, mystery, and environmental preference. *Environment and Behavior*, **20**, 320–344.

Hudspeth, T. R. (1986). Visual preference as a tool for facilitating citizen participation in urban waterfront revitalization. *Journal of Environmental Management*, **23**, 373–385.

Im, S. (1984). Visual preferences in enclosed urban spaces: An exploration of a scientific approach to environmental design. *Environment and Behavior*, **16**, 235–262.

Kaplan, R. (1975). Some methods and strategies in the prediction of preference. In E. H. Zube, R. O. Brush and J. G. Fabos (eds), *Landscape Assessment: Values, Perceptions, and Resources* (pp. 118–129). Stroudsburg, Pennsylvania: Dowden, Hutchinson, and Ross.

Kaplan, R. (1983). The role of nature in the urban context. In I. Altman and J. F. Wohlwill (eds), *Behavior and the Natural Environment*. New York: Plenum, pp. 127–162.

Kaplan, R. (1984). Impact of urban nature: a theoretical analysis. *Urban Ecology*, **8**, 189–197.

Kaplan, S. (1979). Concerning the power of content-identifying methodologies. In T. C. Daniel and E. H. Zube (eds), *Assessment of Amenity Resource Values* (pp. 4–13). USDA Forest Service General Technical Report RM-68.

Kaplan, S. (1987). Aesthetics, affect, and cognition: environmental preference from an evolutionary perspective. *Environment and Behavior*, **19**, 3–22.

Kaplan, S. and Kaplan, R. (eds) (1978). *Humanscape: Environments for People*. Belmont, California: Duxbury (Division of Wadsworth). (Ann Arbor, Michigan: Ulrichs.)

Kaplan, S. and Kaplan, R. (1982). *Cognition and Environment: Functioning in an Uncertain World*. New York: Praeger Publishers.

Kramer, C. Y. (1956). Extension of multiple range tests to group means with unequal numbers of replications. *Biometrics*, **12**, 307–310.

Lingoes, J. C. (1972). A general survey of the Guttman-Lingoes nonmetric program series. In R. N. Shepard, A. K. Romney and S. B. Nerlove (eds), *Multidimensional Scaling, Volume 1*. New York: Seminar Press, pp. 52–68.

Nunnally, J. (1967). *Psychometric Theory*. New York: McGraw-Hill.

Purcell, A. T. (1986). Environmental perception and affect: a schema discrepancy model. *Environment and Behavior*, **18**, 3–30.

Schroder, H. W. (in press). Environment, behavior, and design research on urban forests. In E. H. Zube and G. T. Moore (eds), *Advances in Environment, Behavior, and Design, Volume 2*. New York: Plenum Publishers.

Talbot, J. F. and Kaplan, R. (1986). Judging the sizes of urban open areas: is bigger always better? *Landscape Journal*, **5**, 83–92.

Ulrich, R. S. (1984). View through a window may influence recovery from surgery. *Science*, **224**, 420–421.

Verderber, S. (1986). Dimensions of person-window transactions in the hospital environment. *Environment and Behavior*, **18**, 450–466.

Wike, E. L. (1971). *Data Analysis*. Chicago: Aldine-Atherton.

Woodcock, D. M. (1982). *A Functionalist Approach to Environmental Preference*. Doctoral dissertation, University of Michigan.
Zube, E. H. (1984). Themes in landscape assessment theory. *Landscape Journal*, **3**, 104–110.
Zube, E. H., Sell, J. C. and Taylor, J. G. (1982). Landscape perception: research, application, and theory. *Landscape Planning*, **9**, 1–33.
Zube, E. H., Simcox, D. E. and Law, C. S. (1987). Perceptual landscape simulations: history and prospect. *Landscape Journal*, **6**, 62–80.

Notes

[1] Appleton's third theoretical concept, hazard or danger, is clearly relevant to environmental preference, as demonstrated empirically by Herzog and Smith (1988), but it is not clearly an affordance. It seems to depend more on one's knowledge of what can happen in certain environments rather than on one's interpretation of specific configurations.

[2] For Older Buildings, there were six significant correlations among predictor variables. Spaciousness was positively correlated with legibility (0·80), complexity (0·62), and typicality (0·61). Legibility was also positively correlated with complexity (0·61) and typicality (0·59). Nature was positively correlated with refuge (0·89). For Concealed Foreground, there were four significant correlations among predictor variables. Legibility was positively correlated with coherence (0·82) and spaciousness (0·75), nature with mystery (0·82), and typicality with complexity (0·72). For each of the remaining two categories, there were two significant correlations among predictor variables. For Tended Nature, typicality was positively correlated with coherence (0·75) and spaciousness (0·76). For Contemporary Buildings, mystery was positively correlated with coherence (0·85) and nature (0·97).

[3] The discussion here implies that the nine predictor variables form three groups, one consisting of mystery and nature, a second of typicality, and the third of the remaining six predictors. This three-group interpretation has been supported empirically by the results of both nonmetric factor analysis and hierarchical clustering analysis of the intercorrelations among the nine predictor variables.

CROSS-CULTURAL COMPARISON OF LANDSCAPE SCENIC BEAUTY EVALUATIONS: A CASE STUDY IN BALI

R. BRUCE HULL IV* and GRANT R. B. REVELL†

*College of Architecture, Texas A&M University, College Station, Texas, U.S.A. and
†Landscape Architect, Urban Planner, Melbourne, Victoria, Australia.

Abstract

Both similarities and differences were observed when comparing scenic beauty evaluations of rural landscapes made by persons from different cultures. *Differences* seem due to the westernized tourists' misinterpretation or ignorance of the meaning associated with certain landscape features by the Balinese. This implies scenic beauty is dependent upon meanings assigned to landscape features, which in turn implies that scenic beauty is, to some extent, learned. *Similarities* between tourists' and Balinese' scenic evaluations are significant and correspond to consistencies found in other landscape preference studies (i.e. natural, verdant, or open landscapes are usually preferred over urban, dry, or enclosed landscapes). Multiple methods were used, including participant photography, rating scales, and a variety of statistical analyses.

A review of the literature reveals evidence and theory which suggests both similarities and differences are to be expected when comparing scenic evaluations made by persons of different cultures. This review also suggests three methodological concerns which should be addressed in landscape studies: a concern for the participant's purpose for evaluating a landscape; a concern for the participant's familiarity with a landscape; and a concern for the criterion's appropriateness to all participants. Research designs which ignore these concerns may mask true cultural differences.

Introduction

Landscape perception research findings suggest that both similarities and differences exist among observers' scenic evaluations. Some authors attribute the similarities to things inherited, some attribute the differences to things learned. Several positions at both extremes of this debate are briefly outlined below and three methodological issues which arise from the inquiry are discussed. This review is followed by results of an empirical study comparing the scenic beauty evaluations made by persons from two cultures: 'westernized' tourists and native residents of a tourist destination in Bali, Indonesia.

The position taken on one side of the debate of similarity versus differences in scenic evaluations is that all persons prefer the same sorts of landscapes, that there is a universally agreed upon scenic standard, and that there are inherited mechanisms which are responsible for these similarities. These mechanisms are posited as having adaptive, evolutionary significance. We prefer and rate as scenic those landscapes which evolution has 'taught' our species to be beneficial or worthy of approach (rather than avoidance) behavior. Appleton's (1975) prospect-refuge theory, Kaplan's and

---

*The research was conducted while Hull was a post doctoral fellow at the School of Environmental Planning, The University of Melbourne, Australia. Correspondence should be directed to him at Texas A&M University.

Kaplan's (1982) mystery, legibility, and promise of information, and Ulrich's (1983) 'preferenda' are examples of landscape characteristics which are presumably preferred because of evolutionary pressures.

A complementary reason for similarity in scenic beauty evaluations is that all humans have and use similar information-processing mechanisms. Kaplan (1973) suggests that all humans share a common nature. 'Man gained his selective advantage in a difficult and dangerous world in large part through the development of quick and efficient mechanisms for handling information' (Kaplan, 1973: 63). Thus similarities in information-processing capabilities lead to similarities in the use and interpretation of environmental information and hence similarities in scenic evaluations of landscapes.

There is support from several sources for the position that persons are similar in their reactions to landscapes. Several lines of research indicate marked similarities in emotion. Mehrabian and Russell (1974) cite physiological evidence and logical argument for the existence of pleasure, arousal, and dominance responses in all humans. Russell and Pratt (1980) extend this work and show that persons tend to evaluate all environments with respect to these emotions and that beauty is a component of the pleasure dimension. Osgood's findings of cross-cultural similarity in use of affective language lead him to conclude that the 'semantic differential technique measures certain affective features of meaning, closely related to the dimensions of emotion or feeling, which appear to be universal in the human species' (1969, p. 194). Izard's (1977) theory of emotion suggests that emotions are innate and cross-cultural. He notes cross-cultural similarities in emotional facial expressions and similarities in emotions expressed by babies. More specifically, similarities in scenic beauty evaluations of landscapes have been empirically found among persons of different professions, socio-economic status, and culture (e.g. Shaffer & Tooby, 1973; Zube & Mills, 1976; Daniel & Boster, 1976; Ulrich, 1977; Buhyoff *et al.*, 1983; Tips & Savasdisara, 1986*b*).

The position at the other extreme of this debate is that people have somewhat different aesthetic criteria and thus will differ in the scenic beauty they ascribe to a landscape. Landscape preference is something learned, dependent upon a person's past experiences and current purposes. It is culturally dependent. There are a host of potential explanations for this position. Two are briefly discussed. The first is that people build an image of their environment using information from their past experiences. This image is used as a template to form expectations, structure incoming information, and evaluate environments. Kelly (1955) theorizes that a person derives constructs from past experience and uses them to interpret, construe, and structure environmental information. Constructs are used to abstract and extract the essence of a situation using knowledge gained from experience with similar situations. Brunswik (1956) also theorizes that relationships between environmental features and personal outcomes are learned. Learning occurs through sampling the environment with perception and testing the interpretation of perceptions by action in the environment. The feedback from the testing becomes the basis of interpreting and testing future situations. Both Kelly and Brunswik suggest humans have dynamic and active perceptual systems and constantly test the learned constructs and probabilities of outcomes to improve the system. Because the means of interpreting and evaluating environments is learned, we would expect a person's scenic beauty evaluations to be highly dependent upon prior experience. More recent, and perhaps more closely related work on 'place identity' (Canter, 1973; Proshansky *et al.*, 1983) similarly suggest the importance of past experience on evaluations of environmental quality.

A second related reason for individual and cultural differences in the evaluation of landscapes is that environments are evaluated by persons with a particular purpose in mind (Canter, 1984; Ittelson *et al.*, 1974; Russell & Snodgrass, 1987). A person's immediate purpose in an environment influences the type of information sought and the criteria used to evaluate that environment. A person looking at a landscape with the purpose of raising a family will evaluate it differently from a tourist looking for two to three days of excitement. Both Kelly's theory of personal constructs and Ittelson's theory of perception (e.g. Ittelson *et al.*, 1974) consider the impact of purpose to be a critical determinant of reactions to or evaluations of environments.

Based on this rationale, individuals from different backgrounds would be expected to have different experiences and purposes, and thus different scenic evaluations of a given environment. Several studies have reported significant differences (e.g. Sonnenfeld, 1967; Duncan, 1973; Buhyoff *et al.*, 1978; Zube & Pitt, 1981; Buhyoff *et al.*, 1983; Lyons, 1984; Tip & Savasdisara, 1986*a*). There is, however, a larger body of literature demonstrating remarkable homogeneity in scenic evaluations of landscapes (see Daniel & Vining, 1983; Zube *et al.*, 1982 for reviews of the literature). Several alternative explanations for the commonly reported finding of similarities in scenic evaluations are discussed in light of the aforementioned reasons for expecting individual differences. Many of the studies which found similarities in individuals' scenic beauty evaluations were concerned with evaluations of *natural* landscapes. Most of these studies used urban or suburban residents as subjects. These subjects are likely to have similar experiences with rugged, natural environments; it will be limited to a few camping trips, scenic drives, television shows, and coffee table picture books. Likewise these subjects are likely to have evaluated these natural environments with the purpose of recreation in mind rather than the purpose of wheat farming, sheep grazing, or residential suitability. Since the subjects would have had similar purposes and similar experiences with the landscapes being evaluated it would be expected that similarities would be found in their evaluations of landscape scenic beauty. Thus the limited between-person variation reported in the bulk of the landscape assessment literature may not be due to an inherited scenic preference function but to research designs which limit examination of potential between-person differences.

When comparing landscape evaluations made by different observers, several issues must be addressed. Previous studies have not always successfully done so. First, it is important that subjects be asked to evaluate landscapes using a valid construct. Individuals of different backgrounds may not use the construct 'scenic beauty' in their day to day lives; it may not be relevant to their purposes in the landscape nor may it have been necessary in their past experiences with landscapes. Therefore, if asked to evaluate landscapes with respect to a vague term like 'preference', or 'quality', people of different backgrounds may apply different constructs (e.g. preference for recreation, for farming, for exercise, or for residential purposes). Or, conversely, if forced to use a specific construct, such as 'scenic beauty', they may do so only to appease the researcher. But, instead of using the specific construct provided by the researcher, the subjects may instead be focusing on some more tangible characteristic of the landscape which they do understand; such as the degree of a man-made versus natural areas, the extent of the vista, or the size of the trees in the forest of concern. Thus, it is likely their responses may not be valid (see Nisbett & Wilson, 1977).

A second problem arises when selecting which landscapes to evaluate. If the selected landscapes are different from landscapes normally experienced then respondents will be forced to respond to something outside the realm of their experiences. While they may do so to appease the researcher, their evaluation may be invalid since they will not have 'learned' how to interpret and evaluate these landscapes. Respondents unfamiliar with the landscapes will be less sensitive to subtle differences among landscapes. They also will not have the experience to interpret the meanings of landscape features. Some argue the environment is full of meaning (Rapoport 1982; Fenton 1985). This meaning arises from a person's past experiences and current purposes with environments. It is likely that this meaning is influential in determining a person's scenic evaluations of a landscape. The use of unfamiliar landscapes drastically reduces the meaning persons can 'read' in a landscape and hence removes an important source of between-person variance in scenic beauty evaluations. Thus, cross-cultural comparisons which use abstract stimuli or landscapes unfamiliar to either culture are ignoring a potential cause of differences in landscape evaluations.

A third potential problem concerns the purpose persons have when evaluating an environment. Purpose influences perception (Brunswik, 1956; Ittelson et al., 1974) and evaluation (Canter, 1984; Russell & Snodgrass, 1987) and so it is likely to influence scenic preference evaluations. However, an individual's purpose is largely ignored in experimental designs which take the subjects out of their 'normal' day-to-day lifestyle, place them in a laboratory, read them instructions, show them photographs of landscapes, and ask them to evaluate the surrogate landscapes for scenic beauty or landscape preference using a Likert scale. The validity of evaluations made under these conditions is in doubt. A major objective of *environmental* psychology is to get people to respond to valid environments in a valid way (Ittelson et al., 1974; Proshansky, 1976). This implies that respondents must have a valid *purpose* when making their responses. Testing scientific hypotheses often makes it necessary to use environmental surrogates and obtrusively elicit specific responses. The validity of these efforts is difficult to establish but has been recognized in the literature as a potential problem and opened to rigorous study.

To what extent, then, do persons agree with one another in their evaluations of landscape scenic beauty? Based upon theory and evidence presented above there seems ample reason to expect both similarities and differences. Several studies have noted that within the general agreement commonly found among observers there often exist some differences (Dearden, 1980; Schroeder, 1983; Purcell & Lamb, 1983; Fenton, 1985; Abello' et al., 1986, for example). We expect that there is substantial agreement among persons of different cultures in their scenic evaluations of landscapes, there is simply too much evidence to suggest otherwise. However, we do not expect complete agreement. We expect that there are differences and that some of these differences can be explained by differences between the cultures, by things learned about the landscape. More specifically, we expect some landscape features to mean different things to persons of different cultures and for these differences in meaning to result in different scenic evaluations. In particular, we expect the Balinese, because of their familiarity and close ties with the Balinese landscape, to have different interpretations of the landscape and hence different scenic beauty evaluations from tourists.

Method

Bali Indonesia is a 'tropical island paradise' renowned for its exotic culture, music, art, people, and landscape. As a research setting for the study of cultural differences in scenic evaluations of landscapes, Bali offers several advantages. It allows us to consider the methodological concerns addressed above. Both the Balinese and the tourists are capable and experienced in using 'scenic beauty' as a construct to evaluate landscapes: the Balinese because of their cultural orientation towards beauty, art, and spiritual symbolic harmony in the landscape (Covarrubius, 1972; Powell, 1982) and the tourists because they are touring, in search of new, different, and beautiful settings (Pearce, 1982). Both the Balinese and the tourists will have legitimate, although not identical, purposes for being in the landscape: the Balinese because they live there and the tourist because they are there with the purpose of seeing and understanding Bali, its culture and its landscape. Nonetheless, both groups will have real purposes. Both the Balinese and the tourists will be familiar with the landscape because they are both *in* the landscape.

Participant photography will be used in the research design to select the specific landscape scenes used to make comparisons between cultures. Participant photography facilitates the selection of landscape scenes which are meaningful to participants rather than meaningful to the experimenter and thus increase the likelihood of finding differences among subjects.

The village of Ubud was selected as the research location in Bali. It is situated in the southern foothills of the central volcanic highlands, slightly south of the island's center. It is one of three major tourist destinations in Bali, Indonesia. It is somewhat removed from the more popular seaside resorts and is typically visited by tourists who seek the 'real Bali' experience (although the numerous restaurants, hotels, and tourist shops makes it unlikely that they will find it). The village is preferred by visitors who wish to share the life style of a Balinese rural community. It is known throughout Bali (and the world) as an artists' village, specializing in paintings. Ubud's landscape and culture are still intact, despite growing pressures from the primary tourist industry located at the seaside resorts four to five hours drive away and pressure from industrial and retail developments in the island's major city, only an hour or so away. It was assumed that tourists and residents at Ubud would be more aware of the Balinese landscape than those at the more tourist-oriented resorts found in the south.

The first task of the study was to identify an instructional set which could be interpreted by the Balinese and convey the notion of 'landscape scenic beauty' as understood by westernized, English-speaking tourists. If an appropriate Balinese phrase could not be found then a more general term such as 'liking' or 'preference' would be tried. Assistance was sought from Balinese linguistic experts. In addition, a questionnaire soliciting phrases used to describe landscapes was administered to Balinese residents. The Balinese use the phrases 'pemandangan indah' and 'negara indah' frequently; these phrases mean 'beautiful scenery' and 'beautiful landscape', respectively. This finding suggested there would be little trouble communicating the research task to the Balinese. The assumption that Balinese normally evaluate landscapes with respect to beauty seems substantiated.

Sampling the landscape

Participant photography (see Chenoweth, 1984) was conducted during 12 days in May of 1985. Seventy persons, 35 from each cultural group, participated. They were asked to 'photograph the most beautiful landscape features that [they could] see in the Ubud village' and to return the cameras after two days. Each person was allowed up to 10 photographs. Participants were recruited as they passed by stations set up along well used travel routes. The stations were visited by the researcher at a variety of times during the 12 days. At the time of the visit, the fourth person in view was identified as a participant. Everyone who was approached agreed to participate. Fourteen male and 21 female tourists participated. Their age ranged from 15 to 70 with an average in the mid-20s. Most tourists were from Australia and the United States; the remaining were from Europe and Canada. Twenty-three of the Balinese were male, 12 were female and the average age was in the early 20s.

The primary purpose of participant photography was to obtain a sample of landscape scenes familiar and meaningful to both Balinese and tourists. Photographs of landscape scenes taken by participants were sorted by the researchers to identify those scenes most frequently photographed by each cultural group. While taking photographs, participants were instructed to write down the principal feature in each scene and the reason for its significance. This information made the sorting task straightforward since there was little room for confusion. Scenes photographed by at least 10% of the members of a cultural group were considered representative of that group's perceptions of Ubud's landscape. They are called 'consensus' landscapes for the group. The 10% consensus cut-off is arbitrary but is consistent with previous uses of participant photography (e.g. Cherem, 1983; Cherem & Driver, 1976; Chenoweth, 1984). The consensus landscapes were rephotographed by the researcher using a 35 mm. SLR camera with a 1:1.4 50 mm lens, U.V. filter and Kodak color print 200 ASA film. Twenty landscapes, representing a wide range of Ubud's landscape, were photographed in addition to those scenes identified as consensus landscapes. This was planned prior to collecting data because it was felt that the scenes sampled using participant photography might not fully represent all available scenes: participants might not have their cameras available to sample every scene they thought relevant, some scenes would be difficult to photograph (e.g. an evening sky) and some places might be difficult to visit. Therefore participants were asked to write down scenes which they could not photograph. This information and the researchers' knowledge of the area were used to identify scenes not identified as consensus landscapes but still 'representative' of Ubud. Twenty of these scenes were included in the analysis of scenic beauty evaluations. More details of the methods and the people sampled can be found in Revell (1985).

Evaluating scenic beauty
The third task was to obtain some quantitative measure of scenic beauty so that differences between groups could be more rigorously compared. Again tourists and Balinese were approached as they were for the participant photography exercise and asked to participate. Another 35 people from each cultural group participated; everyone who was approached, except two tourists, agreed to participate. Participants were shown, one at a time, 50 3" by 5" photographs and asked to rate the landscape depicted by each photograph for scenic beauty. The order of presentation was randomized. The 50 photographs consisted of the 30 consensus landscapes and 20 additional representative landscapes. The scenic beauty rating procedure and instructions were similar to those used by Daniel and Boster (1976). Participants were asked, in English or Balinese, to rate the scenic beauty of the landscape scene depicted by a photograph. They were to use a 10-point scale; 10 being most scenic. Ten photographs representative of the 50 scenes to be rated were shown to each participant prior to the actual rating task in order to familiarize the participants with the rating task and with the type of landscape to be rated.

Each person's ratings were 'standardized' by the mean and standard deviation of his/her rating of all 50 scenes (as recommended by Schroeder, 1984). This created scenic beauty measures which were relative to the set of landscape scenes being rated and somewhat independent of the style which raters used the 10-point rating scale. Differences in the use of the rating scale were not of interest in this study (e.g. whether a rater used all high numbers or all low numbers or the whole scale). What was of concern was the relative difference among landscapes as evaluated by the raters. Thus the resulting measures should be interpreted as a relative difference in scenic beauty. The average of these standardized ratings across members of each group was calculated for each scene and used to represent the scenic beauty evaluation for each group.

Testing extent of similarity

The rating procedure produced, for each landscape scene, a scenic beauty rating for each participant and a group average for each of the Balinese and Tourists groups. Similarity between groups was examined several ways. First, a simple correlation between the group metrics was calculated. Second, a factor analysis on the participants' ratings was conducted as recommended by Schroeder (1983). The participants were treated as variables and the scenes as cases. Thus observers who load highly on the same factor are similar to one another in how they rated the fifty landscape scenes. Finally, an ANOVA was used to test whether the agreement among participants within each culture was more than the agreement across cultures. Using a computer program to manipulate the ratings obtained from participants, 20 observers were sampled, randomly and with replacement, from each group. Average scenic beauty values for each of the 50 scenes were calculated for each sample of 20 participants. This was done 20 times for each cultural group. Thus, there were 20 scenic beauty metrics for the tourist group and 20 for the Balinese group. All possible Spearman rank order correlations were calculated (190 for each culture and 400 across cultures) and compared using a oneway ANOVA. Data for one 'treatment' of the ANOVA were the 190 correlations between all the 20 generated Balinese metrics, data for the second treatment were the 190 correlations between all the 20 generated tourists metrics, and the data for the final treatment were the 400 correlations among the 20 Balinese metrics and the 20 tourist metrics.

Testing specific differences

An attempt was made to identify specific landscape features which might be the cause of differences between the scenic evaluations of the Balinese and tourists. It was hypothesized that certain features in the landscape would have different meanings to the Balinese than to the tourists and that this culturally dependent information would influence the Balinese and tourists differently in their scenic evaluations. Discussions with Balinese and experts on Balinese culture along with a review of the reasons participants gave for selecting the landscapes they did in the participant photography exercise lead to five hypotheses, or more specifically, to five landscape features which might mean different things to Balinese than to tourists and hence have different impacts on their scenic evaluations. The first two landscape features were identified *a priori* as things which should convey meaning to Balinese but not to the tourists. The last three features were identified *a posteriori* and reflect our belief that tourists would be more impressed with novel and authentic landscape features (e.g. landscape features not commonly encountered in Australia, United States, or Europe).

The first hypothesis was that Balinese would rate as more scenic those landscapes with traditional Balinese architectural forms. This follows from the belief by Balinese of an intense religious and spiritual order which exists between Balinese architectural design and human well-being. More specifically, Balinese believe they participate in the universal order of their environment. Thus, construction of a traditional house follows certain strict requirements of custom and religion to insure the universal order is maintained (Timuraan, 1973). These ancient building codes govern the manner of building measurement and craftsmanship. Thus we hypothesized that traditional architecture would have important and significant meaning for the Balinese and this in turn would positively influence their scenic evaluations of landscapes containing these architectural features and negatively influence scenic evaluations of landscape with nontraditional architecture. The tourists would not be aware of these differences.

The second hypothesis was that Balinese would rate as more scenic those landscapes which allowed direct public access (roads, walking tracks etc.). This follows from certain religious rules and Balinese' beliefs about relationships between the environment and themselves. For example, Balinese religious custom gives rise to rules about a sacred wind source. This wind source has cosmic, magical qualities and governs building spacing, building orientation, village and roadways layouts, as well as zoning controls (Timuraan, 1973). Thus the direction of the roads and tracks and the orientation of the buildings would have significant meaning for the Balinese. Presumably this would influence the Balinese's scenic evaluations of scenes containing these features, such as walking tracks or roads leading in the 'correct' direction. An additional reason for the Balinese to prefer visible access to landscapes may be because they tend to be very proud of their public-communal spaces and modern construction methods characteric of roads and pedestrian pathways.

The third, fourth, and fifth hypotheses are that tourists would rate as more scenic those landscapes with features which were novel to the western eye, in particular scenes with Balinese people, scenes with a tropical blue sky with large clouds, and scenes with terraced rice fields. This follows first from the belief that novelty tends to raise arousal, interest and hence increases liking. In addition, Pearce (1982) discusses theoretical models which suggests that holidays are cultural sanctioned escapes for western man seeking spiritual encounters and thus many tourists seek authenticity in the environments they tour. Tourists, therefore, would get more pleasure from landscape characteristics which they deem novel and authentic. Often the simple reason for travelling is to experience new places. Seeing the ancient sculptured landscape of the Balinese ricefields, the Balinese themselves, and/or the majestic tropical sky would certainly be regarded as novel and authentic experiences for most tourists. Note that the last three hypotheses were motivated more by observation of the results from participant photography (including respondents' comments) and the scenic beauty evaluations than *a priori* knowledge.

For each landscape feature, the 50 landscapes were sorted by the researcher into two groups: those landscapes with the feature and those without. There was no ambiguity in the sorting task. The aggregate group metrics were then compared. The scenic beauty rating of the landscapes with the feature were compared to the ratings of landscapes without the feature using a t-test to test whether the scenes containing the feature were rated, by Balinese or tourist, as significantly more scenic than scenes without the feature. More specifically, the comparison was between (a) the difference between tourists' and Balinese' scenic beauty evaluations for the landscape with the feature; and

(b) the difference between tourists' and Balinese' scenic beauty ratings of landscapes without the feature. If the difference, (a)–(b), is large and positive then it follows that the Balinese rated landscapes with the feature as more scenic than did the tourists.

Results

Participant photography

There were 15 consensus landscapes for each cultural group. The numbers of persons photographing each 'consensus landscape' varied; a 54% consensus was the highest for the Balinese, 34% for the tourists. Average across all 15 consensus landscapes was 20% for both groups. The tourists tended to select scenes with Balinese people, perhaps because the people and their ways of life were novel to the tourists. The Balinese selected scenes with features of the home, traditional temples, public buildings and gardens, including banyan and coconut trees. Five scenes were identified by both the Balinese and tourists: two views of rice fields, two views of the Campuan Valley, and one of a person and a native cow in a field. The major difference between groups seems to be the significance given to architectural features in the landscape by the Balinese and the significance given to Balinese people by the tourists. Thus there were more differences (20) than similarities (5) between the Balinese and the tourists in the landscape scenes they selected using the participant photography technique.

Extent of similarity in scenic evaluations

The correlation between Balinese and tourist group scenic beauty metrics was moderate yet significant (Pearson's correlation coefficient = $+0.64$; Spearman's correlation coefficient = $+0.56$; $p < 0.001$ for both; $n = 50$). This suggests there was both agreement and disagreement. The largest difference between groups in the rank order to landscape scenes was 36 (rated as sixth most scenic by the Balinese and 42nd by the tourists—a low rank suggests high scenic quality). It was a scene of a paved road disappearing into the distance with ricefields either side. Other large differences in scenic evaluations occurred. A scene of a straight paved road with thick roadside trees was ranked 13 by Balinese and 44 by tourists. A view of the tropical sky at dusk with large cloud formations was ranked 41 by Balinese and 20 by tourists. A distant view of the village residential area containing both houses and trees was ranked 10 by Balinese and 33 by tourists. And, a scene of steps leading down a hill with lots of vegetation on either side of the steps and a temple in the background was ranked 12 by Balinese and 37 by tourists. Three scenes had identical rankings. They were scenes of a roadside restaurant, a heavily commercialized, 'tourist trap' artist studio entrance with paintings displayed and the Campuan River Valley. The first two scenes were rated low in scenic quality and the third scene was rated as highly scenic. Seventeen scenes differed in rank order by less than three. The average difference in rank order between Balinese and tourists for all scenes was 11.

The differences in rankings seems due to differences in how the scenes were interpreted rather than due to a bias introduced through the participant photography sample or the rating method. The magnitude of the difference in rank order was consistent across scenes rated in the top, middle, and bottom thirds of the scenic beauty metrics. Thus disagreement seemed no more extreme at the ends of the metric than it was in the middle. The magnitude of the difference in rank order was also consistent across the consensus scenes selected by tourists, Balinese, and the extra scenes selected by the researcher.

The agreement (on scenic beauty ratings of landscape scenes) among tourists was compared to the agreement among Balinese and these were compared with the agreement across cultures. An ANOVA of Spearman correlations between group metrics generated by randomly selecting 20 observers at a time from each group allowed a test of whether the agreement across cultures was significantly different than the agreement among observers within a culture. The results of the ANOVA suggest that there were significant differences in the levels of agreement ($F = 1671$, $p < 0.0001$, $df = 2,777$). Duncan's multiple comparison test at a 0·05 level of significance found the average correlation among tourists ($+0.86$) was significantly higher than the average correlation among Balinese ($+0.79$) which was significantly higher than the average correlation across cultures ($+0.52$). The average within group correlation of Balinese and tourists ($+0.79$, $+0.86$, respectively) is typical of the level of agreement found among groups of the same culture. The cross cultural correlation was significantly less.

A factor analysis of scenic beauty ratings of observers from both groups was conducted to further examine the extent of similarity among Balinese and tourists. Three interpretable factors emerged accounting for 25%, 7% and 7% of the similarities among all participants. The first factor contained both Balinese and tourists. The second factor seemed to represent the tourists' perspective and the third factor represented the Balinese perspective (as evidenced by the type of person who loaded highly on each factor). This suggests, as do the other results, that there is significant agreement among the participants in their scenic beauty evaluations but within this general agreement there exist differences. Factor scores were calculated for factors 2 and 3. They represent the scenic beauty metrics for the tourist and Balinese perspectives after the common variance has been factored out. Scenes identified as most scenic by the Balinese factor contained animals (cow, dog, duck etc.). Perhaps this represents the animistic aspects of their culture (i.e. the Balinese attribute consciousness and privilege to most features of nature) and/or preferences for evidence of agricultural productivity. Scenes with evidence of commercial tourism such as vendor stalls were rated as not scenic by this factor, perhaps indicating some animosity of the Balinese towards tourism and commercialism, as well as a dislike for nontraditional architectural design. Scenes identified as most scenic by the tourist factor contained obvious signs of Balinese culture, such as fighting cocks in their cages, religious temples, and street vendors. It did not require any special familiarity with the Balinese

TABLE 1
Factor analysis of all Balinese and tourists' ratings: factor loadings sorted by magnitude, sign and cultural group

Loading	Factor 1		Factor 2		Factor 3	
	Balinese	Tourists	Balinese	Tourists	Balinese	Tourists
>0.3	22	31	1	11	9	1
<-0.3	0	0	8	4	1	3

Factors 1, 2, and 3 accounted for 25, 7·4, and 7% of the variance in scenic ratings. Factor loadings larger in absolute magnitude than 0·3% were tallied for each factor and sorted by whether the respondent was a Balinese or a tourist. Factor 1 is mixed and illustrates the general agreement across cultures. Factors 2 and 3 demonstrate minor yet significant cultural differences. Factor 2 appears to represent the tourist group in a positive fashion and the Balinese in a negative one. Factor 3 represents a Balinese perspective. Some people loaded on two factors and were counted as members of both.

culture to realize that these features were culturally relevant. Their prominent location in the landscape makes them 'tourist attractions'. The greatest difference between the two factors were in scenic ratings of scenes with street shops (e.g. tourist traps). The Balinese group rated these scenes as much less scenic. The next greatest difference occurred in scenes with contained Balinese people. The scenes were more preferred by the tourists. The tourist group also rated as more scenic scenes of wide, expansive, and lush green field landscape, in particular the contoured ricefields.

Specific differences in scenic evaluations
The first two hypotheses examined the impact on scenic beauty of two landscape features thought to have meaning interpretable by the Balinese but not the tourists. The data rejected both null hypotheses indicating that these features may significantly contribute more to the Balinese evaluations of scenic beauty than to the tourists' evaluations. The difference in scenic beauty evaluations was positive and moderately significant for both hypotheses. Thus the Balinese preferred scenes with traditional Balinese architecture more than tourists ($t = 2.89$, $p < 0.01$; df = 48). And, the Balinese did rate as more scenic scenes which exhibit direct access into the landscape ($t = 2.06$, $p < 0.045$, df = 48).

The third, fourth, and fifth hypotheses were that tourists would rate as more scenic landscapes containing novel and authentic features, specifically Balinese people, tropical sky, and terraced rice fields. The support for these hypotheses was moderate, at best. Thus these features may not contribute more to a tourist's evaluations of scenic beauty. The difference in scenic evaluations for scenes with Balinese people was moderate but not significant ($t = +1.16$; $p < 0.25$; df = 48). The positive value of the t-test suggests, in contrast to our hypothesis, that seeing Balinese people in the landscape enhanced scenic beauty more for the Balinese than the tourists. Either the hypothesized effect did not occur or it was negated by other factors. The difference between the Balinese and tourists' scenic evaluations of scenes with lots of tropical sky was moderate ($t = 1.38$; $p < 0.17$; df = 48). This suggests that the tourists rated as more scenic those scenes with the expanse of tropical sky, although not significantly. The difference for the scenes with terraced rice fields was negligible but in the hypothesized direction ($t = -0.57$; $p < 0.57$; df = 48).

Discussion

There exists substantial agreement between the Balinese and the tourist populations in their scenic evaluations of Ubud's landscape. There was a moderate yet significant Spearman correlation between the Balinese and tourist scenic beauty metrics ($+0.56$) and the dominant factor in the factor analysis contained both Balinese and tourists. In the participant photography exercise many of the same scenes were photographed by both Balinese and tourist participants; five of these scenes were selected by more than 10% of each group, indicating cross-cultural similarities exist in the image of Ubud. It is remarkable that so many persons from both cultures photographed the same scenes. It was expected that the Balinese intimate knowledge of Ubud and the various walkways, roads, nooks and crannies would have resulted in a sample of views unavailable to the tourist. Although this may have happened, it did not materialize to the extent we expected.

Both the tourists and the Balinese rated as scenic those landscapes containing obvious features of cultural relevance, such as temples. Perhaps, because of their obviousness, these landscape features enhanced the scenic beauty for tourists who normally would be unaware of such positive connotations present in the Balinese landscape. Both groups tended to rate natural scenes with open, distant views of hills or valleys as scenic and to rate enclosed, urban, commercial scenes as less scenic. This finding is often reported in landscape research. Natural, green, or open landscapes are usually preferred over urban, dry, or enclosed landscapes.

It is possible that some of the similarities found between cultures are caused by the Balinese adopting the values of western culture due to the influences of western tourism and western development, both of which are becoming more and more obvious in many Balinese locations. Also, in the 1920s, European sculptural and landscape painting traditions were introduced into Bali by students of European expatriates. Nonetheless, the Balinese culture is strong and intact, most tourism is contained in the southern region of the island, and the traditional Balinese art style is unique, unlike anything western. Thus there is good reason to believe that inculturation is only a minor cause of the similarities. Perhaps the real reason for the observed similarities is that some genetically preferred scenic beauty exists, such as the genotypical preference for particular landscape types as hypothesized by Balling and Falk (1982). Or, perhaps there is an innate preference for landscapes with certain levels of complexity, legibility, focality, ground surface texture, depth, mystery, and threat as suggested by Ulrich (1983, 1986). Note, however, that if the latter were true there would not necessarily be a preferred landscape type but instead a preferred combination of abstract landscape features (e.g. moderate levels of complexity and some mystery). The specific landscape features which contribute to the preferred levels of the landscape features may differ from person to person and culture to culture. Thus both differences and similarities would be expected. Obviously there is a need for more research.

The ANOVA suggests that there was considerable agreement among persons within each cultural group. Thus there is consistency in the ratings and the observed differences are not due to errors in the rating task. The tourists actually were in more agreement with one another than were the Balinese, which is surprising given that people from *different* western cultures made up the tourist group. Perhaps the high level of agreement is a result of tourists having the same overriding purpose (tourism) and being equally unfamiliar with the Balinese culture and landscape. Thus the high level of agreement among tourists might be due to the purpose and familiarity methodological issues mentioned in the introductory section of this paper. In any case, the level of agreement within a culture (as evaluated by the average correlation among scenic beauty metrics) is similar to that reported in other studies.

Given the only moderate level of agreement reported above, it follows that there must also exist substantial disagreement among participants. The ANOVA results suggest significant differences do exist between cultures. The factor analysis and the *t*-test results suggest that some of the differences can be explained. However, there is still 61% of the variance in the factor analysis of scenic beauty evaluations not explained by these three factors and not easily interpreted in its own right. With more knowledge of variables which influence scenic beauty evaluations this variance might be explained. Potential but untested causes of the differences include the strong agricultural ties the Balinese have with land. They relate human well-being with agricultural processes and religious ritual. For example, Balinese use leaves and other agricultural products in religious offerings and have intense respect for the tallest mountain in the north—*Gunung Aoung* (spindle of the universe)—and to the seas in the south (areas of evil spirits and hell). Therefore, scenes of agriculture, banyan trees, mountains, or views towards or away from 'evil' or 'good' may be preferred by the Balinese. These meanings in the landscape would be unavailable to most tourists and hence would not influence their scenic assessments. This suggests, as do Fenton (1985) and Rapoport (1982), that meaning influences aesthetic evaluations of environments. Hence, to some extent, scenic beauty is learned.

Conclusions

In the literature on scenic beauty and landscape preference research there is evidence and theory suggesting that both similarities and difference exist when comparing scenic evaluations of different persons. This is not necessarily contradictory. It suggests that there are perceptual/judgmental mechanisms, shared by all humans, which underlie scenic beauty evaluations and cause similar ratings. It also suggests that things learned through common experiences (e.g. culture) influence scenic beauty evaluations. Since people are unique in their personal experience, everyone will have a slightly different basis from which to evaluate scenic beauty. Our findings support the suggestion that differences exist since scenic beauty evaluations were to some extent dependent upon culture.

Despite enormous cultural differences, the westernized tourists and the native Balinese exhibited considerable similarity in their evaluations of Ubud's landscape. In fact, the results suggest that there was perhaps more similarity than difference between two groups in their scenic evaluations of Ubud. This is remarkable given the enormous differences which exist between the Balinese and western culture with respect to an individual's values, beliefs, and purpose in life. For example, one would expect the Balinese' animistic beliefs, alone, to color strongly any value judgment regarding the physical environment. Apparently scenic beauty evaluations are based on things that transcend strong cultural differences.

We identified several methodological issues which, if ignored, would reduce the sensitivity of scenic beauty evaluation studies to differences among participants. We suggest that one reason differences were found in our study is because these issues were taken into account. The first issue is that all participants need a valid purpose for evaluating the environment. In our study both tourists and Balinese had legitimate *purposes* for evaluating the landscapes: the Balinese because they live there and are concerned about aesthetics and the tourists because they are visiting Bali to experience new and beautiful settings. However, we have no guarantee and did not try to insure that the Balinese and tourists were using the exact same purpose when evaluating the landscapes. The Balinese, for example, might have been more concerned about how the scenic beauty of the landscape would influence the residential quality of Ubud and thus evaluating a slightly different construct. The second methodological issue is that all participants should be *familiar* with the landscapes being assessed. This was insured in our study by using participants who were already in the landscape and by using participant photography to identify landscape scenes which have meaning to the participants but not to the experimenter. The importance of this issue is highlighted by our findings that meaning in the landscape influences scenic beauty: unfamiliar landscape features are less likely to have meaning and thus this important determinant of scenic beauty would be ignored. Finally, it is important that all participants use a meaningful and familiar *construct* to evaluate the landscapes. In this study scenic beauty seemed appropriate for both groups.

References

Abello', R. P., Berna'ldez, F. G. & Galiano, E. F. (1986). Consensus and contrast components in landscape preference. *Environment and Behaviour*, **18**, 155–178.

Appleton, J. (1975). *The Experience of Landscape*. London: John Wiley.

Balling, J. D. & Falk, J. H. (1982). Development of visual preference for natural environments. *Environment and Behavior*, **14**, 5–28.

Brunswik, E. (1956). *Perception and the Representative Design of Psychological Experiments*. Berkeley: University of California.

Buhyoff, G. J., Wellman, J. D., Harvey, H. & Fraser, R. A. (1978). Landscape architects' interpretations of people's landscape preference judgments. *Journal of Environmental Management*, **6**, 255–262.

Buhyoff, G. J., Wellman, J. D., Kock, N. E., Gauthier, L. & Hultman, S. (1983). Landscape preference metrics: an international comparison. *Journal of Environmental Management*, **16**, 181–190.

Canter, D. (1977). *The Psychology of Place*. New York: St. Martin's.

Canter, D. (1984). The purposive evaluation of places: a facet approach. *Environment and Behavior*, **15**, 659–698.

Chenoweth, R. (1984). Visitor employed photography: a potential tool for landscape architecture. *Landscape Journal*, **3**, 136–143.

Cherem, G. (1973). *Visitor Responsiveness to a Nature Trail Environment*. The University of Michigan Unpublished Ph.D. dissertation, Ann Arbor, Michigan: University Microfilm.

Cherem, G. & Driver, B. (1976). *Visitor Employed Photography: a Technique for Measuring Communality in Perception of Natural Environments*. Fort Collins, CO: USDA Forest Service Rocky Mt. Forest and Range Experiment Station.

Covarrubias, M. (1972). *Island of Bali*. Oxford: Oxford University Press.

Daniel, T. C. & Boster, R. S. (1976). *Measuring Landscape Aesthetics: the Scenic Beauty Estimation Method*. USDA Forest Service Research Report RM-167.

Daniel, T. C. & Vining, J. (1983). Methodological issues in the assessment of landscape quality. In I. Altman & J. F. Wohlwill, Eds., *Behaviour and the Natural Environment*, Vol. 6. New York: Plenum. pp. 39–83.

Dearden, P. (1980). *Consensus and the Landscape Quality Continuum: a Research Note*. Landscape Research, 6, 31.

Duncan, J. S. (1973). Landscape taste as a symbol of group identity: a Westchester County village. *Geographical Review*, **63**, 334–355.

Fenton, D. M. (1985). Dimensions of meaning in the perception of natural settings and their relationships to aesthetic response. *Australian Journal of Psychology*, **37**, 325–339.

Hull, R. B. & Revell, G. R. B. (1988). Sampling scenic beauty. *Landscape and Urban Planning*. (In press.)

Ittelson, W. H., Proshansky, H. M., Rivlin, L. G. & Winkel, G. H. (1974). *An Introduction to Environmental Psychology*. New York: Holt, Rinehart and Winston.

Izard, C. E. (1977). *Human Emotions*. New York: Plenum.

Kaplan, S. (1973). Cognitive maps in perception and thought. In R. M. Downs & D. Stea, Eds., *Image and Environment*. Chicago: Aldine

Kaplan, S. & Kaplan, R. (1982). *Humanscape: Environments for People*. Ann Arbor, MI: Ulrich's.

Kelly, G. (1955). *The Psychology of Personal Constructs*. New York: Norton.

Lyons, E. (1983). Demographic correlates of landscape preference. *Environment and Behavior*, **15**, 487–511.

Mehrabian, A. & Russell, J. A. (1974). *An Approach to Environmental Psychology*. Cambridge: MIT Press.

Nisbett, R. E. & Wilson, T. D. (1977). Telling more than we can know: Verbal reports on mental processes. *Psychological Review*, **84**, 231–259.

Osgood, C. E. (1969). On the whys and wherefores of E, P, and A. *Journal of Personality and Social Psychology*, **12**, 194–199.
Pearce, P. L. (1982). *The Social Psychology of Tourist Behaviour*. Oxford, Pergamon Press.
Proshansky, H. M. (1976). Environmental Psychology and the Real World. *American Psychologist*, **31**, 303–350.
Powell, H. (1982). *The Last Paradise*. Oxford: Oxford University Press.
Proshansky, H. M., Fabina, A. K. & Kammoff, R. (1983). Place Identity: Physical World Socialization of Self. *Journal of Environmental Psychology*, **3**, 57–83.
Purcell, A. T. & Lamb, R. J. (1984). Landscape perception: an examination and empirical investigation of two central issues in the area. *Journal of Environmental Management*, **19**, 31–63.
Rapoport, A. (1982). *The Meaning of the Built Environment*. Beverly Hills, CA: Sage.
Revell, G. R. B. (1985). *Cross-cultural Explorations in Scenic Beauty Perception: An Indonesian Experience with Tourism*. School of Environmental Planning Masters Thesis. Parkville, Vic., Australia: The University of Melbourne.
Russell, J. A. & Pratt, G. (1980). A description of the affective quality attributed to environments. *Journal of Personality and Social Psychology*, **38**, 311–322.
Russell, J. A. & Snodgrass (1987). Emotion and the environment. In D. Stokols & I. Altman. *Handbook of Environmental Psychology*, **1**, 245–280.
Schroeder, H. W. (1983). Variations in the perception of urban forest recreation sites. *Leisure Sciences*, **5**, 221–230.
Schroeder, H. W. (1984). Environmental perception rating scales: a case for simple methods analysis. *Environment and Behavior*, **16**, 573–596.
Shaffer, E. L. & Toby, M. (1973). Landscape preferences: and international replication. *Journal of Leisure Research*, **5**, 60–65.
Sonnenfeld, J. (1967). Environmental perception and adaptation level in the Arctic. In D. Lowenthal, Ed., *Environmental Perception and Behaviour*. Chicago: Department of Geography, University of Chicago.
Timuraan, H. (1973). Housing and planning in Bali: a survey of the literature. *Masalah Bangunan*, **18**, 5–15.
Tips, W. E. J. & Savasdisara, T. (1986a). The influence of environmental background of subjects on their landscape preferences evaluations. *Landscape and Urban Planning*, **13**, 125–133.
Tips, W. E. J. & Savasdisara, T. (1986b). The influence of socio-economic background of subjects on their landscape preferences evaluations. *Landscape and Urban Planning*, **13**, 225–230.
Ulrich, R. S. (1977) Visual landscape preference: a model and application. *Man-Environment Systems*, **7**, 279–293.
Ulrich, R. S. (1983). Aesthetic and affective responses to natural environments. In I. Altman & J. F. Wohlwill, Eds., *Behaviour and Natural Environment*, **6**, New York: Plenum, pp. 85–125.
Ulrich, R. S. (1986). Human responses to vegetation and landscape. *Landscape and Urban Planning*, **13**, 29–44.
Wohlwill, J. H. (1973). The environment is not in the head! In W. F. E. Preiser, Ed., *Environmental Design Research*, Vol. 2. Stroudsburg: Dowden, Hutchinson, and Ross.
Zube, E. H. & Mills, L. V. (1976). Cross-cultural explorations in landscape perception. In E. H. Zube, Ed., *Studies in Landscape Perception*. Amherst: Institute for Man and Environment, University of Mass.
Zube, E. H. & Pitts, D. G. (1981). Cross-cultural perceptions of scenic and heritage landscapes. *Landscape Planning*, **8**, 69–87.
Zube, E. H., Sell, J. C. & Taylor, J. G. (1982). Landscape perception: research, application and theory. *Landscape Planning*, **9**, 1–33.

THE PREDICTION OF SCENIC BEAUTY FROM LANDSCAPE CONTENT AND COMPOSITION

MICHAEL R. PATSFALL and NICKOLAUS R. FEIMER

Department of Psychology

GREGORY J. BUHYOFF and J. DOUGLAS WELLMAN

Department of Forestry

Virginia Polytechnic Institute and State University

Abstract

Two studies were conducted to examine distance classes of vegetation (foreground, middleground and background) and scene composition (presence of vegetation in left, center or right section of the image) as predictors of perceived scenic beauty. In study one, 41 students rated 63 landscape scenes with regard to scenic beauty. The Scenic Beauty Estimation Method was used to derive interval scale beauty values (SBEs). For each landscape image, areal measures of vegetation in each distance class and for each vertical section were taken and used as predictors. Presence of haze, clouds and human impacts were also recorded. Among the most important contributors to scenic beauty were amount of center middleground vegetation, and center background vegetation. Left foreground vegetation and right foreground vegetation were found to have significant and opposing regression weight signs—negative for the left and positive for the right. Study two was conducted to determine whether these opposing regression weight signs for foreground vegetation were due to a perceptual right-left bias or to some specific content in the image itself. In the second study, the photographic slides used to present landscape scenes to subjects were reversed so that the content which was previously on the right was now left, and vice versa. Thirty-nine students rated the reversed slides with regard to their scenic beauty. The signs of the regression weights in study two shifted such that left foreground was now positively valued and right foreground was negatively valued. This finding suggests that viewers are sensitive to foreground content and its placement in the image, and not simply to one side of the field of vision.

Introduction

The visual aesthetic quality of the natural environment has become a topic of increasing interest and importance in recent years, as is evidenced by the inclusion of visual amenities into environmental law and policy (Zube, 1976; Zube *et al.*, 1982). As a result, a substantial literature has developed concerning the prediction of human responses to the visual environment with objective, systematic measurement methods. The scope and form of these methods are quite varied*, but can generally be

---

*For a review of the pertinent concepts and methods see Wohlwill (1976); Zube (1976); Arthur *et al.* (1977); Feimer (1983); Daniel and Vining (1983), and Zube *et al.* (1982).

The work reported here was supported by the Southeast Region of the United States National Park Service. The findings and opinions expressed herein are those of the authors and not necessarily those of the Park Service.

Requests for reprints should be sent to Michael Patsfall, Department of Psychology, Virginia Polytechnic Institute and State University, Blacksburg, VA 24061, U.S.A.

characterized as employing a verbal measure of preference or aesthetic quality as a criterion, and predictors which are either concrete, physicalistic attributes (e.g. Shafer *et al.*, 1969; Zube *et al.*, 1975; Daniel and Boster, 1976; Arthur, 1977; Briggs and France, 1980; Buhyoff and Wellman, 1980; Shroeder and Daniel, 1980) or relatively abstract, transactional constructs (e.g. Wohlwill, 1968; Kaplan *et al.*, 1972; Kaplan 1973, 1975; Wohlwill and Harris, 1980; Feimer *et al.*, 1981).

Studies using physicalistic variables as predictors of visual aesthetic landscape quality have commonly included a set of distance classes for vegetation. A tripartite division of distance classes is most common, with visible vegetation classified as being in the foreground, middleground, or background of the scene based upon general criteria of visual resolution. However, efforts to test the utility of such delineations of vegetation distance have met with mixed success. For example, Shafer *et al.* (1969) found that the areal perimeter of immediate (i.e. foreground) vegetation in landscape photos was a significant predictor of preference for the scenes. They also reported a number of significant higher order terms, such as the perimeter of immediate vegetation multiplied by the perimeter of distant vegetation, the perimeter of immediate vegetation multiplied by the area of intermediate (i.e. middleground) vegetation, and the perimeter of immediate vegetation squared. Brush and Palmer (1979) found that the use of distance classes increased prediction of scenic quality by ten percent over sum total indices. Arthur (1977), on the other hand, included the presence of foreground, middleground, and background (measured on a five point rating scale from 'presence of foreground only' to 'presence of all distance classes") and found it failed to predict an index of perceived scenic beauty of Arizona forest landscapes. Similarly, Propst and Buhyoff (1980) employing a regression procedure known as policy capturing, found foreground vegetation to be a relatively inconsequential predictor of landscape preferences.

Adding to the uncertainty surrounding the role of vegetation distance classes is Weinstein's (1976) caveat concerning the application of multivariate statistical procedures in studies such as the one reported by Shafer *et al.* (1969). He points out that environment-behavior researchers are at times unduly insensitive to problems of model overfitting which result from chance variation in the data set or loss of degrees of freedom. As a result, one can expect the generalizability of such studies to be limited.

Another question of interest with respect to vegetation distance is whether or not the particular placement of these landscape elements in the image field has any impact on perceived scenic beauty. That is to say, does it matter if the background imagery is located in the left, center, or right portion of the image? Traditional notions about aesthetic composition would suggest that it might. One often used convention of aesthetic composition, for example, is to have the elements of primary importance centrally placed, and surrounded by secondary elements.

Alternatively, the importance of relative placement of elements in the visual field might result from a cognitive-perceptual bias. There is evidence that individuals may attend to, and process, information differentially in the left and right parts of the visual field due to hemispheric brain specialization (Gazzaniga, 1970; Harcum, 1978). Depending upon both differential lateral functions (i.e. differing stimulus and processing emphases for the right and left hemisphere) and individual lateral dominance (i.e. the degree to which the right or left brain functions are emphasized in the individual), a general preference, or bias for one side of the visual field will emerge. A clear concensus concerning a general tendency, or bias, has not yet emerged, with evidence pointing to both left and right bias under certain circumstances (see Harcum, 1978; Heron, 1957; Wickelgren, 1967; Gazzaniga, 1970; Gur et al., 1975).

The present study attempts to examine further the elements comprising the perceived scenic quality of natural landscapes, with particular emphasis on an appraisal of the effects of the relative placement of vegetation. The data for the study are scenic quality responses to designated scenic vista overlooks along a major tourist parkway. The importance of this investigation is two-fold. First, public exposure to such settings is quite high, making the effects of management actions both visable and potentially meaningful in terms of visitor experience. Second, the role of distance zones and relative lateral placement of vegetation is largely unknown in such settings. Middleground and background vegetation should be important in scenic overlooks since these are assumed to be the focal points of interest. However, the role of foreground vegetation is much less clear. It is, nonetheless, a significant issue, since the manipulation of foreground vegetation is one of the few interventions which may be practically and economically viable to maintain and enhance scenic vistas.

Also of interest in this context was the elucidation of recent findings by Buhyoff et al. (1982), who reported that there was a non-monotonic relationship between the amount of area of sharp mountains in a scene and scenic beauty. They reported scenic beauty increased with increasing area of sharp mountains up to a moderate point, after which scenic beauty dropped as the area of mountains increased. Although they measured sharp mountains across all distance classes, such terrain in vista scenes typically falls into the background. The findings of Buhyoff et al. raise the question of whether such a relationship holds for a related, but more general content class, such as the amount of background vegetation.

Study 1

Method

Stimuli. The stimuli were a sample of 63 vista scenes selected from a larger set of 299 photo-slides sampled along the entire length of the Blue Ridge Parkway in the states of Virginia and North Carolina in the United States of America. The total number of scenes selected for the study was to be less than 100 in order to avoid subject fatigue during the rating procedure. Scenes were evaluated for inclusion in the sample according to three criteria: (1) representativeness; (2) quality of scenic characteristics, and (3) photographic quality. Sites were also chosen not to be extreme in terms of the quality of their scenic characteristics. That is, the scenes should not have been atypically high or low in scenic quality. This selection criterion was used to ensure that the models developed were applicable to conditions most generally found along the parkway. However, few scenes were excluded on that basis. The vistas were photographed from positions and perspectives that were as nearly equivalent as possible, and under relatively similar atmospheric conditions (i.e. under generally clear skies with only minor haze and cloud cover). Scenes which were excessively cloudy were re-photographed at a later time. Finally, the photographs selected for use in the study had to be of good photographic quality. Selection and elimination was by consensus of three of the co-authors.

Scaling of scenic beauty. Forty-one introductory psychology students at Virginia Polytechnic Institute and State University rated each of the 63 scenes on a 10 point scale. The ends of the scale were semantically anchored at one with 'low' and at ten with 'high'. the subjects were instructed to rate each scene according to its 'scenic beauty', defined simply as 'the overall scenic quality of the landscape, its general beauty'. Each 35 mm color transparency was projected for eight seconds, with a period of eight seconds between each slide in which the screen was blank but lit. The scenes were presented in a randomized order. The Scenic Beauty Estimation (SBE) method (Daniel and Boster, 1976) was used to derive an interval scale of scenic beauty from the scenic beauty ratings. This method employs Thurstonian scaling procedures (Guilford, 1954; Torgerson, 1958) and signal detection theory (Green and Swetts, 1966) to transform the rating distributions of a group of individuals into an interval scale of perceived beauty. The Scenic Beauty Estimate (SBE) produced for each scene is the dm value (multiplied by 100) in signal detection theory. These values were termed SBE1 to distinguish them from the SBEs derived in study two.

Scene feature analysis. For each photograph, a number of physical features were measured by digitizing landscape elements from outlines projected on 8·5 by 11 inch paper. The digitizing process uses a computer-connected stylus which can, among other things, produce areal measures from tracing over any two-dimensional figure or outline. Foreground, middleground, and background were delineated for each photograph. Foreground consisted of that area of the photograph for which individual leaves of the vegetation were discernable. Middleground was that portion of the scene for which forms, or outlines, of trees and other vegetation were distinguishable but lacking fine detail. Background was that area of the photo for which the crown shapes of individual trees were not distinguishable.

For the purpose of examining the importance of compositional qualities each outline was also divided vertically into equal left, center, and right sections. The area in each photo of foreground (FV), middleground (MV), and background (BV) vegetation was digitized for each section. This horizontal and vertical division resulted in nine such variables: left foreground vegetation (LFV), center foreground (CFV) vegetation, and so on (see Table 1 for the complete list of variables). All variables were recorded in units of square inches. Also recorded were the total area of cloud cover (TCL), the number of discrete clouds (NC), and dichotomous measures of the presence of man-made impacts (MI), the presence of haze (H), and the presence of clouds (CL), and the geographic section (indicating north/south location) of the parkway from which the scene was sampled (AREA). The human impacts were generally views of residential and commercial areas in the far middleground or background, were small in scale relative to the entire scene, and revealed little detail. Because the focus of the study was principally directed to a delineation of the effects of vegetation, the measures of clouds and human impacts were not measured with regard to lateral placement in the scene. The AREA variable was included to provide an indicator of the effects of general topographic and vegetative features which might not be fully represented by the digitized variables. The distance from one end of the Parkway to the other represents an ecosystem gradient which varies with respect to topography and vegetation. The terrain at the northern end of the parkway is relatively

TABLE 1

Variables	Mean	S.D.
Variable definitions*		
BV = Total area of background vegetation	8·92	5·34
FV = Total area of foreground vegetation	26·97	14·22
MV = Total area of middleground vegetation	13·26	9·90
LBV = Area of background vegetation in left section	2·72	2·20
CBV = Area of background vegetation in center section	3·62	2·11
RBV = Area of background vegetation in right section	2·57	1·87
LFV = Area of foreground vegetation in left section	10·10	5·89
CFV = Area of foreground vegetation in center section	7·48	3·99
RFV = Area of foreground vegetation in right section	9·39	5·34
LMV = Area of middleground vegetation in left section	3·80	3·27
CMV = Area of middleground vegetation in center section	4·95	3·79
RMV = Area of middleground vegetation in right section	4·50	3·96
NC = Number of discrete clouds	2·05	1·70
TCL = Total area covered by clouds	15·84	11·89
SBE1 = Scenic Beauty Estimate of Scenes in Study 1	0·00	45·00
SBE2 = Scenic Beauty Estimate of Scenes in Study 2	0·00	31·92
Categorical variables	Frequency	
CL = Presence of clouds	59	
H = Presence of haze	33	
MI = Presence of human impacts	29	
AREA = Section of the parkway where scene was sampled		
1	18	
2	5	
3	8	
4	16	
5	16	

* Area is in square inches.

low in altitude and flat in surface variation, with alitidude and 'ruggedness' (or surface variation) increasing as one moves south. Vegetation at the northern end of the Parkway is primarily deciduous, with a gradual and continual increase in coniferous vegetation as one moves south. The AREA variable was created by dividing the parkway into five sections of approximately 95 miles each (running from north to south) and assigning a number from one to five (beginning with 1 for the northernmost section) to the section of the parkway each scene was from. The delineation of the scenes into foreground, middleground, and background, and the digitizing of amounts of vegetation for these distance classes and lateral sections were done by one investigator trained by a senior member of the research team.

Results and discussion
The reliability of the SBE1 ratings was computed using the method delineated by Ebel (1951). Using the mean squares produced from an analysis of variance where scenes are a random independent variable, both the average inter-judge agreement (correlation) and the composite reliability of the group of judges may be ascertained. The former represents the reliability of a single rater, and the latter the reliability of the summed or averaged vector of ratings for a set of judges of the size used in the

analysis. In this instance, the intraclass correlation is 0·23, and the composite reliability is 0·92. Thus, the average degree of agreement among individual subjects is relatively low, but the reliability of the composite scores for scenes, which were used for subsequent analysis, is quite high. This latter measure of reliability is much more relevant to the current study than is the former, since the purpose of the study is to predict the general pattern of responses in a rather diverse population.

Because the measurement of these image properties was conducted by one trained researcher, a direct appraisal of the reliability of the independent variables was not possible. Due to the substantial time and expense involved in the measurement of these variables, their duplication for a large enough sample of scenes to derive a reasonable estimate of reliability is normally not feasible. However, the criteria for the delineation of distance classes and the measurement of image features are highly circumscribed, requiring a minimum of subjective judgment. The reliability of such measures has generally been regarded to be extremely high, and is rarely appraised or reported.

Descriptive statistics for all variables are presented in Table 1, and zero-order intercorrelations among them in Table 2. Regression models were formulated using a best subset procedure. Initially, all possible combinations of up to six predictors were constituted. No more than six predictors were examined in any one model to insure no greater than a 10% ratio of predictors to observations (i.e. to avoid overfitting the data). Since the analyses were for exploratory as well as predictive purposes, a family of models is examined rather than a particular one. The family of models was initially chosen on the basis of the highest R square. Subsequently, models were compared with regard to their F ratios, PRESS statistic, coefficient significance, and variance inflation factors (Draper and Smith, 1981; Montgomery and Peck, 1982).

The best models for the sectioned (left, center and right vegetation) variables are presented in Table 3, and the best models for the unsectioned (total area) variables are presented in Table 4. The sectioned and unsectioned variables were analyzed separately, since the latter are a linear combination of the former.

In general, it appears that breaking down the scenes and using measurements from left, center, and right sections improved the predictive power of the models. The R^2 value from the best six predictor unsectioned model was 0·39, ($P < 0.0001$), while for the best six predictor sectioned model the R^2 was 0·55, ($P < 0.0001$). Among the findings for the sectioned models, it is interesting to note that LFV and RFV consistently appear as significant predictors of scenic beauty. Foreground vegetation might have been considered irrelevant to the perceived quality of scenic vistas or overlooks, unless it simply blocked the vista, but this was not the case. In addition, the regression models for the sectioned variables (see Table 3) suggest that there does seem to be a preferred composition. Middle and background vegetation are preferred in the center, and foreground vegetation has an impact on the sides. It should be noted, however, that total foreground vegetation was not a significant predictor of scenic beauty. An examination of the signs of the regression weights for RFV and LFV suggests an explanation for this finding; RFV has a positive weight while LFV has a negative one, indicating that they nullified each other with regard to the overall foreground effect on scenic beauty.

The stability of the signs of the regression weights for LFV and RFV was assessed by recalculating models with those two variables eight times while substituting other

TABLE 2
Correlations among predictor and criterion variables

	MV	RV	LFV	CFV	RFV	LMV	CMV	RMV	LBV	CBV	RBV	TCL	NCL	SBE1	SBE2	AREA
FV	-0.82	-0.56	0.92	0.92	0.94	-0.73	-0.71	-0.75	-0.64	-0.27	-0.55	-0.07	-0.25	-0.38	-0.11	0.02
MV		0.30	-0.68	-0.85	-0.78	0.83	0.94	0.90	0.37	0.07	0.32	-0.10	0.12	0.46	0.22	-0.06
BV			-0.57	-0.51	-0.49	0.31	0.21	0.29	0.88	0.84	0.86	-0.00	0.11	0.26	0.04	0.11
LFV				0.76	0.79	-0.76	-0.53	-0.57	-0.65	-0.30	-0.52	-0.07	-0.26	-0.44	-0.16	0.07
CFV					0.86	-0.67	-0.84	-0.77	-0.57	-0.26	-0.49	-0.04	-0.23	-0.40	-0.16	0.01
FVR						-0.60	-0.68	-0.81	-0.55	-0.19	-0.53	-0.07	-0.20	-0.24	0.10	-0.03
LMV							0.70	0.58	0.32	0.14	0.37	-0.13	0.21	0.51	0.28	-0.14
CMV								0.81	0.29	-0.02	0.28	-0.12	0.12	0.42	0.21	-0.09
RMV									0.39	0.10	0.24	-0.02	0.01	0.34	0.13	0.04
LBV										0.58	0.68	0.04	0.06	0.19	0.00	0.09
CBV											0.59	0.03	0.09	0.31	0.18	0.09
RBV												-0.10	0.14	0.16	0.08	0.11
TCL													-0.15	-0.08	-0.15	0.15
NCL														0.36	0.30	-0.62
SBE1															0.82	-0.36
SBE2																-0.40

$n = 63$.
$r = 0.248$ significant at $P = 0.05$.

variables into the model with RFV and LFV. The regression weight signs and their significance were stable across all trials. Thus the signs of the coefficients for RFV and LFV were not spurious functions of other variables present in the models. However, it is also conceivable that the countervailing signs of LFV and RFV are a result of a suppressor relationship between these two variables*. An examination of the correlation matrix (see Table 2) does in fact suggest such a possibility. In this case, both right and left foreground vegetation are negatively correlated with scenic beauty, while positively correlated with one another. In addition, the zero order correlation between RFV and SBE is not significant ($P > 0.05$). Thus, the change in the RFV regression sign could indicate that LFV and RFV are mutually inhibiting nonpredictive variance. If this is indeed the case, and not a function of other variables, then the relationship should emerge even when no other variables are present in the regression equation. To test this hypothesis, SBE1 was regressed on LFV and RFV alone. The results of this computation are equivocal, but do indicate that any suppression effect between these two predictors is relatively weak. The regression weight signs are the same as in the other equations (standardized coefficients are -0.68 and 0.30 for LFV and RFV, respectively), but the significance test on the RFV regression weight is not significant ($P > 0.05$). Further supporting the assertion that any suppressor effects are weak are the multicollinearity diagnostics reported in Table 3. The variance inflation factors in all models are well below prescribed standards (see Belsley et al., 1980; Montgomery and Peck, 1982), indicating that multicollinearity, of which suppression is a special case, is not a problem.

It is also seemed possible that the differences in signs of the regression weights for RFV and LFV could reflect differences in the distribution of amount of foreground vegetation between the left and right sections in the landscape scenes. Inspection of the means (10·10 and 9·39) and standard deviations (5·89 and 5·33) for LFV and RFV, respectively, suggests that this was not the case.

It is conceivable that right and left foreground vegetation differed in ways not adequately assessed by the measures used in this study. For example, it is possible that the type of vegetation (e.g. coniferous versus deciduous) is not evenly dispersed over right and left foreground. The landscape scenes were visually inspected for obvious content differences (i.e. factors such as shape or form, or the presence of coniferous versus deciduous vegetation) once by two of the co-authors, and once independently by a third co-author. However, no apparent differences were detected simply by visual inspection.

As noted earlier, previous research (Buhyoff et al., 1982) has suggested a non-monotonic relationship between perceived scenic beauty and the area of sharp mountains in a scene. The reason for this is unclear. One possibility may be that the greater the area taken up by background the further those elements are from the viewer, and consequently, they may lose positive visual qualities associated with scenic beauty, such as detail and texture. In the present study it was hypothesized that such a non-monotonic relationship might represent the pattern of covariation between total background vegetation and scenic beauty as well. Visual inspection of the plot of residual SBE values versus total background area suggested that such a curvilinearity might be present. To test this, a regression analysis was done on one

---

*For a discussion of suppressor effects, see Darlington (1968), Conger (1974), and Cohen and Cohen (1975).

TABLE 3
Study 1 best regression models for sectioned variables

Model	R^2	Overall F	PRESS	Variable	Standardized coefficient	$P > \lvert t \rvert$	Variance inflation factor
1	0.55	11.28 ($P < 0.0001$)	69075.81	Left Foreground (LFV)	−0.627	0.0005	3.54
				Right Foreground (RFV)	0.510	0.006	3.96
				Center Middleground (CMV)	0.524	0.0001	2.03
				Left Backgroud (LBV)	−0.333	0.024	2.56
				Center Background (CBV)	0.456	0.002	1.64
				AREA	−0.258	0.008	1.09
2	0.53	10.22 ($P < 0.0001$)	73483.62	Left Foreground (LFV)	−0.504	0.003	3.09
				Right Foreground (RFV)	0.486	0.012	4.18
				Center Middleground (CMV)	0.530	0.0002	2.03
				Center Background (LBV)	0.414	0.001	1.70
				Right Background (RBV)	−0.202	0.141	2.14
				AREA	−0.272	0.0065	1.08
3	0.54	10.73 ($P < 0.0001$)	71473.42	Left Foreground (LFV)	−0.754	0.001	3.66
				Right Foreground (RFV)	0.739	0.0015	5.91
				Right Middleground (RMV)	0.619	0.0003	3.13
				Left Background (LBV)	−0.338	0.023	2.56
				Center Background (CBV)	0.393	0.0012	1.60
				AREA	−0.313	0.0016	1.07
4	0.53	10.38 ($P < 0.0001$)	74571.08	Left Foreground (LFV)	−0.555	0.0016	3.29
				Right Foreground (RFV)	0.768	0.0011	5.87
				Center Middleground (CMV)	0.351	0.0425	3.39
				Right Middleground (CBV)	0.345	0.1058	5.21
				Center Background (CBV)	0.297	0.0047	1.20
				AREA	−0.304	0.0025	1.09

of the sets of total variables, including total background area (BV), while adding a total background area squared (BV2) term to the model with which to test the quadratic effect. Both BV and BV2 were significant predictors of scenic beauty (standardized $b = 1.21$, $P < 0.0003$ and $b = -1.07$, $P < 0.0007$, respectively), suggesting that both linear and non-monotonic nonlinear relationships are present in the data.

The findings of experiment 1 suggest that landscape elements that are general with regard to their content (e.g. amount of background vegetation) are significant predictors of perceived scenic beauty. In addition, the spatial arrangement of these elements were factors in the prediction of scenic beauty. However, other variables, including various measures of clouds, and the presence of haze and human impact were not predictive. The lack of relationship between these latter variables and perceived scenic beauty may be a function of restriction of range (i.e. extreme values on the continuum were not represented in this sample) or lack of measurement sensitivity. For example, in our sample of scenes human impacts tended to be in the background and not predominant in the scene. In contrast, prior research has revealed significant effects when human artifacts are primary elements in the scene (Kaplan et al., 1972).

To understand better the nature of the differential weighting of left and right foreground in the prediction of perceived scenic beauty, a second experiment was conducted. The question addressed by this second experiment was whether differential preference for the left and right foreground of the image was a function of image content, or due to a perceptual bias, discussed earlier. In the present study, if such a right–left bias persists in monochotic presentations, it is conceivable that differential perception might result. Furthermore, since the majority of the population can be characterized by left side brain specialization (perceptual right side emphasis), right side preference might emerge in a random sample drawn from the population. This bias can be tested by simply reversing the image of the landscape (i.e. by turning the slide around) so that the content on the right side would now appear on the left, and vice versa. If the opposing regression weights are due to the specific content of the image, the new regression weight signs should be opposite to those in study 1. That is, LFV should change from negative to positive, and RFV should shift from positive to negative. If, on the other hand, the opposing regression weights are due to perceptual bias, such as differential processing of information from the left and right fields of vision, it would be expected that the regression weight signs for left and right foreground would remain stable.

Study 2

Method

The data in study 2 were collected using procedures identical to those in study 1, with one exception. In this replication the stimuli (images) were reversed with regard to their right–left orientation, so that what was previously left was now right, and vice versa. Thirty-nine introductory psychology students at Virginia Polytechnic Institute and State University rated the reversed slides. None of these subjects had

TABLE 4
Study 1 best regression models for unsectioned variables

Model	R^2	Overall F	PRESS	Variable	Standardized coefficient	$P > |t|$	Variance inflation factor
1	0·39	5·99 ($P < 0.0001$)	96734·06	Foreground (FV)	0·244	0·288	4·76
				Middleground (MV)	0·613	0·004	3·82
				Background (BV)	0·284	0·044	1·76
				Human Impact (MI)	−1·25	0·367	1·73
				Haze (H)	−0·091	0·441	1·26
				AREA	−4·04	0·004	1·71
2	0·39	5·92 ($P < 0.0001$)	98180·40	Foreground (FV)	0·274	0·256	5·25
				Middleground (MV)	0·615	0·004	3·98
				Background (BV)	0·310	0·034	1·86
				Area of Clouds (TCL)	0·089	0·450	1·25
				Haze (H)	−0·140	0·244	1·28
				AREA	0·339	0·003	1·13
3	0·39	5·88 ($P < 0.0001$)	96433·02	Foreground (FV)	0·284	0·243	5·29
				Middleground (MV)	0·633	0·003	4·03
				Background (BV)	0·278	0·050	1·77
				Human Impact (MI)	−0·135	0·330	1·73
				Presence of Clouds (CL)	0·051	0·660	1·21
				AREA	−0·430	0·001	1·56
4	0·38	5·84 ($P < 0.0001$)	97327·98	Foreground (FV)	0·266	0·272	5·23
				Middleground (MV)	0·623	0·004	4·09
				Background (BV)	0·273	0·055	1·77
				Area of Clouds (TCL)	0·025	0·826	1·22
				Human Impact (MI)	−1·42	0·305	1·72
				AREA	−0·443	0·001	1·49

participated in the first study. The SBE values derived from this study were termed SBE2.

Results and discussion

SBE2 reliability was computed in the same manner described in study 1, and the outcome was largely the same. The intraclass correlation for SBE2 is 0·19 (compared with 0·23 for SBE1) and the composite reliability is 0·90 (compared with 0·92). Thus, once again, there is substantial variation at the individual level, but the composite scores are extremely reliable.

To make more direct comparisons between the two studies, the first set of regression models formulated using the replication data contained identical predictors to those in the best models of study 1. These models are presented in Table 5. For ease of interpretation, the variables for study 2 are named for their new orientation. That is, what was formerly right foreground vegetation (RFV) in study 1 is now termed new left foreground vegetation (NLFV). The other left and right variables are correspondingly identified. Comparing the two sets of models in Tables 3 and 5, it is apparent that prediction is less effective in study 2. The average R^2 in the second set of models is 0·36 (compared with 0·53 for the original models), and even the best sectioned models from study 2 had only an average R^2 of 0·42 (see Table 8).

A comparison of regression weight signs for the best study 1 models and the corresponding study 2 models is given in Table 6. These results suggest that the right–left bias in study 1 indicated by the contrasting regression weight signs for LFV and RFV, is not manifest in the corresponding models in study 2. Instead, the regression weight signs for RFV and LFV reverse with the reversal of the scene. All other coefficient signs remain the same between study 1 and 2 models, although some of these predictors are not significant within all models. These findings suggest that the sign of the predictors seems to be associated with the actual content (on the right or left side) of the image rather than with a perceptual bias for the right side of the visual field. That is, people seem to be responding to something specific in the scene, and if it is valued on the right side of the image, it will be similarly valued on the left side. This would suggest that individuals making global evaluations of these scenes are responding to specific features regardless of their placement in the image.

Support for this latter inference derives from the finding that the correlation between the study 1 and study 2 SBEs was 0·83 ($P < 0.0001$). While this is a reasonably high correlation, Buhyoff *et al.* (1982) report that SBE intercorrelations among four heterogeneous groups (two different student groups, a church group, and a PTA group) ranged from 0·89 to 0·97. While the Fisher's Z transformation for the difference between an r of 0·83 and 0·97 is highly significant ($z = 5.01$; $P < 0.0001$), the difference between an r of 0·83 and 0·89 is not ($z = 1.30$; $P < 0.10$). The difference between those correlations among SBEs and the one found here represents, in the most conservative case, about a twelve percent difference in the amount of variance that can be explained in one set of SBEs from the other. It is also possible that the observed differences are a function of the reliabilities of the values used in estimating the correlations. However, in this study, the composite reliabilities of the SBEs were quite high (0·92 and 0·90, for SBE1 and SBE2, respectively), indicating that unreliability is likely to be only a minor constraint on the attained magnitude of the

TABLE 5
Study 2 regression models using same predictors as best experiment 1 models

Model	R^2	Overall F	PRESS	Variable	Standardized coefficient	$P > |t|$	Variance inflation factor
1	0·39	5·99 ($P<0·0001$)	47531·96	New Left Foreground (NLFV)	0·456	0·03	4·17
				New Right Foreground (NRFV)	−0·322	0·08	3·09
				Center Middleground (CMV)	0·432	0·005	2·03
				New Left Background (NLBV)	−0·348	0·026	2·14
				Center Background (CBV)	0·429	0·002	1·69
				AREA	−0·322	0·004	1·09
2	0·37	5·42 ($P<0·0002$)	49008·8	New Left Foreground (NLFV)	0·537	0·14	3·96
				New Right Foreground (NRFV)	−0·414	0·04	3·53
				Center Middleground (CMV)	0·424	0·007	2·03
				Center Background (CBV)	0·382	0·006	1·64
				New Right Background (NRBV)	−0·291	0·09	2·55
				AREA	−0·322	0·005	1·09
3	0·36	5·16 ($P<0·0003$)	50783·0	New Left Foreground (NLFV)	0·130	0·49	3·14
				New Right Foreground (NRFV)	−0·016	0·94	4·74
				New Right Middleground (NRMV)	0·379	0·03	2·53
				New Left Background (NLBV)	−0·362	0·02	2·15
				Center Background (CBV)	0·404	0·005	1·68
				AREA	−0·341	0·003	1·07
4	0·34	4·73 ($P<0·0006$)	52290·73	New Left Foreground (NLFV)	0·557	0·027	4·73
				New Right Foreground (NRFV)	−0·217	0·41	5·88
				Center Middleground (CMV)	0·375	0·068	3·44
				New Right Middleground (NRMV)	0·090	0·69	4·27
				Center Background (CBV)	0·250	0·03	1·19
				AREA	−0·345	0·003	1·08

TABLE 6
Comparison between experiment 1 best models and corresponding experiment 2 models

	Experiment 1		Experiment 2	
	Variable	Beta sign	Variable	Beta sign
Model 1	LFV	−	NLFV	+
	RFV	+	NRFV	−
	CMV	+	CMV	+
	LBV	−	NLBV	−
	CBV	+	CBV	+
	AREA	−	AREA	−
	$R^2 = 0.54$		$R^2 = 0.39$	
Model 2	LFV	−	NLFV	+
	RFV	+	NRFV	−
	CMV	+	CMV	+
	CBV	+	CBV	+
	RBV	−	NRBV	−
	AREA	−	AREA	−
	$R^2 = 0.52$		$R^2 = 0.36$	
Model 3	LFV	−	NLFV	+
	RFV	+	NRFV	−
	RMV	+	NRMV	+
	LBV	−	NLBV	−
	CBV	+	CBV	+
	AREA	−	AREA	−
	$R^2 = 0.53$		$R^2 = 0.35$	
Model 4	LFV	−	NLFV	+
	RFV	+	NRFV	−
	CMV	+	CMV	+
	RMV	+	NRMV	+
	CBV	+	CBV	+
	AREA	−	AREA	−
	$R^2 = 0.52$		$R^2 = 0.33$	

correlation. In fact, correcting for attenuation (see Cohen and Cohen, 1975) increases the correlation between SBE1 and SBE2 to only 0·91.

As was noted, the best initial models account for somewhat more variance in SBEs than do the best replication models—an average R^2 of 0·39 vs. 0·29 for the unsectioned models, and an average of 0·53 vs. 0·42 for the sectioned models. Comparing the best unsectioned models in studies 1 and 2, there seems to be considerable consistency (see Tables 4 and 7). The models from each experiment with the highest R^2 values contain the same elements (both models 1) as do model 2 in study 1 and model 3 in study 2. With regard to specific predictors, it is interesting to note that in the initial models presence of haze (H) was not a powerful predictor, while in the replication models it was. And as in the initial study, the models using the replication data indicate that total foreground did not add to the power of the models.

Unlike the study 1 models however, the replication models show total background not to be a significant predictor. This is enigmatic since background is the *sine qua non* of vistas. It is possible that part of the reason background vegetation was such

TABLE 7
Study 2 best regression models for unsectioned variables

Model	R^2	Overall F	PRESS	Variable	Standardized coefficient	$P > |t|$	Variance inflation factor
1	0·30	3·91 ($P<0·0025$)	55978·36	Foreground (FV)	0·321	0·19	4·76
				Middleground (MV)	0·422	0·05	3·82
				Background (BV)	0·210	0·16	1·75
				Human Impact (MI)	0·138	0·35	1·73
				Haze (H)	−0·278	0·03	1·26
				AREA	−0·252	0·09	1·71
2	0·29	3·76 ($P<0·003$)	55783·43	Foreground (FV)	0·312	0·23	5·32
				Middleground (MV)	0·451	0·04	3·81
				Background (BV)	0·201	0·19	1·80
				Haze (H)	−0·267	0·04	1·28
				Presence of Clouds (CL)	−0·059	0·63	1·22
				AREA	−0·334	0·007	1·12
3	0·29	3·74 ($P<0·0034$)	55732·62	Foreground (FV)	0·390	0·13	5·25
				Middleground (MV)	0·512	0·02	3·99
				Background (BV)	0·226	0·14	1·87
				Area of Clouds (TCL)	0·049	0·69	1·25
				Haze (H)	−0·265	0·04	1·29
				AREA	−0·337	0·006	1·13
4	0·28	3·64 ($P<0·004$)	57027·09	Middleground (MV)	0·193	0·13	1·26
				Background (BV)	0·104	0·40	1·19
				Human Impact (MI)	0·144	0·34	1·78
				Haze (H)	−0·302	0·02	1·30
				Presence of Clouds (CL)	−0·087	0·47	1·12
				AREA	−0·246	0·10	1·73

TABLE 8
Study 2 best regression models for sectioned variables

Model	R^2	Overall F	PRESS	Variable	Standardized coefficient	$P > |t|$	Variance inflation factor
1	0·42	6·85 ($P < 0·0001$)	45178·19	New Right Middleground (NRMV)	0·318	0·007	1·30
				New Left Background (NLBV)	0·396	0·005	1·83
				Center Background (CBV)	0·459	0·0007	1·59
				Human Impact (MI)	0·225	0·09	1·66
				Haze (H)	−0·271	0·01	1·23
				AREA	−0·154	0·24	1·70
2	0·42	6·69 ($P < 0·0001$)	46022·40	New Left Foreground (NLFV)	0·865	0·0009	5·85
				New Right Foreground (NRFV)	−0·522	0·005	3·14
				New Left Middleground (NLMV)	0·522	0·006	3·23
				Center Background (CBV)	0·234	0·03	1·15
				Human Impact (MI)	0·315	0·004	1·08
				Haze (H)	−0·366	0·001	1·07
3	0·42	6·64 ($P < 0·0001$)	45832·77	Center Middleground (CMV)	0·120	0·43	2·20
				New Right Middleground (NRMV)	0·250	0·10	2·19
				New Left Background (NLBV)	−0·433	0·002	1·85
				Center Background (CBV)	0·494	0·0004	1·67
				Human Impact (MI)	0·298	0·0089	1·16
				Haze (H)	−0·324	0·003	1·07
4	0·42	6·63 ($P < 0·0001$)	45106·73	New Left Foreground (NLFV)	0·109	0·44	1·95
				New Right Middleground (NRMV)	0·378	0·006	1·72
				New Right Background (NRBV)	−0·369	0·01	2·15
				Center Background (CBV)	0·455	0·0009	1·61
				Human Impact (MI)	0·307	0·006	1·13
				Haze (H)	−0·312	0·004	1·07

a relatively weak predictor is that it was somewhat restricted in range (0·0–23·03) relative to foreground (0·6–70·39) and middleground vegetation (0·0–42·97). However, these same variables were used in the study 1 regressions, wherein background vegetation was at least marginally significant for all four models.

Given the study 1 best sectioned models (see Table 3) previously discussed, the best sectioned models for study 2 (see Table 8) are most notable for the failure of geographic area of the parkway to be included, except in model 1 where it was a weak predictor. In addition, the foreground variables that were prominent in the original models (see Table 3) were not as prominent in the replication models, though they did appear in model 2, and to a lesser degree in model 4. In these models from the second study, nonvegetative variables appeared to be relatively more powerful than in the best study 1 models, which contained only vegetative variables, except for AREA. For study 2 presence of human impacts (MI) had a positive effect on SBEs, while the presence of haze (H) had a negative impact.

General Discussion and Conclusions

The present findings support previous work (Shafer *et al.*, 1969; Brush and Palmer, 1979) which demonstrated the ability of general content classes of vegetation to predict scenic beauty. Of particular interest is the finding that foreground vegetation can have a substantial impact on the perceived scenic beauty of vistas. Unfortunately, the nature of this impact is complex, as indicated by both the differential regression weights found for LFV and RFV, and the lack of impact of total foreground vegetation. In addition, in the best study 2 models left and right foreground were strong predictors in one of the four models. In this instance, the weights are consistent with the weights found in the other models. There was no support for the notion that a perceptual left–right bias was responsible for the differential weights of LFV and RFV.

The stability of the weights for foreground vegetation suggests that particular foreground content and its placement within a scene are significant predictors of scenic quality. It is somewhat enigmatic that while viewers perceive specific content (i.e. left and right foreground) positively or negatively no matter what side of the image it is on, the correlation between SBEs for the original and reversed scenes was only 0·83. This suggests that the perceived quality of the original and reversed scenes is similar but far from identical.

Until the basis for the differential effects of LFV and RFV are better understood, it is difficult to make specific recommendations for management actions. It would obviously be unwise to generalize from the weights found here for left and right foreground, to suggest left foreground be inhibited and right foreground be enhanced for any particular scenic overlook. In addition, as Weinstein (1976) has noted, the generalizability of any prediction model must be established by demonstrating its accuracy in other contexts. Thus, efficacy and utility of these predictors must be evaluated for other sets of landscape scenes and other samples of observers.

The regression models examined in the present study explained a respectable but moderate amount of criterion variance. Nonetheless, a considerable amount of variance in the SBEs went unaccounted for as well. Given that the findings regarding LFV and RFV remain somewhat enigmatic, it may be that other relevant variables or attributes of the scenes went unrecognized, and that these variables may have been able to account for more of the SBE variance. That is, the variables used in these studies (e.g. LFV and RFV) may have been surrogates for these unrecognized other variables. The nature of these 'other' variables remains unclear, but more complex formulations of environmental attributes must be considered as one viable alternative. As noted earlier, relatively abstract transactional constructs such as complexity, congruity, and mystery have been used effectively in research on environmental aesthetics (Wohlwill, 1968, 1976; Kaplan et al., 1972; Kaplan, 1973, 1975; Wohlwill and Harris, 1980; Feimer et al., 1981; Feimer, 1983), suggesting that a characterization of the inter-relationship among the elements within the scene from within a more holistic framework may add to prediction beyond what is represented by a simple and gross representation of content. On a similar, but somewhat less abstract plane, it is also conceivable that a more discriminating analysis of content, including an examination of vegetation type (e.g. coniferous vs. deciduous), and visually salient physical attributes such as shape, form, and color, might provide a meaningful increment in predictive power. In any case, an examination of these other classes of variables in conjunction with the kinds of variables used in this set of studies holds clear promise for providing insight into the complex pattern of relationships that characterize aesthetic responses to natural settings.

In conclusion, the research presented suggests that general content classes of vegetation and their lateral placement within scenes provide moderately good prediction of scenic beauty, but that the nature of the relationships which emerged requires further exploration before they are clearly understood. An interesting research agenda presents itself, which includes at least three items of immediate priority: (1) a cross-validation of the findings from these studies to other samples of scenes and observers; (2) a more fine-grained analyses of vegetation content, and (3) the concurrent use of more complex variables to provide additional predictive power and provide insight into the nature and meaning of relationships between physicalistic constructs and scenic beauty.

References

Arthur, L. M. (1977). Predicting scenic beauty of forest environments: some empirical tests. *Forest Science*, **23**, 151–160.

Arthur, L. M., Daniel, T. C. and Boster, R. S. (1977). Scenic assessment: an overview. *Landscape Planning*, **4**, 109–129.

Belsley, D. A., Kuh, E. and Welsch, R. E. (1980). *Regression Diagnostics: Identifying Influential Data and Sources of Collinearity*. New York: John Wiley and Sons.

Briggs, D. J. and France, J. (1980). Landscape evaluation: a comparative study. *Journal of Environmental Management*, **10**, 263–275.

Brush, R. O. and Palmer, J. F. (1979). Measuring the impact of urbanization on scenic quality: land use change in the northeast. *Proceedings of Our National Landscape: A conference on applied techniques for analysis and management of the visual resource*. Berkeley, CA.: USDA Forest Service, pp. 358–364.

Buhyoff, G. J. and Wellman, J. P. (1980). The specification of a nonlinear psychophysical function for visual landscape dimensions. *Journal of Leisure Research*, **12**, 257–272.

Buhyoff, G. J., Wellman, J. D. and Daniel, T. C. (1982). Predicting scenic quality for Mountain Pine Beetle and Western Spruce Budworm damaged forest vistas. *Forest Science*, **28**, 827–838.

Cohen, J. and Cohen, P. (1975). *Applied multiple regression/correlation analysis for the behavioral sciences*. New Jersey: Lawrence Erlbaum Associates.

Conger, A. J. (1974). A revised definition for suppressor variables: a guide to their identification and interpretation. *Educational and Psychological Measurement*, **34**, 35–46.

Daniel, T. C. and Boster, R. S. (1976). *Measuring landscape aesthetics: The scenic beauty estimation method*. USDA Forest Service Research Paper RM-167. Rocky Mtn. Forest and Range Experiment Station, Fort Collins, Colo, 66pp.

Daniel, T. C. and Vining, J. (1983). Methodological issues in the assessment of landscape quality. In I. Altman and J. F. Wohlwill (eds), *Human Behavior and Environment*. Vol. 6. New York: Plenum Press.

Darlington, R. B. (1968). Multiple regression in psychological research and practice. *Psychological Bulletin*, **69**, 161–182.

Draper, N. R. and Smith, H. (1981). *Applied Regression Analysis*. New York: John Wiley and Sons.

Ebel, R. L. (1951). Estimation of the reliability of ratings. *Psychometrica*, **16**, 407–423.

Feimer, N. R. (1983). Environmental perception and cognition in rural contexts. In A. W. Childs and G. B. Melton (eds), *Rural Psychology*. New York: Plenum press, pp. 113–149.

Feimer, N. R., Smardon, R. C. and Craik, K. H. (1981). Evaluating the effectiveness of observer-based visual resource and impact assessment methods. *Landscape Research*, **6**, 12–16.

Gazzaniga, M. S. (1970). *The Bisected Brain*. New York: Appleton.

Green, D. M. and Swetts, J. A. (1966). *Signal Detection and Psychophysics*. New York: John Wiley & Sons.

Guilford, J. P. (1954). *Psychometric Methods*. New York: McGraw-Hill.

Gur, R. E., Gur, R. C. and Marshalek, B. (1975). Classroom seating and functional brain asymmetry. *Journal of Educational Psychology*, **67**, 151–153.

Harcum, E. R. (1978). Lateral dominance as a determinant of temporal order of responding. In M. Kinsbourne (ed.), *Asymmetrical function of the brain*. Cambridge: Cambridge University Press.

Heron, W. (1957). Perception as a function of retinal locus and attention. *American Journal of Psychology*, **70**, 38–48.

Kaplan, R. (1973). Predictors of environmental preference: designers and clients. In W. F. E. Preiser (ed.), *Environmental Design Research*. Stroudsburg, PA.: Dowden, Hutchinson & Ross.

Kaplan, R. (1975). Some methods and strategies in the prediction of preference. In E. H. Zube, R. O. Brush, and J. G. Fabos (eds), *Landscape Assessment: Values, Perceptions and Resources*. Stroudsburg, PA.: Dowden, Hutchinson & Ross.

Kaplan, S., Kaplan, R. and Wendt, J. S. (1972). Rated preference and complexity for natural and urban visual materials. *Perception and Psychophysics*, **12**, 354–356.

Montgomery, D. C. and Peck, E. A. (1982). *Introduction to Linear Regression Analysis*. New York: John Wiley & Sons.

Propst, D. B. and Buhyoff, G. J. (1980). Policy capturing and landscape preference quantification: a methodological study. *Journal of Environmental Management*, **11**, 45–59.

Schroeder, H. W. and Daniel, T. C. (1980). Predicting the scenic quality of forest road corridors. *Environment and Behavior*, **12**, 349–366.

Shafer, E. L., Jr., Hamilton, J. F., Jr. and Schmidt, E. A. (1969). Natural landscape preferences: a predictive model. *Journal of Leisure Research*, **1**, 1–19.

Torgerson, W. S. (1958). *Theory and Methods of Scaling*. New York: John Wiley.

Weinstein, N. D. (1976). The statistical prediction of environmental preferences: problems of validity and application. *Environment and Behavior*, **8**, 611–626.

Wickelgren, L. W. (1967). Convergence in the human newborn. *Journal of Experimental Child Psychology*, **5**, 74–85.

Wohlwill, J. F. (1968). Amount of stimulus exploration and preference as differential functions of stimulus complexity. *Perception and Psychophysics*, **4**, 307–312.

Wohlwill, J. F. (1976). Environmental aesthetics: the environment as a source of affect. In I. Altman and J. F. Wohlwill (eds), *Human Behavior and Environment: Advances In Theory and Research*, Vol. 1. New York: Plenum Press.

Wohlwill, J. F. and Harris, G. (1980). Response to congruity or contrast for man-made features in natural recreation settings. *Leisure Sciences*, **3**, 349–365.

Zube, E. (1976). Perception of landscape and land use. In I. Altman and J. F. Wohlwill (eds). *Human Behavior and Environment: Advances in Theory and Research*. Vol. 1. New York: Plenum Press.

Zube, E. H., Pitt, D. G. and Anderson, T. W. (1975). Perception and prediction of scenic resource values of the Northeast. In E. H. Zube, R. O. Brush, and J. G. Fabos (eds), *Landscape Assessment: Perceptions and Resources*. Stroudsburg, PA., Dowden, Hutchinson & Ross, pp. 151–167.

Zube, E. H., Sells, J. L. and Taylor, J. G. (1982). Landscape Perception: research, application and theory. *Landscape Planning*, **9**, 1–33.

PREFERENCE AND MEANING OF ARBORETUM LANDSCAPES: COMBINING QUANTITATIVE AND QUALITATIVE DATA

HERBERT W. SCHROEDER
USDA Forest Service, North Central Forest Experiment Station, Chicago, Illinois, U.S.A.

Abstract

A group of members and volunteers at the Morton Arboretum near Chicago rated their preferences for photographs of landscapes in the arboretum, wrote open-ended descriptions of their favorite arboretum settings, and described the thoughts, feelings, and memories they associated with those settings. Most participants rated densely forested, natural landscapes highest in preference, but some also liked either open, natural fields or maintained, formal landscapes. The open-ended descriptions revealed a variety of significant meanings and experiences, some of which appeared to be associated with specific kinds of environments. The combination of quantitative and qualitative research methods yields a more complete understanding of how people experience arboretum landscapes, than would either method used by itself.

Introduction

Environmental perception researchers have focused much effort on understanding how people respond to different kinds of outdoor environments and landscapes (Daniel & Vining, 1983). One of the basic questions addressed in this research is, what kinds of landscapes do people prefer? A popular approach for answering this question is to show people sets of landscapes (usually represented by photographs) and have them use numerical rating scales to express their degree of liking for each (Daniel & Boster, 1976). These preference ratings can then be related statistically to objective measurements of features contained in the landscapes, to determine how much each feature contributes to the perceived quality of the landscape.

This quantitative approach to studying landscape perception has produced statistical models for predicting landscape quality from measurements of features such as tree density, vegetative ground cover, and built structures (Schroeder & Daniel, 1981; Brown & Daniel, 1984). These models can be used to estimate the impact that various management actions will have on the perceived quality of landscapes. There are, however, important questions that this quantitative approach to landscape perception cannot answer. For example, what kinds of experiences do people have in particular types of landscapes, what are the meanings and values associated with preferred landscapes, and how important are these landscapes in the context of people's lives? To answer these questions a more open-ended, qualitative approach to studying landscape perception is required.

Furthermore, quantitative preference studies do not tell us how people are likely to react if preferred landscapes are altered in specific ways. For example, two individuals might both agree that a particular landscape is the most attractive in a set of scenes. One of the individuals might think of this preferred landscape simply as a pretty backdrop for a picnic. For the other individual, the same landscape might evoke strong feelings about the sanctity of pristine nature. If the visual quality of the landscape were altered, for example by building paved paths or other facilities, the first person might be relatively unconcerned, while the second might react with strong anger and a sense of loss. Thus, knowledge of a person's preference ratings of landscapes is not sufficient to predict how the person will respond to alternative landscape management actions.

This study used a combination of quantitative and qualitative research methods to examine landscape preferences and meanings for a group of arboretum users. I define 'preference' as the degree of liking for one landscape as compared to another, and 'meaning' as the set of thoughts, feelings, memories and interpretations evoked by a landscape. In this study, preference was measured on a rating scale using a quantitative approach similar to earlier studies of landscape preference (e.g. Daniel & Boster, 1976; Schroeder, 1987). Landscape meanings were pursued through open-ended, written responses.

The relative advantages of quantitative and qualitative methods have been debated throughout the history of psychology. Quantitative methods have dominated American psychology with an emphasis on the measurement of objectively observed behavior. Phenomenologists and humanistic psychologists, however, have insisted that psychology must also consider the meanings of events as people experience them in everyday life (Giorgi, 1970; Keen, 1975). In the field of landscape perception and environmental esthetics, some researchers have pursued rigorous quantitative measurement of human response to the environment. Others have followed a qualitative experiential or humanistic approach, seeking to understand the meaning of human–environment interactions from the viewpoint of the experiencer. (See the reviews by Zube *et al.*, 1982; Porteous, 1982; and Daniel & Vining, 1983 for discussion of these different approaches to landscape esthetics research.)

Quantitative and qualitative approaches need not be mutually exclusive. Giorgi (1971, 1975) sees strong parallels between quantitative and qualitative data gathering methods, and advocates using both approaches in any experiment involving human subjects. Similarly, both Porteous (1982) and Zube *et al.* (1982) urge more integration and collaboration between quantitative and qualitative approaches to environmental esthetics and landscape perception research.

A combination of quantitative and qualitative approaches can provide a more complete understanding of human response to landscapes than can either approach used alone. On the one hand, people cannot always explain exactly why they prefer one landscape over another. Using a numerical rating scale to evaluate visual images allows people to express their degree of preference and to make fine discriminations among landscapes without having to justify or explain every evaluation verbally. On the other hand, the preferences expressed in numerical ratings exist within a larger context of feelings, beliefs, values and memories, many of which are easily verbalized. This qualitative context is important for understanding how landscapes are experienced and the significance they have in people's lives.

One situation in which the personal meaning of preferred landscapes becomes particularly important is with respect to scarce or unique recreation and landscape resources. The Morton Arboretum, located in the Chicago suburb of Lisle, Illinois, is an example of a unique landscape resource in a major metropolitan area. The value of the Arboretum's landscape is reflected in the heavy use that the Arboretum receives, especially in the colorful fall and spring seasons. On peak days the Arboretum is filled to overflowing, despite the fact that popular activities such as picnicking and bicycling are not permitted. The Arboretum has a large and dedicated following of members and volunteers. Many of these people have formed strong personal attachments to the Arboretum and its landscapes. The Morton Arboretum staff recognizes that its landscapes have special meaning for many people, but does not fully understand the nature of the experiences people have in these landscapes or how the design of new landscapes, displays, and collections will affect people's perceptions and experiences.

In this research I explored preference for and meaning of Morton Arboretum landscapes with a group of members and volunteers who value the Arboretum highly. The research addressed several questions:

(1) What kinds of landscape scenes are most preferred by this group of Arboretum users?
(2) Do different individuals prefer different kinds of landscapes?
(3) What specific features appear in these people's descriptions of their favorite places in the Arboretum?
(4) What meanings do these people associate with their favorite places?
(5) Are different meanings associated with different kinds of places?

In addition, I examined the convergent validity of the quantitative and qualitative approaches, by testing whether individuals who give high preference ratings to particular scenes tend to describe similar scenes in their open-ended descriptions of favorite settings.

Methods

Participants for this study were contacted through announcements in the Morton Arboretum newsletter and in a volunteer training session. Thirty-four people expressed interest in participating.

A two-part survey was employed. To explore landscape preference, I sent all 34 people a questionnaire containing 20 color photographs of Arboretum landscapes. I included examples of several important landscape types in the Arboretum, for example, natural forests, formal gardens, special collections, and open fields. Brief descriptions of all the scenes are given in Table 1, and some examples of the scenes themselves appear in Figure 1. Participants rated each landscape on a scale of preference ranging from 1 to 10. The physical characteristics of each photo were measured by laying a square grid over the photo and estimating the per cent of the photo image that was composed of each of several important features. The features that were measured are listed in the first column of Table 2.

To investigate landscape meaning, I distributed a second questionnaire to the people who completed the first one. This questionnaire asked people to select from memory, three to five landscapes that characterized the kind of place the Arboretum is for them, and to give a brief verbal description of each selected landscape. The respondents were then asked to explain the meaning of each landscape by describing the thoughts, feelings and memories that they associated with it.

Having people select their own settings for this part of the survey ensured that their descriptions would in fact include places with special significance for them. This would

TABLE 1
Photo clusters

Cluster name	Photo no.	Mean z-score	Description
Formal	8	−1·23	• Geometrically pruned formal hedge garden
	14	−1·24	• Large mowed lawn surrounded by shrubs and conifers
Meadow	4	−0·01	• Savanna-type scene with long grass and openly spaced trees
	12	−0·43	• Natural meadow with yellow/brown grass and trees in background
	20	−0·33	• Natural meadow with green grass and trees in midground
Tree/lawn	2	−0·55	• Mowed grass, formal shrubs, and tall trees, with monument in background (Four Columns)
	6	−0·54	• Mowed grass area bordered with tall conifers
	7	0·01	• Mowed grass and footpath next to ground-cover bed, overhanging tree (Joy Path)
	13	−0·38	• Mowed grass, shrubs, and display beds with tall trees in background
	18	−0·17	• Park-like scene with widely spaced trees, mowed grass and denser vegetation in background
Woods	1	0·56	• Small bridge surrounded by trees and dense vegetation (Lake Marmo)
	5	0·79	• Dense natural forest with large trees, no sign of human influence
	10	0·84	• Dense natural forest with hills, no sign of human influence
	17	0·52	• Footpath through dense natural forest
	19	0·65	• River lined with trees and dense vegetation
Informal/open	3	0·43	• Sloping lawn in front of lake with natural shoreline, trees in background
	9	0·31	• Single crabapple tree in bloom in an open grassy area with dandelions
	11	0·17	• Unmowed grass area in openly spaced conifers
	15	0·06	• Several very large trees in a mowed grass area with dense vegetation behind
	16	0·51	• Footpath through opening with unmowed grass and scattered trees surrounded by denser forest.

TABLE 2
Mean values of photo clusters on physical features: per cent of scene showing features

Physical feature	Photo cluster				
	Formal	Meadow	Trees/lawn	Woods	Informal/open
Sky	19·2	8·0	9·5	0·0	10·0
Deciduous trees	9·9	36·6	34·9	62·9	45·8
Coniferous trees	9·6	0·0	9·7	0·0	8·5
Pruned shrubs	32·2	0·0	5·9	0·0	0·0
Natural shrubs	0·0	1·5	1·1	3·3	5·7
Lawn grass	29·1	0·0	28·7	1·8	15·2
Natural grass	0·0	53·8	0·0	0·4	10·3
Forest floor	0·0	0·0	0·0	20·4	0·6
Gardens, beds	0·0	0·0	7·7	0·0	0·0
Water	0·0	0·0	0·0	7·7	1·0
Paths	0·0	0·0	2·1	1·9	2·9
Structures	0·0	0·0	0·3	1·5	0·0

not necessarily be the case with a set of landscapes chosen for them by the researcher. This self-selection approach is similar to the technique of 'visitor employed photography', in which visitors are given inexpensive cameras and are asked to photograph scenes according to some criterion (Chenoweth, 1984; Cherem and Traweek, 1977). In our study, instead of photographing the real landscape with cameras, people were asked to provide verbal descriptions of landscapes selected from their mental image of the Arboretum.

FIGURE 1a–e. Examples of scenes from the Morton Arboretum.

FIGURE 1a. Example of scene from the 'formal' cluster: photo 8, mean preference = −1·23.

FIGURE 1b. Example of scene from the 'meadow' cluster: photo 12, mean preference = −0·43.

FIGURE 1c. Example of scene from the 'tree/lawn' cluster: photo 18, mean preference = −0·17.

FIGURE 1d. Example of scene from the 'woods' cluster: photo 5, mean preference = 0·79.

FIGURE 1e. Example of scene from the 'informal/open' cluster: photo 11, mean preference = 0·17.

Results

The photo rating questionnaire was mailed to 34 Morton Arboretum members and volunteers. The 32 participants who returned usable questionnaires were then mailed the second questionnaire. Twenty-nine people completed the second questionnaire. Each person described between three and five landscapes, providing a total of 126 separate landscape descriptions.

Analysis of preference ratings

  Landscape clusters. The first step in analyzing the quantitative preference data was a cluster analysis, to reveal groups of photos that were rated similarly by the viewers[1]. Five interpretable clusters of scenes were found (Table 1). The most preferred cluster is labeled 'Woods' (mean = 0·678), and contains views within dense natural forests, or views in which natural appearing trees and shrubs predominate. The next highest rated cluster, labeled 'Informal/open' (mean = 0·297) contains scenes that feature trees in more open settings that do not appear highly formal or maintained. The next most preferred cluster is called 'Meadow' (mean = −0·258) and contains scenes of open areas with tall, natural appearing grass. Slightly lower ratings were given to scenes in the 'Tree/lawn' cluster (mean = −0·326) which show trees in more maintained, park-like settings. The lowest ratings were given to the two highly manicured scenes in the 'Formal' cluster (mean = −1·234).

  The physically measured contents of scenes, averaged within clusters, are given in Table 2. These physical features are consistent with the interpretations of the clusters given above. The scenes in the 'Woods' cluster are composed primarily of deciduous trees and natural forest floor. The scenes in the 'Informal/open' cluster are composed mainly of deciduous trees and a combination of lawn and natural grass. Scenes in the 'Meadow' cluster are composed of natural grass with some deciduous trees. The 'Tree/lawn' scenes are composed predominately of a combination of deciduous trees and lawn grass, and the 'Formal' scenes are composed of a combination of pruned shrubs and lawn grass.

  Rater clusters. To see whether there were subgroups of raters with differing preferences, a cluster analysis of raters was performed[2]. Two large clusters emerged with 11 and 17 raters (Table 3). Both of these clusters preferred 'Woods' the most, but the first cluster had a higher preference for 'Meadow' and a lower preference for 'Formal' and 'Tree/lawn' than the second cluster. In addition to these two main clusters of raters, there is a small cluster with three people that gave higher than average ratings to 'Formal' and 'Tree/lawn' landscapes and lower than average ratings to the more

TABLE 3
Mean preference of rater clusters for photo clusters

Rater cluster	No. of raters	Photo cluster				
		Formal	Meadow	Trees/lawn	Woods	Informal/open
1	11	−1·61	0·35	−0·61	0·74	0·30
2	17	−1·24	−0·55	−0·30	0·78	0·34
3	3	−0·09	−0·76	0·17	0·12	0·20
4	1	−0·45	−0·51	0·81	−0·20	−0·13
All raters		−1·23	−0·26	−0·33	0·68	0·30

natural 'Woods' and 'Meadow' scenes. Finally, a fourth cluster consisted of a single rater who gave very high ratings to the 'Tree/lawn' cluster.

Analysis of open-ended responses

Open-ended descriptions of landscapes from the second part of the survey were content analyzed to identify the concepts that figured prominently in respondents' mental images of the Morton Arboretum. Each description was broken down into a series of short phases, and the phrases were sorted into categories that expressed similar concepts or themes. These categories were then organized into a hierarchical outline, in which general concepts are subdivided into more specific concepts. For example, the general concept of 'wildlife' includes the subconcepts of 'birds', 'fish', 'mammals' and 'insects'. The concept of 'birds' is further subdivided into 'waterfowl' and 'other birds'.

TABLE 4
Frequently mentioned environmental features in open-ended responses

General feature	Specific feature	Raters		Landscapes	
		No.	%	No.	%
Built features	Buildings	12	41	19	15
	Bridges	10	34	11	9
	Paths	20	69	37	29
Trees	Forest, woods	23	79	39	31
	Backdrop, border	10	34	12	10
	Tall, large	16	55	24	19
Fall colors		12	41	14	11
Ground cover	Grass	13	45	20	16
	Forest floor	12	41	13	10
Flowers	Wildflowers	15	52	22	17
	Daffodils	10	34	11	9
Gardens, beds		10	34	18	14
Prairie		12	41	12	10
Field, meadow		10	34	11	9
Plant collections		12	41	15	12
Shrubs, bushes		11	38	17	13
Water	Lake, pond	23	79	33	26
	Stream, river	11	38	13	10
Terrain	Valley, ravine	10	34	10	8
	Hill	12	41	12	10
Birds	Waterfowl	10	34	10	8
	Other birds	16	55	23	18
Atmospheric features	Temperature	13	45	16	13
	Sun	12	41	15	12
	Lighting	15	52	22	17
Open space		15	52	21	17
Vistas, views		11	38	12	10
Variety		16	55	25	20
Contrast		13	45	21	17
Colors		23	79	33	26
Seasons	Spring	19	66	32	25
	Summer	13	45	16	13
	Autumn	18	62	27	21
	Winter	12	41	16	13
	Changing	12	41	13	10

TABLE 5

Frequently mentioned subjective experiences in open-ended responses

General experience	Specific experience	Raters		Landscapes	
		No.	%	No.	%
Qualities	Beautiful, pretty	18	62	35	28
	Appealing, satisfying	14	48	24	19
	Quiet, peaceful	23	79	37	29
	Interesting	11	38	14	11
	Natural, native	12	41	15	12
	Special, favorite	12	41	20	16
Values	Novelty	13	45	18	14
	Contact with nature	15	52	19	15
	Experience heritage	13	45	18	14
	Refuge, escape	14	48	17	13
	Solitude	12	41	15	12
	Information source	14	48	17	13
Activities	Walking, hiking	18	62	35	28
	Observation	11	38	14	11
Memories of places, people, events		20	69	32	25

The outline consists of two major sections: one that includes references to objective features of the environment and one that includes references to subjective experiences, qualities, and values associated with the settings. The entire content outline is too long to include here, but Tables 4 and 5 summarize some of the most frequent responses from each main section of the outline. The most frequently mentioned environmental features include forests, paths, lakes or ponds, colors, spring and autumn seasons and large trees. The most frequently mentioned subjective qualities of the environments are quietness and beauty. Walking was frequently mentioned as a part of people's experience of their favorite settings, and memories of people, places, and events were often associated with those settings.

Most people chose several different kinds of settings to represent their mental image of the Arboretum. Forests were among the most frequently selected settings, but 22 of the 23 people who described a forest setting described at least one other type of setting, too. For example, 17 people described a lake or pond setting in addition to a forest setting, 14 people described a prairie or meadow setting, six people described gardens or beds, and six people described lawns or grassy areas. Fifteen of the 22 people who described forest settings included two or more of these other settings in their set of three to five descriptions. Thus the variety of different kinds of settings available at the Morton Arboretum seems to be an important aspect of people's mental images. This is also indicated by the fact that 55% of the respondents explicitly mentioned 'variety' as an important feature of at least one of their preferred settings.

Relation between experiences and the environment
An important question in landscape assessment is, how are perceptions of settings related to particular features of the settings? Earlier studies have usually approached this question using quantitative preference data. The qualitative data in this study offer another way of approaching the same question. First, I specified lists of keywords that express some of the concepts identified in the content analysis (Table 6). A keyword

variable was then defined from each of the keyword lists. A keyword variable takes the value 1 if a landscape description contains one or more of the words in the corresponding list, and the value 0 if the description contains none of the words in the list.

For example, a landscape description would be given the value 1 on the keyword variable 'PATHS' if it contained any of the words 'path', 'paths', 'trail', or 'trails'. It would be given a 0 on this variable if it contained none of these words. All 126 landscape descriptions were assigned values in this way for all of the keyword variables in Table 6.

I performed probit analyses on the keyword variables to see whether the occurrence of keywords for particular qualities and meanings in a landscape description could be predicted from the occurrence or non-occurrence of keywords for particular environmental features[3]. Several significant relationships were found, and are displayed in Table 7. Examples of actual responses that illustrate the relations discovered through this analysis are given in Table 8.

Of the two most frequent subjective qualities, serenity and beauty, only serenity was signficantly related to particular environments. Serenity tended to be mentioned in descriptions of places with water and places described as cool. Expressions of joyful,

TABLE 6
Definition of keyword variables

	Keyword variable	Keyword list
Environmental features	BRIDGE	bridge, bridges
	JOY PATH	Joy path
	PATHS	path, paths, trail, trails
	FOUR COLUMNS	columns, pillars
	FOREST	forest, forests, forested, woods, wooded, woodsy, woodland
	TALL GRASS	tall grass, tall grasses, uncut, unmowed
	WILDFLOWERS	wildflower, wildflowers, wild flower, wild flowers
	HEDGES	hedge, hedges, hedged
	GARDENS/BEDS	garden, gardens, bed, beds
	PRAIRIE	prairie, prairies
	MEADOW	field, fields, meadow, meadows
	LAKE MARMO	Marmo
	LAKE/POND	lake, lakes, pond, ponds
	WATER	water
	COOLNESS	cool, coolness
	WARMTH	hot, warm, warmth
	SUN	sun, sunshine, sunny
	SHADE	shade, shady, shaded
Subjective qualities and values	BEAUTIFUL	beautiful, beauty, pretty, lovely
	SERENE	calm, serenity, peaceful, quiet, peace, restful, tranquility, relaxing, tranquil, quietness, stillness
	ACTIVE	active, alive, activity
	JOYFUL/HAPPY	joyful, happy, happiness, uplifting
	NATURE	native, natural, naturally, nature, wildness
	ORDERLINESS	orderly, manicured, orderliness, elegance, formal, maintained, order, stately
	HISTORY	history, pioneer, heritage, settlers
	SOLITUDE	private, privacy, alone, secluded, isolated

TABLE 7
Probit analyses of keywords

Dependent variable	N[a]	Log likelihood chi square[b]	Independent variables	Coefficient	t
SERENE	35	13.6[c]	(Constant)	−0.825	−5.88[c]
			WATER	0.929	2.67[c]
			COOL	1.183	2.57[d]
BEAUTIFUL	38		(no significant predictors)		
JOYFUL/HAPPY	6	8.8[d]	(Constant)	−2.084	−7.21[c]
			WARM	1.147	2.12[d]
			SUN	0.901	2.02[d]
NATURE	29	7.1[d]	(Constant)	−0.986	−5.94[c]
			WILDFLOWERS	0.593	1.60
			FOREST	0.415	1.55
ORDERLINESS	9	15.6[c]	(Constant)	−1.732	−8.46[c]
			HEDGES	2.162	3.81[c]
HISTORY	9	7.8[c]	(Constant)	−1.703	−8.23[c]
			PRAIRIE	1.201	2.87[c]

[a] Number of descriptions (out of 126) with dependent variable = 1.
[b] A measure of the overall significance of the probit model.
[c] $p < 0.01$.
[d] $p < 0.05$.

happy feelings tended to occur in places described as warm or sunny. Experiencing nature tended to occur most often in places where wildflowers and forests are found together. The quality of orderliness was associated with hedges, and the theme of history or heritage was most often mentioned in connection with the prairie restoration area.

Relation between quantitative and qualitative responses
An additional question is whether there is a relation between people's qualitative and quantitative responses. That is, did people who rated certain types of landscapes as highly preferred in the photo preference section of the survey tend to describe those types of landscapes in the open-ended section of the survey? A test of the correspondence between quantitative and qualitative responses was made in the following way. For each photograph, I selected the keyword variables that seemed intuitively to apply most directly to that photo. For example, photo number 17, which shows a footpath through a dense natural forest, was assigned the keyword variables 'PATHS' and 'FOREST'. (Four of the photos were omitted from this test because none of the keyword variables clearly applied to them.)

Probit analysis was then used to see whether the people who gave high ratings to a particular photograph were more likely to mention the keywords corresponding to that photo in their open-ended descriptions. By hypothesis, all the coefficients in these analyses should be positive, because the keyword variables were deliberately selected to represent features present in the photos. Table 9 shows the results of the analysis. Of the 28 coefficients, all but four have the expected positive sign. Eleven of the coefficients (39%) are significant at the 0.05 level or beyond, and seven (25%) are significant at the 0.01 level. This is a far greater number than would be expected by chance.

Five of the 11 significant coefficients are for MEADOW or TALL GRASS,

TABLE 8
Examples of relationship between environment and experience

Experience	Environment	Examples
SERENE	COOLNESS	'A forest represents to me cool, calm, a place to regain composure'.
		'Grove of large pine trees, ... Coolness, calm, mystery'.
	WATER	'Lily pond area in front of library. ... water in pond—tranquil'.
		'There's something very peaceful and calm about Lake Marmo'.
JOYFUL/HAPPY	WARMTH	'It was the first warm day in March. We had my two older boys ... When they saw the green grass and the broad sloping lawn they rolled and turned somersaults all the way down. They were just that happy'.
	SUN	'This is an open, sunny place ... This place is exciting and JOYFUL to me'.
		'Open field scattered with large trees ... Sunshine, happiness'.
NATURE	FOREST,	'Native woods ... haven for wild flowers in the spring. ... nature controlling the environment'.
	WILDFLOWERS	'The floor of the forest is covered with decomposed leaves and spring wildflowers are popping through the leaves. ... I love to experience the awakening of nature'.
		'Path leading through forested area. Trees overlapping road. Wildflowers. ... A natural view of the earth'.
ORDERLINESS	HEDGES	'The orderly clipped hedge gardens. ... It has the appearance of orderliness'.
		'The hedge garden ... Majestic, measured, rhythmic beauty—the ability of the plant to survive the whims of man and still survive in elegance'.
HISTORY	PRAIRIE	'My first experience with prairie plants and animals and what settlers must have thought of Illinois'.
		'Prairie—open sky, unusual plants ... History'.
		'I remember the history I've heard and the accounts I've read about prairies'.

indicating that there is a consistent tendency for people who rated natural meadow scenes high to describe meadow scenes in their open-ended responses as well. Several significant coefficients also occur for photos 1 and 2. These photos represent clearly identifiable landmarks in the Morton Arboretum: a unique bridge at Lake Marmo and the 'Four Columns' monument. The significant coefficients show that people who rated these photos of landmarks high in preference were more likely to include the landmarks in their open-ended landscape descriptions.

None of the negative coefficients are significant. The two largest negative coefficients are both for the keyword PATHS. The photos for which these coefficients occurred both showed scenes of unpaved trails through natural appearing forest. A significant positive coefficient for PATHS occurs, however, for a third photo of a paved path in a more maintained setting. Perhaps the people who were most likely to mention paths

TABLE 9
Probit coefficients for individual slide ratings predicting keywords

Photo no.	Keywords predicted	Probit coefficient
1	BRIDGE	0·067
	WATER	0·202
	LAKE/POND	0·212
	LAKE MARMO	0·582[a]
2	FOUR COLUMNS	0·600[a]
	HEDGES	0·577[a]
	ORDERLINESS	0·478[a]
3	LAKE/POND	0·297
	WATER	0·367
4	TALL GRASS	0·274
	MEADOW	0·408[a]
5	FOREST	0·305[b]
6	ORDERLINESS	0·068
7	PATHS	0·385[b]
	JOY PATH	0·155
8	HEDGES	−0·065
	ORDERLINESS	0·285
10	FOREST	0·096
11	TALL GRASS	0·775[b]
12	TALL GRASS	0·198
	MEADOW	0·230[b]
14	ORDERLINESS	0·191
16	PATHS	−0·350
17	PATHS	−0·334
	FOREST	−0·180
19	WATER	0·089
20	TALL GRASS	0·457[a]
	MEADOW	0·309[a]

[a] $p < 0.01$.
[b] $p < 0.05$.

and trails in their setting descriptions were thinking in terms of a developed rather than a natural forest context.

Discussion

The quantitative preference ratings showed that this group of arboretum users had a strong preference for natural-appearing settings, although a few people liked the more formal, managed scenes better. On average, natural deciduous woods were the most preferred. The least preferred scenes were formal landscapes with pruned shrubs and mowed lawns. There was significant variation among individuals in their degree of preference for open meadows and fields. These results are consistent with past studies of visual preference for recreation sites, which have shown scenes with dense natural vegetation to be the most preferred. Earlier studies have also shown that preferences often vary along the dimensions of vegetation density and naturalness (Schroeder, 1987), and the variations observed in this study with respect to meadows and formal landscapes are consistent with these earlier findings.

Forests figured prominently in the qualitative descriptions of preferred landscapes, along with lakes and ponds, paths, large trees and colors. These results are consistent with earlier research which shows that natural vegetation, large trees and water are among the most preferred features of landscapes. Serenity, beauty and contact with nature were among the most frequently mentioned experiential aspects of the settings. The prominence of peace and serenity in people's open-ended responses is very interesting in view of the physiological research by Ulrich and his colleagues (Ulrich, 1981; Ulrich & Simons, 1986). This research has shown that natural environments with vegetation and water induce relaxed and less stressful states in observers compared with urban scenes with no vegetation. This ability of trees, other vegetation, and bodies of water to function as 'natural tranquilizers' may be one of the most significant human benefits of preserving nature, especially in urban areas where stress is an all too common aspect of daily living.

These arboretum users also associated their favorite settings with walking, contact with nature, and memories of people, places, and past events from their lives. It seems that arboretum settings are not experienced simply as esthetic scenes to be viewed in a stationary, detached way. The settings help people to feel connected with the processes of nature and with their natural and historical heritage. The ability to move through the settings and experience their variety is important, as are the memories which tie the settings into the individual's life context.

Quantitative research on landscape preference has focused on predicting how ratings of landscape quality vary between settings having different kinds of physical features. The results of this study suggest that a similar approach would be worth pursuing with qualitative data, focusing on how experiential qualities and meanings vary across settings with different physical characteristics. The experience of beauty occurred across a wide-range of environments and did not appear to be associated with certain kinds of settings rather than others. This is not surprising since the landscape descriptions were all self-selected and would be unlikely to include scenes with low aesthetic quality. Other experiential qualities and meanings did seem to be associated with particular types of settings, however. Serenity was most often mentioned in connection with cool settings and water. Joyful, happy feelings on the other hand, seemed most associated with sunshine and warmth. Forests and wildflowers evoked thoughts of nature, while a prairie restoration area was associated with pioneer history.

The convergent validity of the quantitative and qualitative approaches is supported by the fact that both approaches found natural forests to be among the most preferred settings. Forest settings were rated highest on average in the preference rating photo survey and were one of the most frequently chosen settings in the qualitative survey. A more exacting test of convergent validity is whether the two approaches reflect similar variations in preferred settings across individuals. The results of our analysis showed that people who gave higher preference ratings to scenes of natural meadows or to more developed, formal scenes were more likely to include these kinds of scenes in their self-selected landscape descriptions. Thus the two approaches provide different kinds of information, but when taken together they give a consistent picture of people's landscape perceptions and experiences.

Recommendations for arboretum management

The Morton Arboretum calls itself a 'museum of woody plants', and regards a major part of its mission to be the provision of information, through research and extension, to promote the planting and care of trees. This study shows that, beyond its role as an information source, the Arboretum also provides landscape settings in which people can have a variety of important and meaningful experiences. An improved understanding of the meaning of the Arboretum's landscapes for the people who enjoy and value them could help the Arboretum itself to design new landscapes that enhance users' experiences, and to develop educational and interpretive programs that will enable more people to enjoy and appreciate the unique features of its setting. Natural settings, particularly forests, are very important in this regard, as are the several lakes and ponds found in the Morton Arboretum. Paths that lead through diverse environments could enhance the experience of variety. These kinds of settings should receive special attention in future arboretum management.

The prominence of serenity as a quality in people's explanations of the meaning of their preferred settings highlights the unique contribution of this arboretum setting in a highly urbanized metropolitan area. Many of our respondents viewed the Arboretum as a place of refuge where they can escape from daily routine and urban hassles to find solitude and peace. Research has shown that esthetic experiences occur more often in solitude than in the company of other people (Gobster & Chenoweth, 1990). The Morton Arboretum is a particularly good place to provide settings for solitude, because its control on entry and exclusion of more active recreation, greatly reduces safety concerns and the noise which can intrude on solitude in more traditional urban outdoor recreation sites. Serenity, refuge and solitude could be provided in areas away from roads and congestion, by inconspicuous trails leading to cool, shaded places near lakes or ponds.

A final recommendation concerns the fact that preferences varied significantly among different people in our study. Most of our participants liked natural woods the best, but several preferred more formally landscaped settings. There was also considerable variation in preference for scenes with open, natural meadows. By providing a variety of natural and landscaped settings with varying densities of vegetation, the Arboretum can appeal to a public with diverse landscape preferences.

Recommendations for future research
As a preliminary attempt to combine quantitative and qualitative approaches in landscape assessment, this study suffers from several shortcomings. The results are based on a limited group of respondents in a single arboretum. This provides an in-depth view of how these devoted users experience this particular arboretum, but it is not clear whether the results would generalize to other, less serious users of the Morton Arboretum or to users of other types of landscape areas such as city, county and state parks. Additional research is needed to generalize these findings, and to explore further how experiences in the landscape are related to particular landscape features.

A further problem relates to the time required to analyse and categorize the open-ended responses. In this case, the content analysis in Tables 4 and 5 was performed by a single investigator. Because of the time required for categorizing all the landscape descriptions on all the concepts, the task could not be replicated with another coder to test the reliability of the categories. The keywords in Table 6 were introduced in order to have more objectively defined variables for the subsequent analyses. The keywords, however, do not capture the whole range of concepts and themes in the responses, and is some instances may lead to misinterpretations of the descriptions due to the context-sensitive meanings of words. For example, the keyword 'SHADE' is intended to refer to places shaded from the sun, but the word 'shade' could also refer to a particular 'shade of green' in the foliage. Future research will need to seek an acceptable trade-off between the objectivity of the analysis, the validity of the interpretations, and the time demanded of the investigators.

Conclusion

Qualitative responses provide useful information about landscape perception that is not obtained through quantitative preference ratings. Asking people to select scenes from memory tells us which particular landscapes are most significant in forming a mental image of a place like the Morton Arboretum, and which features of these landscapes are most important. Asking people to tell what meanings they associate with specific landscapes helps us to understand why these landscapes are preferred and what benefits they provide to people. Combining the precision and analytic power of quantitative ratings with the richness and depth of qualitative responses provides a much fuller understanding of user responses to landscapes than could be gained from either method alone.

Notes

(1) Before clustering, each respondents' ratings of landscape scenes were transformed into z-scores by subtracting the mean and dividing by the standard deviation of that respondent's ratings. The scenes were clustered with the complete linkage (farthest neighbor) method. The similarity measure between scenes was the euclidean distance between the vectors of z-scores for scenes across raters.

(2) The similarity measure between raters in this cluster analysis was the euclidean distance between vectors of z-scores for raters across scenes, and the clustering method was complete linkage.

(3) Probit analysis is conceptually similar to multiple regression analysis. The dependent variable is a dichotomous categorical variable coded as 0 or 1. The analysis estimates coefficients of an equation that predicts the probability that the dependent variable will take the value '1':

$$P(d = 1) = F(k + a_1 x_1 + a_2 x_2 + \cdots + a_n x_n)$$

where P = probability
F = cumulative normal probability distribution function
d = dependent variable
k = constant
$a_1 \ldots a_n$ = coefficients
$x_1 \ldots x_n$ = independent variables.

The coefficients are derived using maximum likelihood estimation.

Acknowledgements

I wish to thank Charles Lewis and Susan Klatt of the Morton Arboretum for their assistance in carrying out this research.

References

Brown, T. C. & Daniel, T. C. (1984). *Modeling Forest Scenic Beauty: Concepts and Application to Ponderosa Pine*, USDA Forest Service Research Paper RM-256. Rocky Mountain Forest and Range Experiment Station, Fort Collins, CO.

Chenoweth, R. (1984). Visitor employed photography: a potential tool for landscape photography. *Landscape Journal*, **3**, 136–143.

Cherem, G. J. & Traweek, D. E. (1977). Visitor employed photography: an aid in planning guided activities. *Interpreter*, **9**, 13–15.

Daniel, T. C. & Boster, R. S. (1976). *Measuring Landscape Esthetics: the Scenic Beauty Estimation Method*, USDA Forest Service Research Paper RM-167. Rocky Mountain Forest and Range Experiment Station, Fort Collins, CO.

Daniel, T. C. & Vining, J. (1983). Methodological issues in the assessment of landscape quality. In I. Altman & J. S. Wohlwill, Eds., *Behavior and the Natural Environment*. New York: Plenum, Vol. 6, 39–84.

Giorgi, A. (1970). *Psychology as a Human Science: A Phenomenologically Based Approach*. New York: Harper and Row.

Giorgi, A. (1971). The experience of the subject as a source of data in a psychological experiment. In A. Giorgi, W. F. Fischer & R. Von Eckartsberg, Eds., *Duquesne Studies in Phenomenological Psychology*. Pittsburgh: Duquesne University Press, vol. 1, pp. 50–57.

Giorgi, A. (1975). Convergence and divergence of qualitative and quantitative methods in psychology. In A. Giorgi, C. T. Fischer & E. L. Murray, Eds., *Duquesne Studies in Phenomenological Psychology*. Pittsburgh: Duquesne University Press, Vol. 2. 72–79.

Gobster, P. H. & Chenoweth, R. E. (1990). Peak aesthetic experiences and the natural landscape. In *proceedings of EDRA 21*. Oklahoma City: Environmental Design and Research Association, pp 185–191.

Keen, E. (1975). *A Primer in Phenomenological Psychology*. New York: Holt, Rinehart and Winston.

Porteous, D. (1982). Approaches to environmental aesthetics. *Journal of Environmental Psychology*, **2**, 53–66.

Schroeder, H. W. (1987). Dimensions of variation in urban park preference: a psychophysical analysis. *Journal of Environmental Psychology*, **7**, 123–141.

Schroeder, H. W. & Daniel, T. C. (1981). Progress in predicting the perceived scenic beauty of forest landscapes. *Forest Science*, **27**, 71–80.

Ulrich, R. S. (1981). Natural versus urban scenes: some psychophysiological effects. *Environment and Behavior*, **13**, 523–556.

Ulrich, R. S. & Simons, R. F. (1986). Recovery from stress during exposure to everyday outdoor environments. In proceedings of EDRA 17. Washington, D.C.: Environmental Design and Research Association, pp 115–122.

Zube, E. H., Sell, J. L. & Taylor, J. G. (1982). Landscape perception: research, application, and theory. *Landscape Planning*, **9**, 1–33.

PERSPECTIVES ON WILDERNESS: RE-EXAMINING THE VALUE OF EXTENDED WILDERNESS EXPERIENCES

JANET FREY TALBOT and STEPHEN KAPLAN

Psychological Laboratories, The University of Michigan, Mason Hall, Ann Arbor, Michigan 48109, U.S.A.

Abstract

This paper presents results from the final phase of a ten-year research program dealing with the dynamics and the impacts of wilderness experiences. Although these data are from participants in shorter trips than those reported on previously, questionnaire data indicate that responses to the different trips were similar, and that responses from participants of different ages and sexes were also similar. Theoretical issues which emerged from earlier analyses of participants' journals are also re-examined in light of the current data. These earlier results had suggested that an individual's growing perceptual understanding of the surrounding wilderness environment was connected to a wide range of personal insights as well as other psychological benefits. Results from the current data concur with this finding. Furthermore, contrary to alternative hypotheses, feelings of control over the environment were not evident either in the original data or in the current participants' journals. These data suggest that an alternative stance, described as feeling 'at one with' or 'part of' the environment, is more frequent and is generalized to non-wilderness surroundings. Other categories of individual response which complement this non-dominant environmental orientation are also documented in the current data.

Introduction

Wilderness experiences have long been thought to have special impacts on people. Biblical as well as other literary and historical sources include numerous examples of individuals whose encounters with wilderness environments have left them with enhanced perceptions and strengthened feelings of commitment to various causes (James, 1902; Scott, 1974).

A number of recent psychological surveys have illustrated popular beliefs which roughly correspond with these images. Both wilderness users and non-users have been found to share perceptions that experiences in natural environments can be highly satisfying and can offer valuable psychological benefits not often found elsewhere (for reviews see Heimstra and McFarling, 1974; Iso-Ahola, 1980; Kaplan and Talbot, 1983).

While such evidence may be intriguing, it does not, in itself, constitute convincing proof of the value of wilderness experiences. However, efforts to examine the nature and the impacts of these experiences directly by collecting data from participants in wilderness programs have been fraught with methodological difficulties (for reviews see Turner, 1976; Gibson, 1979; Kahoe, 1979; Kaplan and Talbot, 1983). While the combined weight of several studies suggests that some beneficial responses can result from such experiences, most efforts to clarify the nature of these benefits and to demonstrate the dynamics of their emergence have achieved only limited success.

The following report describes the results of the last in a sequence of research studies which have been somewhat more successful in quantifying the elements of individual response to wilderness experiences. This research has been conducted over a period of ten years, and encompasses a number of distinct phases in which related issues have been examined independently. Perhaps the most interesting theoretical issues raised by the earlier results of this research concern the direct connections between individuals' perceptions of their physical surroundings and their evolving perceptions of themselves and their own purposes. This network of results had not been anticipated, but emerged repeatedly in content analyses of the participants' journals. This finding of the central role of the natural environment in prompting individual changes was central to theoretical discussions questioning the appropriateness of control orientations in everyday environmental interactions (Kaplan and Talbot, 1983). It also figured in the subsequent development of the concept of compatibility as describing person–environment interactions, in which the individual's capabilities and purposes are well-balanced with the pattern of opportunities and constraints found in the physical environment (Kaplan, 1983).

This report focuses on data from participants during two final years of the wilderness program on which this research has been based. Before examining the more theoretically interesting data from the current participants' journals, questionnaire data comparing the responses of participants in both the longer and shorter trips will be compared and examined for differences in response by age and sex. Then, analyses of the participants' journals will be presented. These both support the earlier finding that environmental perceptions prompted significant psychological changes in individuals, and provide further insights regarding control issues raised by the previous results.

Research methods

The Outdoor Challenge Program has been conducted for 12 years in an extensive wilderness area in Michigan's Upper Peninsula (Hanson, 1973). Following an initial two years as a survival course for teenage boys, the program incorporated an explicit research agenda in 1972. Besides spending two weeks in a large wilderness setting and acquiring wilderness–survival skills, the 129 participants between 1972 and 1979 wrote daily journals and filled out brief questionnaires both during the trips and afterwards. Participants were recruited without reference to the extent of any prior backpacking experience, and fees were kept low in an effort to include as wide a variety of individuals as possible (further details on this phase of the program are available: Kaplan *et al.*, 1979; Kaplan and Talbot, 1983).*

In its earliest years, the Outdoor Challenge Program was conducted in a manner quite similar to the popular Outward Bound system, emphasizing risks and physical hardships. In response to early research findings, however, a number of adjustments were made in the way the program was being conducted. Some endurance tasks and risk-related exercises were dropped, and participants were given food and shelter materials for use during their solos. Such changes gradually altered the program

---

* The Outdoor Challenge Program as well as the associated research effort has been funded throughout the project by the Forest Service, North Central Experimental Station, USDA. Rachel Kaplan has had a central role in these research efforts, and Robert Hanson has guided the Outdoor Challenge Program since its earliest years. We are grateful for their collaboration throughout this project.

from being a survival-dominant experience into one more centered on the natural environment and more closely similar to a typical backpacking excursion.

The initial research done in conjunction with this program dealt with comparisons between wilderness trips and other activities, using pre- and post-measures collected at roughly 6-month intervals. Initial findings indicated that wilderness program participants experienced a variety of benefits, including the development of greater concerns for others, increased self-sufficiency, and more realistic self-assessments, which were not found within control groups (Kaplan, 1974). A subsequent study showed similar findings, and also illustrated that participants in other outdoor programs reflected positive impacts but also some differences in response (Kaplan, 1977), with greater positive changes in self-perceptions found among the wilderness program participants than among either the controls or the participants in the other outdoor programs studied. During later research the comparison groups were dropped, and data collection and analyses focused on the participants' day-to-day responses in an attempt to explore the dynamics of individual response to wilderness. Analyses of these data illustrated that personal benefits developed only gradually and were very broad in scope, and also clarified the central roles which perceiving and functioning in the natural environment played in the development of the benefits which individuals experienced (Kaplan and Talbot, 1983).

During 1980 and 1981, due to financial constraints and time considerations, the trips were shortened from two weeks to nine days in total length. Backpacking and orienteering remained the primary daily activities, and the latter portion of the trips again included a solo experience lasting approximately 48 hours. As in earlier years, the 49 program participants contributed to the final phase of this research effort by writing journals and filling out questionnaires during their trips.

Responses to Wilderness Experience

Immediate assessments
In both the shorter and the longer versions of the program, participants filled out a set of questionnaires immediately before returning home. Four open-ended items were included in these questionnaires, asking participants to describe the best, the worst and the hardest things about their trip, and asking them how they felt they were changed, if at all, by this experience. In order to compare the immediate assessments of this experience, summaries reflecting the answers of all the participants in the shorter trips were compared with summaries from a representative sample of 35 of the 129 participants in the longer trips.

The answers to each of these four questions were summarized according to the six most frequent response categories.* Statistical tests were then conducted for all responses which were mentioned by at least 20% of the participants. The responses from participants on the shorter and longer trips were compared, as were the responses of adult and younger participants, and males and females.

The answers to these questions, as presented in Table 1, illustrate that these trips have many positive qualities, but that they encompass significant difficulties as well. Among the best elements, participants mentioned the beauty of their surroundings, their experiences during solo, and the lack of time pressures during the trips (ap-

---
* Two individuals coded these short-answer responses independently. The reliability coefficient for the two codings was 0·99.

TABLE 1
Comparisons in last day assessments of wilderness trips[a]

	Statistical comparisons[b]		
Response Categories	Shorter/Longer (47/35)	Adults/Teens (36/46)	Males/Females (30/52)
What were the best things?			
Coping with things, learning	—	Adults	—
Trip activities	—	—	Males
The natural surroundings	—	—	—
The solo	—	—	—
The peacefulness, relaxed pace	—	—	—
What were the worst things?			
Trip activities	—	—	—
Natural elements (bugs, etc.)	—	—	—
The hiking	—	—	—
What were the hardest things?	—	—	—
The solo		—	
The hiking	Short trips	—	Males
Will you be different now?			
Try to slow down and simplify	—	—	—
Greater nature involvement	Long trips	—	—
Be closer to, kinder to others	—	—	—
Be more independent and decisive	Short trips	—	—

[a] The table includes all responses which were given by at least 20% of the samples. Significant differences were the results of Student's t-tests, with table entries indicating those whose responses were statistically higher.

[b] Cases are indicated at the top of each column. Questionnaire responses were only available for 47 of the 49 participants in the shorter trips. For statistical comparisons, responses were summarized over eight subsamples; df = 3,3; $P < 0.10$.

preciating 'the peace and calm', and feeling 'no time-consciousness'). A variety of camping activities (setting up camp, eating, telling stories around the fire) were recalled as being the best parts of the trip, and various personally difficult experiences were valued as demonstrating the individual's growing ability to cope with daily challenges.

Not all memories were so positive, however. In mentioning the worst elements, participants frequently noted some of the more mundane camping chores (washing dishes, having to cook) and the more irritating environmental elements such as insects, the swamps ('muddy, wet, smelly and bored') and the rain. Hiking that was too strenuous or too lengthy was mentioned as being both among the worst and among the most difficult or challenging aspects of the trips. And the solo experience, besides being among the best parts of the trip, was also mentioned as among the most difficult for a number of participants.

Finally, when asked if they felt these experiences had changed them, many of the participants reflected a sense that they wanted to live life more simply and slowly in the future because of these experiences (to 'look more closely, take my time', to 'consume less, and simplify'). Many also felt a more compelling interest in the world of nature, and felt they would be more considerate of their family and friends ('just an opener and nicer person'). They also wanted to be careful to make decisions about their lives which reflected their own priorities rather than others' values ('a lot of things I thought were important really are not', I'm 'more determined to change what I don't like').

The results of statistical comparisons between the shorter and longer trips and between participants of different ages and different sexes are also shown in Table 1. These reveal both a large number of similarities and a few differences in response to these experiences. Responses concerning the best and worst elements of the shorter and longer trips were quite similar: both the type of answer given and the frequencies of each different response were equivalent for participants on all the trips. However, there were a few differences in response to the two remaining questions. Participants in the shorter trips identified hiking as one of the hardest aspects of the program significantly more often than did the participants in the longer trips. And in evaluating the difference they felt the program would make in their lives, participants in the shorter trips mentioned more often than the others an increased desire to choose and to control their own activities. In contrast, participants in the longer trips more frequently mentioned perceiving a larger and more valued involvement with nature as resulting from their trip experiences.

Comparisons of the responses of adults and teenagers resulted in only one finding of a significant difference in response. Adults were more likely than the younger participants to say that coping with daily problems was among the best elements of the trip for them. All other evaluations of these experiences and their impacts were equivalent for the older and younger participants.

Statistical comparisons between males and females also reflected a largely similar pattern of response to these experiences. Males made more concrete assessments of their experiences in two instances, being more likely to say that specific trip-related activities were among the best things in the trip, and that hiking was among the most challenging elements for them. In other categories of response, no significant differences were found between male and female participants.

Taken together, the answers to these questions illustrate the many ways in which wilderness experiences are valued. Such trips take place in fascinating physical surroundings, and involve enjoyable activities. But enjoyment is not the only value which is perceived in these experiences. They also offer opportunities to learn, to cope with difficulties, and to reflect on one's character and future plans. These data suggest that wilderness experiences can prompt some change in the participants' overall perspectives on life and their own priorities, as well as their preferred involvements. The results of statistical comparisons suggest that the impacts of these experiences are largely similar for different individuals, and for participants in somewhat different programs as well.

Data collected from additional questionnaires completed by the participants in the current trips (R. Kaplan, 1984) give further evidence of individuals' positive responses. These data illustrate high levels of appreciation for the solo and other aspects of the trip, as well as the development of increased sensitivity to nature, and positive changes from the trip's beginning to its end in individual ratings of self-confidence, psychological energy and general well-being.

The development of individual response to wilderness
The kinds of individual response to wilderness experiences which are discussed above seem to approximate those so eloquently spoken of in literary and historical accounts. These trips offer enjoyable and compelling learning experiences which have

implications for individuals' views of themselves and the world. Beyond re-examining the effects of these experiences, a further examination of the development of individual response over the course of the trips was also undertaken, in order to validate and to expand on the earlier results.

For these examinations, a content analysis of the journals written during the shorter trips was conducted, using methods similar to those used in analysing journals from participants during one year (1976) of the longer trips. For the earlier analysis, categories representing comments which appeared in at least one-third of the journals had been defined. Coded summaries of the journals were then prepared, indicating the frequency with which each topic was mentioned. Clusters of topics were subsequently identified, using the criterion that the correlations between each pair of topics within the cluster was at least 0·50. *Alpha* values (Cronbach, 1951), representing the internal consistency or coherence of a cluster of items, were computed for these dimensions of individual response.

For the current analysis, the previous list of topics was repeated, and the list was expanded to express a number of more abstract issues raised by the previous analysis. By repeating the previous topics, the elements of individual response which were related to the emergence of psychological benefits could be revalidated. In addition, by examining new concepts defined as the result of the previous analysis, the network of theoretically related concepts might be enriched. Even though these other responses might not be found as frequently as those studied initially, documenting their presence and studying the relationships among them might offer new theoretical insights, and might augment the understanding of the dimensions of response identified initially.

Of particular interest in this expanded inquiry was the possibility of exploring individual feelings of control over the environment. This response was not investigated earlier, both because it was outside the scope of the initial investigation and because it was not found to be a frequent response among the program participants. However, others conducting research on the impacts of wilderness programs have claimed that the individual's increased ability to control the environment is a critical outcome upon which the benefits of such experiences depend (Newman, 1980). Further evidence on the participants' feelings about control might be helpful in responding to these claims.

Additional topics which were investigated in the current participants' journals described an alternative to the control position, described as feeling a part of or 'at one with' the environment. This category of response was found in some of the journals originally, and seemed more likely to emerge from the wilderness experience than feelings of control over the environment. While this non-dominant environmental orientation and its hypothesized correlates were not among the most frequent topics in the earlier journals, the journal analysis had suggested they might be conceptually related to some of the more common categories of individual response.

Enhanced perceptions of the environment and the individual
The previous journal analysis had suggested that a wide range of individual benefits emerged directly from the development of enhanced environmental perceptions in the wilderness. Despite many early feelings of apprehension, the participants were fascinated by an environment which was radically different from their everyday surroundings, and upon which they had to depend for their comfort and safety. They began to notice more of the physical details of their environment, and developed an

TABLE 2
Comparisons in perceptual response to wilderness

Categories in dimension (with examples from journals)	Journal entries			
	Shorter Trips (Alpha = 0·70)		Longer Trips (Alpha = 0·86)	
	% of sample	Mean/ journal	% of sample	Mean/ journal
Notice nature details (I could begin to see, noticing how trees creak, ripples in the water, the sun's progression)	86	2·2	69	3·2
Comfortable in the woods (feel really at home, could stay here forever, this is real)	55	1·2	45	2·2
Awe and wonder about nature (a special thrill, so hard to believe, the bear was incredible)	62	2·1	42	2·2
Self-insights (really feel like yourself here, learning about me, I really grew, surprised at my feelings)	84	3·7	42	2·7

enhanced appreciation for their surroundings. In time, daily functioning in these surroundings came to be accompanied by a strong sense of comfort—described not as physical ease but rather as an appreciation for the ease of fitting in with the wilderness environment. The participants' growing environmental awareness was often accompanied by similar increases in perceived levels of self-knowledge, and by sensations of awe in relation to the natural environment and the events observed there.

From a theoretical perspective, these responses themselves are not as interesting as are the interrelationships which were discovered among them. The correlational structure found within the earlier journal data suggested that neither the specific enjoyments of the trips nor the difficulties which the trips encompassed were connected to the more internalized levels of response. While both enjoyments and stresses were present, as the questionnaire data discussed above indicate, the structure of the journal data indicated that it was the individual's developing perceptions which were directly related to each other, that the ways of perceiving which were acquired through experiences in wilderness surroundings had direct consequences for individuals' views of their own abilities and interests and for their views of the larger world as well.

Table 2 presents the *Alpha* coefficient of the 'Perceptual Change' cluster of response, both as reflected in the current journals and as originally found in journals kept by the participants in the longer trips, along with a description of the contents of this dimension.* This dimension of response clearly expresses the connection

---

* Two individuals coded the current journals independently. The reliability coefficient for the two codings was 0·69. The frequencies used in constructing Table 2 were obtained by taking the average of the two independent coding sets.

between the participants' interactions with their surroundings during the wilderness experience, and their feelings about themselves. As individuals began to notice new and sometimes subtle details in their surroundings, their feelings of personal comfort increased. This often occurred despite individuals' expectations that their time in the woods would be an anxious and disturbing one, and to some this new sense of comfort was an 'amazing' development. The participants' emotional response to the natural environment—both these feelings of comfort and the emerging feelings of awe and wonder—gradually generalized to include their feelings about themselves as well. As one participant expressed it, 'those feelings and rhythms transfer themselves to us without our ever being aware of the process'. The participants felt more self-aware, sometimes expressed simply as feeling 'more like myself' but at other times expressed more fully (e.g. 'maybe this is the secret, what is most dramatic is quiet and it escapes us because we expect great and preponderous things. I think the real giving is quiet and the real sharing is quiet').

Table 2 also presents information on the percentage of participants mentioning each of the categories in the 'Perceptual Change' cluster, along with the frequencies with which each of the topics was mentioned. The relatively stable findings in reference to this dimension, which connects individuals' environmental- and self-perceptions, lend additional empirical support to the analytic framework developed earlier. There seem to be certain patterns of psychological response, involving the development of environmental sensitivity and the implications of this learning for one's self perceptions, that are basic to extended encounters with wilderness surroundings.

Control orientations, and some alternatives

Evidence regarding the participants' control feelings, although not found often enough in the earlier journals to permit systematic analysis, was investigated in the journals kept by the current wilderness program participants. However, comments reflecting feelings of control over one's surroundings were again found only infrequently, being present in only 7% of the current participants' journals.* Again, this was not considered to be sufficient to justify further analysis. The implication of this result, as suggested also by the results of earlier phases of this research effort, is that feelings of control are not common elements of individuals' response to wilderness experiences, and are not central to the emergence of psychological benefits.

However, as mentioned above, the earlier analysis had suggested that an alternative response, described as feeling 'at one with' or 'part of' one's surroundings, might be found with some frequency among the participants. This non-control orientation towards the environment might also be related to other potential responses which had been identified as the result of the theoretical analysis of the earlier journals' structure.

Table 3 presents the *Alpha* coefficient and describes the contents of a cluster of items which were found in the current journals and which were related to this feeling of oneness with the environment.† As the contents of this table

---

* Regarding the occurrence of control-related sentiments, there was agreement between the two coders on 95% of the current participants' journals.

† The reliability coefficient between the two coders for the categories included in this cluster was 0.68. Frequencies given reflect the average of the two coding sets. This cluster of response was identified through the combined use of the SSA-3 Nonmetric Factor Analysis Program (Lingoes, 1972) and the ICLUST Clustering Algorithm (Kulik *et al.*, 1970).

TABLE 3
Perceptions of oneness with the environment

Categories in dimension (with examples from journals)	Journal entries for shorter trips ($Alpha = 0.88$)	
	% of sample	Mean/ journal
Oneness with environment (feel close to the earth, not an intruder, related to the earth and the animals)	26	1·6
Feelings of awe and wonder[a] (so sacred and mysterious, spiritual, a sanctuary)	57	1·4
Environmental coherence (everything in harmony, simple yet complex, nothing's either good or bad, it's all part of a system)	17	1·6
Simplicity of woods living (things get basic, days reduced to a few simple tasks, no frills, just living and enjoying the world)	24	1·1
Feel refreshed, restored (feel better than I have in years, mentally and physically renewed, very relaxed and alive)	24	1·2
Nature/city comparisons (quickly adapt to not having phones & cars, the commotion of society, the frustrations)	67	1·4

[a] This category represents a slightly narrower coding of the 'Awe and wonder about nature' category as shown in Table 2, including only specific references to a somewhat spiritual quality in the surroundings.

indicate, the participants' feelings of awe and wonder and their sensitivity to the spiritual elements of the environment were related to this 'oneness' response. Their awareness of environmental coherence, of the increasingly apparent harmony within the environment ('things are not as haphazard as they appeared to me originally'), is also related to this feeling, as are an appreciation of the simplicity of living in the woods; strong sensations of physical and mental renewal; and specific comparisons between one's experience in the woods and the irritations of daily life (activities here are 'very strenuous yet less frustrating; at home, there are few physically strenuous activities but many mentally strenuous ones').

Conclusions and Implications

These findings are largely in agreement with results from earlier phases of this research program. Participants with varied backgrounds have found their experiences in this wilderness hiking program to be enjoyable and compelling. They also indicate that their orientations to life have been affected by these experiences. They see their lives afterwards as being different from before—less cluttered, more mindful of those to whom they are close, and more focused on what they personally consider valuable.

The findings based on journals kept by participants in the current trips are also in agreement with earlier results. A crucial outcome of these wilderness trips appears to be the emergence of a shift in perceptual awareness which encompasses more than the acquisition of knowledge about a specific type of physical environment. Again, the evidence suggests that the processing of environmental perceptions has generalized to include individuals' feelings about themselves.

Accompanying this response, the data from the current participants' journals also suggest that a non-control-oriented approach to life and to one's surroundings has developed through the course of this experience. This orientation is perceived both as being quite comfortable and as being harmonious with what has come to be understood as an awesome physical reality.

In analysing the meaning and functions of cultures, Kluckhohn (1953) proposed that gaining an understanding of the proper relationship between man and nature is one of five inevitable questions to which cultures must provide answers. The answers to this question are varied: humans can be perceived as subjugated to nature, as being in harmony with natural forces, or as dominating nature. The data presented here suggest that wilderness hiking experiences can deeply affect individuals and their understanding of this critical issue. For these individuals the answer to this question is often clear and compelling. Far from concluding that humans should dominate or 'control' natural forces, as others have suggested, they become convinced that living with nature is both more appropriate and more satisfying.

The data presented here give ample evidence that a compelling set of psychological responses to wilderness occur; they do not, however, address whether similar benefits might be experienced in other environments. Czikszentmihalyi (1975) has analysed certain experiences which share many properties with the psychological events which have been described here. He has used the terms 'autotelic' and 'flow' to describe experiences which are pursued for their own intrinsic rewards rather than for any resultant outcomes. These are activities in which one loses track of time; feels a loss of self and a sense of oneness; and senses a coherence or a lack of contradictions in the type of actions required. Czikszentmihalyi's analysis focuses on the pursuits of highly skilled individuals, such as surgeons, chess experts and gifted athletes. His description of autotelic activities is similarly limited, concentrating on certain pursuits which have explicit rule systems and in which the perceptual field is limited to a narrow range, such as a gameboard or an artist's canvas. The analysis of wilderness experiences which has been presented here, in contrast, deals with ordinary individuals pursuing commonplace activities within a particular kind of environment. Rather than being a response to a constrained or limited sensory field, in this situation the psychological effect appears to be dependent upon the unlimited scope of the environment itself.

The evidence presented here suggests that the wilderness environment is one where the experience of compatibility, the harmonizing of one's own capabilities and inclinations with the opportunities and limitations present in the physical surroundings, is particularly likely (Kaplan, 1983). To a large degree, this is the result of qualities which are inherent both in the individual and in this particular type of environment. The wilderness is composed of fascinating content, and it presents a coherent world of considerable scope, one that readily captures one's full attention. The individual is inclined to take an active part in the functioning of this environment, and to become immersed in observing its physical details. The richness of this experience, the satisfying quality of functioning within a supportive physical setting, often leads individuals to deeper levels of personal understanding, and to convictions that the ways in which they conduct their lives in their ordinary surroundings should also be different.

The data reviewed in this report echo the descriptions of others who have spoken perhaps more eloquently from personal experience. A trip to the woods has the potential to be more than an enjoyable vacation or, as non enthusiasts would view it, a grueling physical endurance test. The commonplace experiences of ordinary individuals in these surroundings seem to lead to psychological effects which the participants themselves may not have anticipated. Individuals with unusual talents or unusual training apparently are able to control events within a limited stimulus field and to achieve a heightened and beneficial psychological state, characterized by strong feelings of coherence and compatibility. Wilderness seems to offer the same or similar benefits to individuals ranging considerably more widely in ability and background.

References

Cronbach, L. J. (1951). Coefficient alpha and the internal structure of tests. *Psychometrika*, **16**, 297–335.
Czikszentmihalyi, M. (1975). *Beyond Boredom and Anxiety*. Washington, D.C.: Jossey-Bass.
Gibson, P. M. (1979). Therapeutic aspects of wilderness programs: a comprehensive literature review. *Therapeutic Recreation Journal*, **13**, 21–33.
Hanson, R. (1973). Outdoor Challenge and mental health. *Naturalist*, **24**, 26–30.
Heimstra, N. W. and McFarling, L. H. (1974). *Environmental Psychology*. Monterey, CA: Brooks/Cole.
Iso-Ahola, S. E. (1980), *The Social Psychology of Leisure and Recreation*. Dubuque: William C. Brown.
James, W. (1902). *The Varieties of Religious Experience*. New York: Holt.
Kahoe, R. D. (ed.) (1979). Wilderness therapy. *Wilderness Psychology Newsletter*, **2**.
Kaplan, R. (1974). Some psychological benefits of an Outdoor Challenge Program. *Environment and Behavior*, **6**, 101–116.
Kaplan, R. (1977). Summer outdoor programs: their participants and their effects. In *Children, Nature and the Urban Environment: Proceedings of a Symposium-Fair* (USDA Forest Service General Technical Report NE-30). Upper Darby, PA: USDA Forest Service Northeastern Experimental Station, pp. 175–179.
Kaplan, R. (1984). Wilderness perception and psychological benefits: an analysis of a continuing program. *Leisure Sciences*, **6**, 271–289.
Kaplan, R., Kaplan, S. and Frey, J. (1979). Final report: assessing the benefits of a natural area experience, and orientation to a wilderness area experience. Cooperative agreements 13–451 and 13–452, North Central Forest Experimental Station, Forest Service, USDA.
Kaplan, S. (1983). A model of person–environment compatibility. *Environment and Behavior*, **15**, 311–332.
Kaplan, S. and Talbot, J. F. (1983). Psychological benefits of a wilderness experience. In I. Altman and J. F. Wohlwill (eds), *Behavior and the Natural Environment*, Vol VI of *Human Behavior and Environment*. New York: Plenum.
Kluckhohn, F. R. (1953). Dominant and variant value orientations. In C. Kluckhohn, H. A. Murray and D. M. Schneider (eds), *Personality in Nature, Society and Culture*. New York: Knopf.

Kulik, J. A., Revelle, W. R. and Kulik, C-L. (1970). Scale construction by hierarchical cluster analysis. Unpublished, University of Michigan.

Lingoes, J. C. (1972). A general survey of the Guttman-Lingoes nonmetric program series. In R. N. Shepard, A. K. Romney and S. B. Nerlove (eds), *Multidimensional Scaling* Volume I. New York: Seminar.

Newman, R. S. (1980). Alleviating learned helplessness in a wilderness setting: an application of attribution theory to Outward Bound. In L. J. Fyans, Jr. (ed.) *Achievement Motivation: Recent Trends in Theory and Research*. New York: Plenum.

Scott, N. R. (1974). Toward a psychology of wilderness experience. *Natural Resources Journal*, **14**, 231–237.

Turner, A. L. (1972). The influence of Outward Bound School experience on the self-concept of adolescent boys. Ph.D. Dissertation, Boston University. Ann Arbor: University Microfilms International.

STRESS RECOVERY DURING EXPOSURE TO NATURAL AND URBAN ENVIRONMENTS[1]

ROGER S. ULRICH*, ROBERT F. SIMONS†, BARBARA D. LOSITO†,
EVELYN FIORITO†, MARK A. MILES† and MICHAEL ZELSON†

*College of Architecture, Texas A & M University,
College Station, Texas 77843-3137 and
† Department of Psychology, University of Delaware,
Newark, Delaware, U.S.A.

Abstract

Different conceptual perspectives converge to predict that if individuals are stressed, an encounter with most unthreatening natural environments will have a stress reducing or restorative influence, whereas many urban environments will hamper recuperation. Hypotheses regarding emotional, attentional and physiological aspects of stress reducing influences of nature are derived from a psycho-evolutionary theory. To investigate these hypotheses, 120 subjects first viewed a stressful movie, and then were exposed to color/sound videotapes of one of six different natural and urban settings. Data concerning stress recovery during the environmental presentations were obtained from self-ratings of affective states and a battery of physiological measures: heart period, muscle tension, skin conductance and pulse transit time, a non-invasive measure that correlates with systolic blood pressure. Findings from the physiological and verbal measures converged to indicate that recovery was faster and more complete when subjects were exposed to natural rather than urban environments. The pattern of physiological findings raised the possibility that responses to nature had a salient parasympathetic nervous system component; however, there was no evidence of pronounced parasympathetic involvement in responses to the urban settings. There were directional differences in cardiac responses to the natural vs urban settings, suggesting that attention/intake was higher during the natural exposures. However, both the stressor film and the nature settings elicited high levels of involuntary or automatic attention, which contradicts the notion that restorative influences of nature stem from involuntary attention or fascination. Findings were consistent with the predictions of the psycho-evolutionary theory that restorative influences of nature involve a shift towards a more positively-toned emotional state, positive changes in physiological activity levels, and that these changes are accompanied by sustained attention/intake. Content differences in terms of natural vs human-made properties appeared decisive in accounting for the differences in recuperation and perceptual intake.

Introduction

The growing interest in environmental stress has been accompanied by a rapid accumulation of evidence indicating that environmental stressors (e.g. crowding, community noise, air pollution) can elicit substantial stress in large groups of people (for surveys see Cohen et al., 1986; Evans & Cohen, 1987). Much previous stress research has been concerned primarily with person-based variables in responses to situations, such as coping and perceived control. Many studies also reflect an increasing emphasis on physical properties of environments (e.g. high stimulation levels) that increase demands on coping resources (e.g. Evans *et al*., 1986). Whether concerned with person-based variables or environmental characteristics, the vast majority of research to date has focused on situations that challenge resources or threaten well-being and accordingly elicit stress. Also, most studies have been concerned with extreme or unusual environmental conditions such as heat stress or loud aircraft noise. A different, though complementary perspective on stress and environments is evident in the question of whether different everyday, non-extreme physical environments have different influences in terms of fostering or hampering recovery from stress (Ulrich & Simons, 1986). If individuals are experiencing uncomfortable stress, due to either environmental conditions or other factors (e.g. illness, bereavement), do encounters with some types of common environments have restorative effects, while other everyday settings hamper or even work against recovery? To help answer these questions, an understanding of the concepts of stress and restoration is required.

Stress is the process by which an individual responds psychologically, physiologically, and often with behaviors, to a situation that challenges or threatens well-being (Baum *et al*., 1985). The psychological component includes cognitive appraisal of the situation, emotions such as fear, anger, and sadness, and coping responses. The physiological aspect consists of activity responses in numerous bodily systems, such as the cardiovascular, skeletomuscular and neuroendocrine, that mobilize the individual for coping or dealing with the situation. This mobilization uses resources or energy and, if prolonged, contributes to fatigue. The behavioral component includes a wide range of manifestations—for instance, avoidance, alcohol or cigarette use, and declines in cognitive performance on tasks such as proof reading (e.g. Cohen *et al*., 1986). Also, after cessation of a stressor, after-effects may be observed such as a decline in frustration tolerance and lower task performance (e.g. Glass & Singer, 1972).

A second concept central to the theory and research described in later sections is 'stress recovery' or 'restoration'. These terms will be used here interchangeably, although restoration can be construed as a broader concept that is not limited to stress recovery situations, or to recovery from states characterized by excessive psychological and physiological arousal, but could also apply to recuperation, for instance, from understimulation or excessively low arousal (Ulrich, 1981, 1983). 'Restoration' could also pertain to recovery influences that extend to the anabolic recharge of energy expended in the psychophysiological mobilization involved in responding to a stressor. In contrast to a stress response, restoration or recovery from stress involves numerous *positive* changes in psychological states, in levels of activity in physiological systems, and often in behaviors or functioning, including cognitive functioning or performance. Central to the psychological component of restoration are positive changes in emotional states, i.e. reduced levels of negatively toned feelings such as fear or anger, and increases in positively-toned affects (Zuckerman, 1977; Ulrich, 1979). Because responses to short-term as well as long-term fatiguing stressors sometimes involve declines in cognitive functioning or performance, recovery may be evident in gains in performance (Hockey, 1983; Hartig *et al*., 1987).

The fact that both stress symptoms and restoration appear in different response modes has led Baum *et al*. (1985), among others, to advocate strongly the use of research approaches that assess responses in more than one mode. An outcome of general synchrony between data obtained from different modes (e.g. psychological and physiological) would suggest convergent validity, and justify greater confidence in the findings. At the most general level, the purpose of the present study was to investigate, using a multi-modal combination of measures—physiological and verbal—the extent to which exposure to different everyday outdoor environments may foster or hinder recovery from stress. A second major objective was to test the notion that exposures to natural settings may promote greater stress recovery than contacts with urban environments, and that such differences in recovery effects should be evident in emotional states and physiological indicators. The physiological measures used in this research can objectively indicate effects of environmental exposures on bodily systems, and yield insights concerning attention or intake responses to settings during stress recovery (e.g. Lacey & Lacey, 1970). Compared with other types of stress measures, physiological procedures offer the important advantage of continuous monitoring of responses during an environmental encounter. Also, the use of physiological measures addresses a conspicuous gap in environment-behavior research; physiological methods have been neglected by investigators, and very little is known about the physiological correlates of experiences with everyday physical settings.

In investigating recovery effects of outdoor environments, this research distinguished broadly between natural and urban environments. This is justified by different theories of human–environment interactions, and by evidence from many studies indicating that natural vs human-made visual properties elicit different patterns of affective responses in unstressed individuals, and have a central role in influencing perception and categorization of outdoor settings (Kaplan et al., 1972; Wohlwill, 1983). Investigations of groups in different countries have employed multivariate procedures such as multidimensional scaling to show that natural vs built groupings of landscape scenes emerge as prominent dimensions when affective ratings are obtained for diverse samples of views (e.g. Kaplan et al., 1972; Bernaldez & Parra, 1979). Visual environments tend to be categorized broadly as 'natural' by American and European groups if the content is predominantly vegetation and/or water, and if human-made features such as buildings and cars are absent or inconspicuous (Ulrich, 1983). Accordingly, we selected for study examples of natural settings that were dominated either by vegetation or a water feature. Consistent with the general natural/urban distinction, various urban settings were selected that had little or no vegetation and lacked a water feature.

Previous findings concerning stress reducing influences of natural settings
Apart from the perceptual categories implicit in individuals' responses to outdoor environments, a consistent finding in well over 100 studies of recreation experiences in wilderness and urban nature areas has been that stress mitigation is one of the most important verbally expressed perceived benefits (Driver, 1976; Knopf, 1987; Schroeder, 1989). Recreation experiences are often complex (Hull, 1990), and apart from possible restorative influences of viewing or experiencing nature, other mechanisms foster stress recovery, e.g. physical exercise and achieving sense of control and other coping advantages through 'temporary escape' (Driver & Knopf, 1975). Although this body of research offers convincing evidence that stress recovery occurs in recreation experiences, the contribution of natural content and configurations *per se* has not been clearly isolated. However, the notion that simply viewing unthreatening nature tends to foster recovery from stress has received empirical support from a study by Ulrich (1979) of students who were experiencing mild stress because of a final exam. This study

used self-ratings to assess recovery produced by viewing color slides of either everyday nature scenes or unblighted city views lacking nature such as vegetation. Findings suggested that the natural scenes held attention more effectively and fostered greater recovery as indicated by higher levels of positive affects and greater reductions in fear. Honeyman (1990) replicated this study with the addition of a recovery condition consisting of urban scenes containing prominent vegetation. Her results suggested that the urban settings with nature produced more recovery than the urban scenes lacking nature. In a study performed in Sweden using unstressed subjects (Ulrich, 1981), findings from self-ratings suggested that slides of unspectacular natural scenes sustained attention much more effectively through a lengthy viewing session, and produced more positively toned feeling states, than did urban scenes. These verbal results were broadly consistent with recordings of brain electrical activity in the alpha frequency range that suggested individuals were more wakefully relaxed during the nature exposures (Ulrich, 1981). These studies suggest that restorative effects of natural, in contrast to urban, scenes involve positive changes in emotional states accompanied by attention.

These positive emotional states elicited by viewing unthreatening nature may be a mechanism underlying the finding that hospital patients recovering from surgery had more favorable recovery courses, including shorter hospital stays, lower intake of potent narcotic pain drugs, and more favorable evaluations by nurses, if their windows overlooked trees rather than a brick building wall (Ulrich, 1984). A questionnaire study of patients who were severely disabled by accidents or illness (and presumably stressed) found that a highly preferred category of window views included scenes of natural content such as trees (Verderber, 1986). In research by Heerwagen and Orians on patient anxiety in a dental fears clinic (Heerwagen, 1990), self-ratings and heart rate data suggested that patients felt less stressed on days when a large mural depicting a natural scene was hung on a wall of the waiting room, in contrast to days when the wall was blank. These findings from studies of health facilities are paralleled by results from prison research suggesting that cell window views of nature are associated with lower frequencies of prisoner stress symptoms such as digestive illness and headaches, and with fewer sick calls (Moore, 1982; West, 1985).

Theoretical Perspectives on Stress Reducing Influences of Nature

The intuitively-based beliefs that exposures to trees, water and other nature tend to foster psychological well-being, and produce restoration from the stresses of everyday urban living, date as far back as the earliest large cities (Ulrich & Parsons, 1990). For instance, residents of ancient Rome wrote that they valued contacts with nature as a contrast to the noise, congestion and other stressors of the city (Glacken, 1967). In the United States in the 19th century, the influential landscape architect and planner Frederick Law Olmsted (1865) wrote insightfully about stresses associated with cities and job demands, and argued that viewing nature is effective in producing restoration or recovery from such stresses (Ulrich, 1979). Olmsted contended that for individuals experiencing stress, viewing nature 'employs the mind without fatigue and yet exercises it; tranquilizes it and yet enlivens it; and thus, through the influence of the mind over the body, gives the effect of refreshing rest and reinvigoration to the whole system' (Olmsted, 1865). Olmsted's intuitively-based ideas about the restorative effect of nature formed an important part of his influential justification for providing pastoral parks and other nature in America's cities, and for preserving wilderness such as the Yosemite Valley for public use. These ideas, along with the many well-known parks he created, such as Central Park in New York City, were influential in shaping the City Beautiful movement in the United States, and had widespread effects on parks and urban design that have carried down to the present (Ulrich & Parsons, 1990).

More recently, social scientists have advanced a number of theoretical perspectives, as widely different as cultural conditioning and evolutionary positions, that converge in predicting that if individuals are stressed, encounters with most unthreatening natural settings will have stress reducing influences, whereas many urban environments will impede recuperation (Ulrich & Simons, 1986). Very briefly, *cultural* and other learning-based perspectives suggest that contemporary Western cultures tend to condition their inhabitants to revere nature and dislike cities (e.g. Tuan, 1974). Also, learned positive associations with natural environments can be acquired, for instance, during vacations and other recreational experiences. *Arousal* theories (e.g. Berlyne, 1971; Mehrabian & Russell, 1974) imply that recuperation from excessive arousal or stress should occur more rapidly in settings having low levels of arousal increasing properties such as complexity, intensity and movement. Consistent with the arousal perspective, studies using abstract, non-environmental visual displays have found that preferred levels of complexity decline when individuals are stressed or anxious (e.g. Berlyne & Lewis, 1963; O'Leary, 1965). Since natural settings may tend to have lower levels of complexity and other arousal properties than urban environments (Wohlwill, 1976), arousal theory implies that nature should have comparatively restorative influences on stress. *Overload* perspectives provide a rather different explanation of why recuperation following a stressor may be more rapid when external stimulation is comparatively low; high complexity and other stimulation place taxing processing demands (Cohen, 1978) that should slow or hamper restoration from stress.

Evolutionary perspectives often contend that because humans evolved over a long period in natural environments, people are to some extent physiologically and perhaps psychologically adapted to natural, as opposed to urban, physical settings. Whereas evolutionary arguments advanced by different authors vary considerably, a theme common to this position is that humans have an unlearned predisposition to pay attention and respond positively to natural content (e.g. vegetation, water) and to configurations characteristic of settings that were favorable to survival or ongoing well-being during evolution (e.g. Stainbrook, 1968; Appleton, 1975; Driver & Greene, 1977; Kaplan & Kaplan, 1989; Ulrich, 1983; Orians, 1986). As an example, Orians (1986) and Orians and Heerwagen (in press) have suggested that aesthetic liking and other positive responding to nature are elicited by specific types of configurations characteristic of environments that were most favorable to pre-modern humans from the standpoint of yielding food and drinking water. In an interesting analysis, Orians (1986) has obtained data suggesting high aesthetic liking for specific vegetation and tree canopy structures that are found in particular types of savannah environments; in turn, scientific measurements suggest that such savannah settings offered to pre-modern humans an especially high potential for obtaining food and water. Another variant of an evolutionary perspective has been suggested by authors who speculate that natural content may be processed with relative ease and efficiency because the brain and sensory systems evolved in natural environments (e.g. Wohlwill, 1983). Because this evolutionary tuning is lacking for urban or built environments, encounters with such settings place greater demands on processing resources, and may overload the individual or require more coping or adaptation effort (Stainbrook, 1968). This argument implies that if an individual is stressed, these processing and/or adaptation demands should hinder recovery. As another example, Kaplan and Kaplan have advanced an evolutionary perspective that asserts preferences and restorative influences are cognitively-based, and are elicited by general contents such as vegetation, by properties of settings that foster movement and exploration, by coherent properties of nature that facilitate comprehension, and by natural objects and configurations that are 'fascinating' or attention holding (Kaplan & Talbot, 1983; Kaplan & Kaplan, 1989).

Attention or fascination and stress recovery
In addition to Kaplan and Kaplan, other authors concerned with natural physical settings as well as with animals and pets have conjectured that strong attention holding properties of natural phenomena play a critical role in stress recovery or restoration (e.g. Katcher et al., 1983). As a prominent example, Olmsted (1865) advanced the position that non-taxing, attention-holding effects of natural views foster restoration from mental 'fatigue', or 'severe and excessive exercise of the mind', associated with work demands that require sustained, effortful attention and thought. Olmsted argued that natural settings 'restore' because they hold attention without mental effort, are pleasureable, and block out the demands and stresses of daily work and urban living. He wrote that when an individual is exposed to a natural view, 'The attention is aroused and the mind occupied without purpose' (1865).

In arguments somewhat similar to Olmsted's, Kaplan and Kaplan have conjectured that people respond with involuntary attention or 'fascination' to nature, and that this is a key mechanism in restoration from 'mental fatigue' stemming from work situations that necessitate prolonged, directed, effortful attention (Kaplan & Talbot, 1983; Kaplan & Kaplan, 1989). In this regard, a study by Hartig et al. (1987) of subjects stressed by a difficult mental task offered some equivocal support for the notion that greater restoration of cognitive performance may be fostered by exposure to nature in contrast to urban settings. However, an assessment of the viability of a restoration explanation that emphasizes fascination should also take into account the fact that several scientific studies have shown that settings containing certain types of natural stimuli, such as snakes and spiders, do elicit strong 'involuntary' attention or fascination, yet the effects are anything but restorative. These studies indicate that along with strong attention (usually assessed by analysis of phasic cardiac deceleration), normal or non-phobic subjects respond to such stimuli as snakes and spiders with negatively-toned emotions and autonomic nervous system activation (e.g. Dimberg, 1986; Dimberg & Thell, 1988). Because automatic attention or fascination can be salient components of responses to stressors, this research implies that a model of restoration or stress recovery should specify other mechanisms in addition to attention or fascination.

At this point it might be argued that whether an environmental encounter involving automatic attention or fascination is restorative or stressful is shaped by elaborated, conscious cognitive appraisals such as 'compatibility' with respect to the individual's inclinations (Kaplan & Kaplan, 1989). However, conditioning studies have shown that nature settings containing snakes or spiders can elicit pronounced autonomic responses (e.g. skin conductance) even when presented subliminally in backward-masking designs (e.g. Öhman, 1986; Öhman et al., 1989). In other words, these findings suggest that *coherent responding to quite specific nature elements, can occur in the absence of recognition or conscious awareness of the elements.* Other studies using exposures of several seconds have found that well-defined positive or negative emotional responses to natural stimuli (assessed by facial electromyography) can occur in 400 ms or less (Dimberg, 1990). This very rapid emotional/physiological responding, which appears relevant to stress and restoration, is difficult to reconcile with a purely 'controlled' cognitive perspective on human–nature interactions and restoration.

Further, a theoretical conceptualization of restoration that focuses heavily on 'mental fatigue' is likely to be inadequate, given the findings of studies that have examined emotional, physiological and cognitive performance indicators while individuals engaged in mental problem solving or other activities that required prolonged, taxing, directed attention. These studies clearly indicate that cognitive 'fatigue' does not occur as an isolated effect, but is usually accompanied by negatively-toned feelings, sometimes by declines in cognitive performance (Holding, 1983), and typically involves recruitment of a variety of physiological systems and responding (electrocortical, autonomic, skeletomuscular, neuroendocrine) (e.g. Frankenhaeuser, 1980). Even prolonged attention to an interesting, comparatively positive mental task is accompanied by physiological mobilization, for instance, in the endocrine system as indicated by release of stress hormones (Lundberg *et al.*, 1990). In view of these findings, it seems appropriate to interpret 'mental fatigue' in more mainstream terms as referring to a stress state of varying intensity elicited by work or mental stressors.

While all the above mentioned conceptual perspectives—evolutionary, arousal and cultural/learning—have implications for the issue of stress recovery, most are not theories of restoration. Whereas Kaplan and Kaplan (1989) have advanced arguments that explicitly address restorative influences of nature, particularly with respect to 'mental fatigue', the foremost concern of evolutionary writings has been to explain patterns of aesthetic preference or judgements of visual quality. With the exception of some arousal and overload formulations, the conceptual positions described above contain very few explicit statements relating to such critical dimensions of restoration as physiological responses and changes in emotional states. For the most part, these theoretical conjectures regarding possible beneficial effects of nature have been grounded on data obtained from verbal indicators that offer at best a limited assessment of restoration from stress (e.g. preferences, satisfactions, attitudes or ratings of self-concept).

A psychoevolutionary theory
Ulrich's (1983) 'psycho-evolutionary' framework is an exception because it encompasses in addition to aesthetic preferences, a broad range of emotional and physiological arousal responses to natural configurations and content, including recovery or restoration. In Ulrich's perspective, preference is considered to be an important affect, but is construed only as one of a broad range of emotions (e.g. fear, interest, anger, sadness) that are central to the psychological component of stress and restoration, a position consistent with a very large research literature in clinical psychology and behavioral medicine. In contrast to, for instance, the Kaplans' cognitive perspective, Ulrich (1983) postulates that immediate, unconsciously triggered and initiated emotional responses—not 'controlled' cognitive responses—play a central role in the initial level of responding to nature, and have major influences on attention,

subsequent conscious processing, physiological responding and behavior (Schriffin & Schneider, 1977; Zajonc, 1980; Öhman *et al.*, 1989). The emphasis on quick-onset affective reactions is reconcilable with the growing amount of scientific evidence suggesting that the initial level of response to natural elements can be preconscious (e.g. Öhman *et al.*, 1989). A fundamental contention of Ulrich's framework is that this multimodal process of responding should be adaptive in the sense that it is appropriate to the situation and motivates approach-avoidance behaviors that foster ongoing well-being or survival. Depending on the characteristics of a natural setting, and the individual's preceding affective/cognitive/physiological state, adaptive responses can range from stress and avoidance behavior to restoration and approach behavior (seeking out, staying in, not avoiding) (Ulrich, 1983, pp. 93–95). An example of a situation where adaptive responding would entail stressful influences, would be an early human encountering a natural setting involving risk or threat (e.g. a venomous snake or the edge of a precipice). In this case the quick-onset emotional reaction comprising fear, dislike, and attention/interest, would initiate adaptive physiological mobilization and very quickly motivate avoidance behavior on the basis of only a minimum of cognitive activity. But the costs of this adaptive process of responding would be evident in, among other modes, negatively-toned emotional states and energy consuming physiological arousal. If the threat situation were resolved, and the individual then encountered a natural setting favorable to ongoing well-being or survival (e.g. a savannah-like area or setting with water), Ulrich's theory suggests the adaptive need is for restoration or a 'breather' from stress, perhaps partly to restore energy to sustain subsequent behaviors to exploit food, water or other advantages of the area. An adaptive constellation of restorative responses would involve, for instance, attention/interest accompanied by liking, reduced levels of negatively toned feelings such as fear, and reductions in physiological arousal from high levels to more moderate ranges (Ulrich, 1979, 1981, 1983). The conceptual arguments suggest, among other testable hypotheses, that restorative influences of unthreatening natural scenes following a stressor should be evident in a shift towards a more positively-toned emotional state, and in decreased levels of physiological arousal. From an adaptive evolutionary perspective, it can further be predicted that such restoration should occur fairly quickly, i.e. often within minutes rather than hours, depending on the intensity of the stress response. In light of the earlier discussion concerning attention or fascination, it should be emphasized that Ulrich's (1983) theory explicitly predicts that attention/interest will be a prominent component of *both* restorative responses to unthreatening natural scenes as well as stress responses to natural settings containing risk or threat. Regarding the latter point, humans should react with automatic 'involuntary' attention to potentially dangerous stimuli as part of the process of motivating avoidance or other adaptive behavior that would occur with sufficient quickness to favor long-term survival.

These arguments imply that acquiring a capacity for restorative responding to certain unthreatening natural contents and configurations had major advantages for humans during evolution including, for instance, rapid attenuation of stress responses following threatening encounters, and fostering recharge of physical energy. Accordingly, modern humans might have a biologically prepared readiness to quickly and readily acquire restorative responses with respect to many unthreatening natural settings, but have no such prepardness for most urban or built contents and configurations. The notion that biological preparedness may be a factor in responding to natural but not urban content has plausibility in light of many studies during the last 15 years on 'biologically prepared learning' (Seligman, 1971). In clinical psychology and psychophysiology, biologically prepared learning has gained some acceptance as an explanation for strong fear responses, avoidance, and phobic reactions with respect to situations and objects that presumably were survival threats throughout evolution (e.g. heights, snakes). Findings from many conditioning experiments indicate that strong aversive or defense responses are often readily acquired, and are consistently resistant to extinction, for certain pre-technological risk stimuli such as snakes and spiders, but not for much more dangerous modern stimuli such as handguns and frayed electrical wires (for survey of studies see Öhman, 1986). In view of these important findings, the speculation seems justified that biological preparedness might also be manifested in positive emotional/physiological/approach responses to natural content and configurations that tended to foster survival and well-being during evolution, but that such preparedness should not be evident for urban or built stimuli. Arguably, the rewards associated with natural settings during a few million years of evolution have been sufficiently critical to favor individuals who very easily learned and then persistently retained two related types of adaptive positive responding to nature: (1) restoration responses following stressful or taxing activities; and (2) in the absence of stress, liking/attention/approach responses for certain contents and classes of situations that favored well-being or survival because of high food potential, low risk and other advantages (e.g. water, savannah-like settings).

Hypotheses of the present study
All of the theoretical perspectives discussed earlier—cultural, arousal and evolutionary—converge in implying that everyday unthreatening natural environments, compared with most urban settings, should tend to foster greater stress recovery. Consistent with this consensus prediction and with the findings from previous empirical research, the main hypothesis of the present study was that exposures to unthreatening natural environments would foster greater recuperation from stress than contacts with various urban settings. Furthermore, the study evaluated hypotheses derived from Ulrich's theoretical framework (1983). Specifically, it was anticipated that following a stressor, restorative influences of unthreatening natural scenes would be evident in a shift towards a more positively-toned emotional state, by declines in physiological arousal, and that these changes would be accompanied by comparatively high levels of attention. In this latter regard, we also evaluated the hypothesis from Ulrich's framework that involuntary or automatic attention can be a salient component of responding to a visual stressor as well as an accompaniment of restoration.

Furthermore, the study design was influenced by the objective of testing an influential conceptual perspective in environmental psychology, arousal theory, from the standpoint of its predictions concerning stress recovery influences and attention-holding effects. Arousal theory predicts that recovery from stress will be especially impeded by urban settings having high levels of intense, unpredictable or arousal increasing stimuli. To make possible a test of this hypothesis, a sample of urban environments was chosen as recovery conditions that varied markedly in stimulation levels, especially in terms of high vs low quantities of traffic and pedestrians. A related expected finding was that least recovery from stress would occur during contact with an urban setting having heavy as opposed to light traffic. This hypothesis is supported by arousal arguments, and is consistent with findings from many studies suggesting that traffic is evaluated as negative or stressful (e.g. Cermak & Cornillon, 1976; Rylander et al., 1976). Furthermore, on the basis of arousal theory and findings from crowding research (e.g. Aiello et al., 1975), we anticipated that more recovery would occur during exposure to an urban setting with few people, rather than many people.

Finally, arousal theory clearly predicts that urban settings with high levels of complexity, intensity and other arousal-increasing properties (i.e. heavy traffic or many pedestrians) would elicit more attention than either nature settings or urban environments with light traffic or few pedestrians. In line with arousal theory, we anticipated that the high stimulation urban settings would prove more attention-holding than the low stimulation urban settings. However, with respect to the nature settings, we followed the prediction suggested by the biological preparedness argument, and by other evolutionary perspectives, in anticipating that nature would prove more effective than the various urban settings in eliciting sustained attention.

Methods

Stressor

The subjects consisted of 120 undergraduate volunteers (60 males and 60 females) at the University of Delaware who were studying in diverse fields. Each individual, while seated in a comfortable armchair, viewed two 10 min videotapes on a 19" color monitor having a supplementary speaker and amplifier system that insured accurate reproduction of sounds. The first videotape was the stressor; this was a black and white film about prevention of work accidents ('It Didn't Have to Happen') that has been found to be an effective stressor in previous studies (e.g. Lazarus et al., 1965). The film depicts several serious injuries, with simulated blood and mutilation, that occur to employees in a woodworking shop as a result of their carelessness or disregard of safety procedures. Other commonly used stressor films that depict, for instance, auto accidents or human violence, were considered inappropriate because such scenes might have biased subjects against either urban settings with cars or people, or natural settings, in terms of stress recovery influences.

Environments

Following the stressor, subjects viewed the second ten minute tape (recovery condition) that was a color/sound display of one of six different everyday outdoor settings (two natural, four urban). Using a random assignment procedure, 20 subjects were exposed to each recovery environment. Table 1 lists the six environments and describes their major properties.

It appears there are no procedures currently available for measuring objectively the information rate over a time period of non-static, audiovisual environmental displays (Mehrabian & Russell, 1974). In this regard, verbal judgements of information rate obtained after a 10 minute video simulation may be misleading because of habituation. However, it seems very likely that the quantity of information or stimulation in the urban setting with heavy traffic was much higher than in the light traffic condition (Table 1). Likewise, stimulation levels were probably higher in the urban setting with many pedestrians compared with the same environment with fewer people. Stimulation in all of the urban videotapes may have been moderately predictable. In the case of the two traffic settings, vehicles could be heard approaching a few seconds

TABLE 1
Environments displayed during stress recovery period

Environment	Visual content	Sounds
Nature		
Vegetation	Setting dominated by trees and other vegetation; some openness among trees; occasional light breeze in background; no people or animals.	Birds, light breeze. Range of dB levels: 42–64.
Water	Setting dominated by trees and a fast-moving stream; waves and ripples visible on stream surface. No people or animals.	Constant 63–64 dB from stream.
Urban		
Heavy traffic	Commercial street with moderately heavy traffic (24 vehicles/min) and no pedestrians or animals. Two-way traffic; wide variety of vehicles (e.g. large and small trucks, buses). Traffic moving at 35–45 mph.	Range of dB levels: 65–93.
Light traffic	Same commercial street as above, but during light traffic conditions (4 vehicles/min). No pedestrians. Two-way traffic moving at 35–45 mph. Less variety in vehicles than during heavy traffic conditions.	Range of dB levels: 64–85.
Urban		
Many pedestrians	Pedestrianized, traffic-free outdoor shopping mall with many people (35 persons passing/min). Two-way movement. Several store facades; moderate depth or openness; no animals.	Voices, footsteps, and other people noises. Range of dB levels: 65–78.
Few pedestrians	Same traffic-free shopping area as above, but with fewer people (7 persons passing/min). No animals.	Range of dB levels: 52–72.

before they appeared; in the shopping mall tapes, predestrians could be seen approaching in a predictable manner from the right and left peripheries of the monitor display. In all of the environments, urban and natural, there was openness in the foreground and middleground; the settings contained no foreground elements that obstructed sight lines or which otherwise might engender uncertainty or risk, thereby eliciting negative affective responses (Schroeder & Anderson, 1984). Sounds and visual stimuli were congruent or fitting in all settings. The natural setting with water may have been higher in overall information rate than the vegetation (forest) conditions, despite having less variation in decibel levels. The water setting displayed constant movement on the surface of the stream, whereas the forest environment was visually static.

The six environments were videotaped and the accompanying sounds were recorded simultaneously by a professional crew from the Office of Instructional and Information Technology of the University of Delaware. The settings were videotaped using a broadcast quality camera (three Saticon tubes) and 0·75" color/sound tape. For all environments, the camera was tripod-mounted and positioned next to an existing public bench that was apparently intended for relaxation. The sound recording microphone was located below and in front of the camera lens. Decibel levels were recorded at 20 s intervals at the sites, and later were used for calibrating sound intensities for each environment in the laboratory. The videotaping was done in clear weather, and only during middle portions of days (10·30 to 14·30 h) in order to reduce shadows and variations in sun angles at the various sites.

The validity of using displays such as color slides and photographs to simulate real outdoor scenes has been supported by several studies (e.g. Shuttleworth, 1980). Also, studies using audiovisual simulation procedures (i.e. color slides or photographs accompanied by audio segments) have found significant similarities between on-site and laboratory ratings for natural and urban environments (Anderson et al., 1983; Zube et al., 1985). In light of these findings, it seems likely that the use in the present study of more realistic color/sound videotapes was a valid simulation procedure.

Procedures concerning subjects

When subjects arrived for their laboratory appointment, an experimenter provided them with a general description of the experimental procedures and familiarized them with the apparatus and recording equipment. The individuals were then asked for their informed consent. After the electrodes for the physiological recordings were attached, and preliminary recordings had been obtained, subjects were given more detailed information and instructions. They were told that after a short rest period a videotape would be presented that dealt with the prevention of workplace accidents. They were advised that a second videotape would follow shortly after the first, but the specific contents of the second film were not revealed. To establish an appropriate cognitive set for the second tape and thereby enhance the validity of the findings (Ward & Russell, 1981), a message was presented on the color monitor just prior to onset of the environmental tape that instructed the subjects to imagine they were relaxing while seated looking at the environment which was to appear.

Measures

The electrocardiogram (EKG), pulse transit time (PTT), spontaneous skin conductance responding (SCR), and frontalis muscle tension (EMG) were recorded from all subjects during a 2·5 min base period that began as soon as all sensing devices were attached and high quality recordings were achieved. These measures were continuously monitored throughout the subsequent stressor and environmental tapes. The EKG and PTT were used to obtain information regarding cardiovascular activity; the EKG would yield rate information (heart period, HP), while PTT correlates highly with systolic blood pressure (Obrist et al., 1979; Marie et al., 1984). Compared with measuring blood pressure using a conventional automated cuff, PTT has the major advantages of continuous (each heart beat) and far less invasive recording. Also, PTT does not require quiet for detecting Korotkoff sounds, and hence is exceptionally suited to environments with high decibel levels, such as some urban settings. Skin conductance is a measure that reflects activity in the sweat glands lying under the recording devices; skin conductance and the number of active sweat glands vary directly. Like the cardiovascular measures, SCR records activity that is controlled by the autonomic nervous system. In view of the concern in this research with both stress and recovery from stress or restoration, it should be mentioned that the autonomic nervous system is subdivided into the sympathetic nervous system and the parasympathetic nervous system. The major function of the sympathetic system is to mobilize the body for action, in order that situations which are challenging or stressful can be dealt with effectively. Sympathetic activation consumes energy and accordingly is physically taxing or non-restorative. By contrast, the parasympathetic system functions to restore and maintain bodily energy resources. Restorative parasympathetically dominated responding can also be associated with non-taxing perceptual sensitivity or attention with respect to the external environment (Lacey & Lacey, 1970).

The EMG measure differs from the other three in that the frontalis muscles are striate muscles located on the forehead, and these are innervated by central rather than autonomic nervous system fibres. Many decades of research have shown that EMG activity is involved both in responding to challenging situations or stressors as well as in relaxation. EMG and SCR normally increase during stress and decrease during recovery; PTT decreases during stress (shorter transit times correlate with higher blood pressure), and increases during recovery. The heart rate response is more complex in that it can accelerate or decelerate depending on particular characteristics of stressor situations. Stressors that involve mental problem-solving, or the storage, retrieval and internal manipulation of information, produce heart acceleration (Lacey & Lacey, 1970). However, a posture of intake, or attention/interest, to external stimuli usually reduces heart rate (Lacey & Lacey, 1970). Both unpleasant and pleasant environmental stimuli, if they elicit intake or attention, result in heart deceleration (Libby *et al.*, 1973). In the present study, a paradoxical heart rate response of deceleration was anticipated during the stressor, because blood and mutilation stimuli are potent in eliciting attention/intake (e.g. Hare *et al.*, 1970; Klorman & Ryan, 1980).

In addition to the physiological measures, subjects were asked to rate their feelings before and after the stressor, and after the recovery videotape, using the Zuckerman Inventory of Personal Reactions (ZIPERS) (Zuckerman, 1977). The ZIPERS is a broad yet brief state affect questionnaire that assesses feelings on five factors: Fear, Positive Affects, Anger/Aggression, Attentiveness/Interest, and Sadness. The subject indicates on a 5-point scale the degree to which each item describes the way he/she feels 'now'. Examples of the items are: 'I feel angry or defiant', and 'I feel elated or pleased'. Two items that assess self-reported autonomic responses were deleted because autonomic data were obtained by physiological measures (e.g. 'My heart is beating faster').

Physiological recording and data reduction
The EKG was recorded from two Beckman Ag–AgCl miniature electrodes placed on the left and right anterolateral rib cage after preparing the skin with alcohol and Redux electrode paste. To obtain heart period (HP) on each beat, the EKG signal was amplified with a Coulbourn High Gain Bioamplifier (S75-01) and fed into a Schmitt trigger which detected the occurrence of the 'R' wave. The output of the Schmitt trigger then started a clock in a Digital Equipment Corporation PDP-11/10 laboratory computer that continued until the next 'R' wave was detected. This inter-R interval was

timed to the nearest millisecond for each beat, and beats were accumulated over 30 s intervals and averaged. HP is the reciprocal of heart rate; that is, longer HP indicates slowing of heart rate.

PTT is obtained by measuring the time between the occurrence of a heart beat (i.e. an 'R' wave) and the arrival of the pulse pressure wave at a site distal to the heart. For the present study, the ear served as the distal site. A Hewlett-Packard photo-electric device was attached to the pinna of the right ear; this sensed changes in the translucence of the ear as the pressure wave from the heart waxed and waned. The voltage output of the photocell was amplified with a Coulbourn Bioamplifier (S75-01) and digitized every millisecond by the computer. A program then detected the beginning of each pressure wave at the ear, and computed the time in milliseconds since the EKG 'R' wave occurrence at the heart. This was done for each heart beat and subsequently averaged across 30 s intervals. Generally, shorter pulse transit times are associated with higher systolic blood pressure and longer PTTs with lower blood pressure. Both PTT and HP were computed on-line.

Skin conductance was recorded directly using a 0·5 volt constant voltage Coulbourn Skin Conductance Coupler (S71-22). Conductance was measured from the non-dominant hand by placing Beckman standard Ag–AgCl electrodes on the second phalange of the ring and middle fingers. An isotonic jelly (Johnson & Johnson K-Y) served as the electrolyte. The data were recorded on FM tape and subsequently played back through a Grass Model 7D polygraph that produced a paper record of the information. The record was hand scored; skin conductance was quantified by counting the number of spontaneous fluctuations which exceeded 0·067 microsiemens in amplitude during each 30 s recording period.

Muscle tension (EMG) was recorded from the two frontalis muscles by affixing Beckman miniature Ag–AgCl electrodes over the muscles, approximately 1" above the left and right eyes. The skin was cleansed with alcohol and mildly abraded with Redux electrode paste prior to electrode application. The raw EMG signal was amplified with a Coulbourn Bioamplifier (S75-01), full-wave rectified, and integrated by a Coulbourn Resetting Integrator (S76-22) which produced pulsed output at a rate proportional to the amount of raw muscle activity. The output was stored on FM tape and subsequently analysed off-line on the PDP-11/10 which was programmed to compute the average number of integrator 'resets' during 30 s recording periods. Further data reduction consisted of combining the five 30 s intervals of the 2·5 min base period into one average for each of the four physiological measures. The data from the stressor and recovery tapes were reduced to yield averages for three 3 min exposure periods. Data for the first minute of each environmental tape were not used because the onset of the videotapes with respect to the on-line computer program varied slightly for each subject.

Statistical analyses

The physiological data were subjected to two sets of mixed-model analysis of variance (ANOVA). The first consisted of the base and the three 3 min stress periods, and the second consisted of the last stress period and the subsequent three 3 min recovery periods. The second ANOVA revealed no general significant differences between the two nature settings (water vs vegetation); nor were there general differences between the heavy and light traffic conditions, or between the mall settings with many vs few pedestrians. Accordingly, the data were collapsed into three broader environmental categories: nature, traffic and pedestrian mall. The structure of the subsequent analyses was 3 (Environment) × 2 (Sex of subject) × 4 (Period), with orthogonal polynomial contrasts applied to the within-subject factor (Period). Significant effects of Environment were not expected to appear in the first ANOVA, because this covered the baseline and stressor periods. Environment was expected to appear in the second ANOVA as a main effect, or as an interaction with Period. Analyses of the ZIPERS self-ratings data were conducted separately for each question, and for items grouped as factors (Zuckerman, 1977). Mixed-model ANOVAs were employed for this purpose with orthogonal polynomials applied to the within-subject (Phase) factor: 3 (Environment) × 2 (Sex) × 3 (Phase). 'Phase' referred to the three times that the ZIPERS was administered to each subject: during baseline, following the stressor, and following the recovery tape displaying an environment. Differential effects of Environment were expected to be revealed in these analyses as interactions with Phase, because no differences were expected during baseline or immediately following the stressor.

Finally, correlation analyses were performed to assess relationships among the physiological measures, and between the ZIPERS items and the physiological measures. The first series of analyses addressed effects related to the stressor; the second focused on recovery. For the first series of correlations, each ZIPERS question was expressed as the change from baseline to post-stressor, and the physiological data were expressed as the changes from baseline for the three 3 min stressor periods. The second series was similar except that changes during recovery were computed from the offset of the stressor rather than from baseline. For all ANOVAs, alpha was set at $p = <0.05$ and the Greenhouse–Geisser correction applied to multiple df within-subject factors.

Effects of Stressor

The first ANOVA performed on the physiological data indicated as expected that there were no significant differences among the groups for either the baseline or stressor periods. The results in Figures 1 to 3 show that the groups were affected in the anticipated direction by the stressor, as evidenced by pronounced increases in skin conductance and muscle tension, and significantly shorter pulse transit time (higher systolic blood pressure) ($p = 0.001$ for all measures). Figure 4 shows that the expected sharp deceleration in heart rate (longer heart period, $p = <0.001$) did in fact occur during the stressor, which is interpreted as indicating high intake/attention for the scenes of work accidents displaying blood and mutilation. This latter finding is important in light of the theoretical discussion in earlier sections, because it shows that strong 'involuntary' attention can be a salient component of responsiveness to a stressor. This in turn suggests that a theoretical position which contends that 'involuntary' attention is the basis for restorative effects of nature is inadequate.

The results from the ZIPERS self-ratings were broadly consistent with the physiological findings. Analyses of the ZIPERS factors revealed that the subjects had much more negatively toned emotional states following the stressor. Post-stressor scores were higher for the Fear factor ($p = <0.01$) and Anger/Aggression factor ($p = <0.01$), and levels of Positive affects were much lower ($p = <0.01$). Also, scores for a Sadness factor rose significantly ($p = <0.01$), and reported levels of Attentiveness/Interest were lower following the stressor than during baseline ($p = <0.01$). The latter result may not be inconsistent with the heart period findings indicating high intake

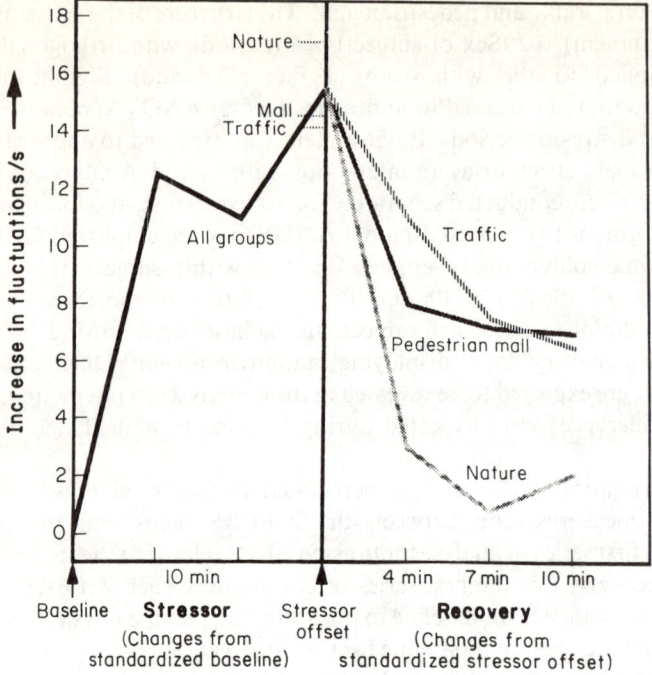

FIGURE 1. Changes in skin conductance (SCR) during stress and recovery.

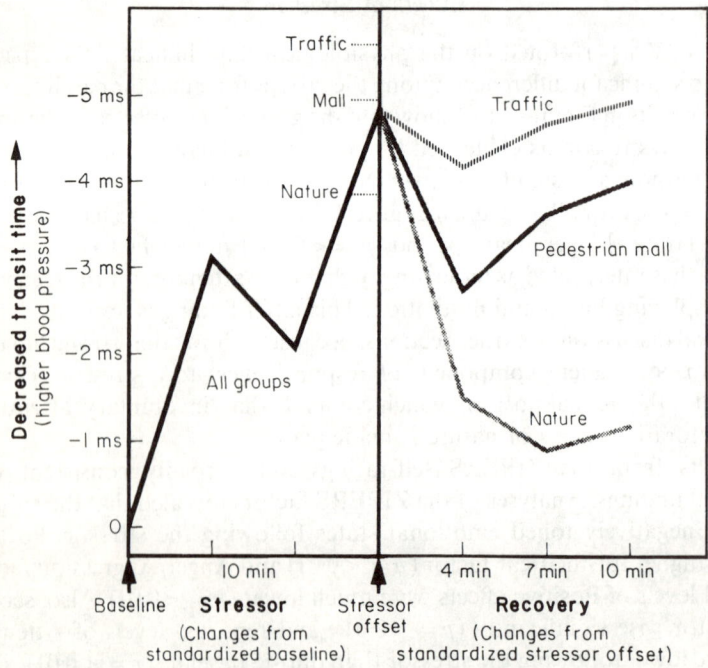

FIGURE 2. Changes in pulse transit time (PTT) during stress and recovery.

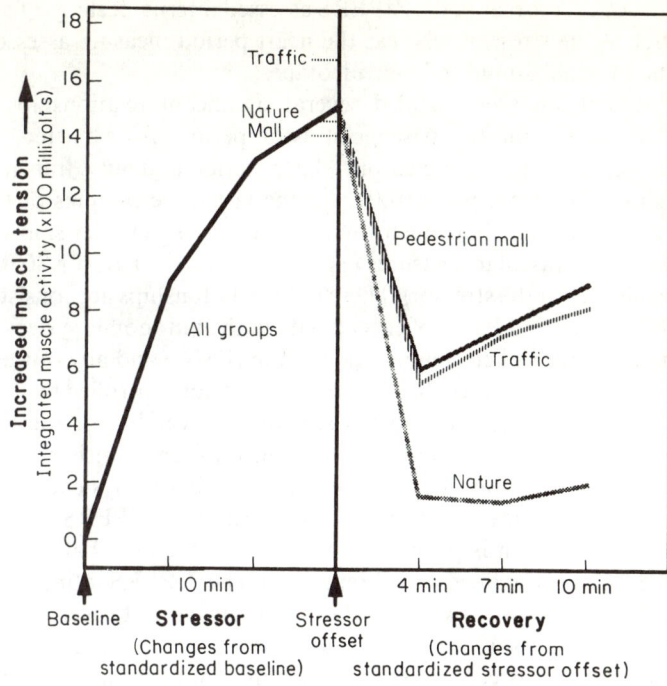

FIGURE 3. Changes in muscle tension (EMG) during stress and recovery.

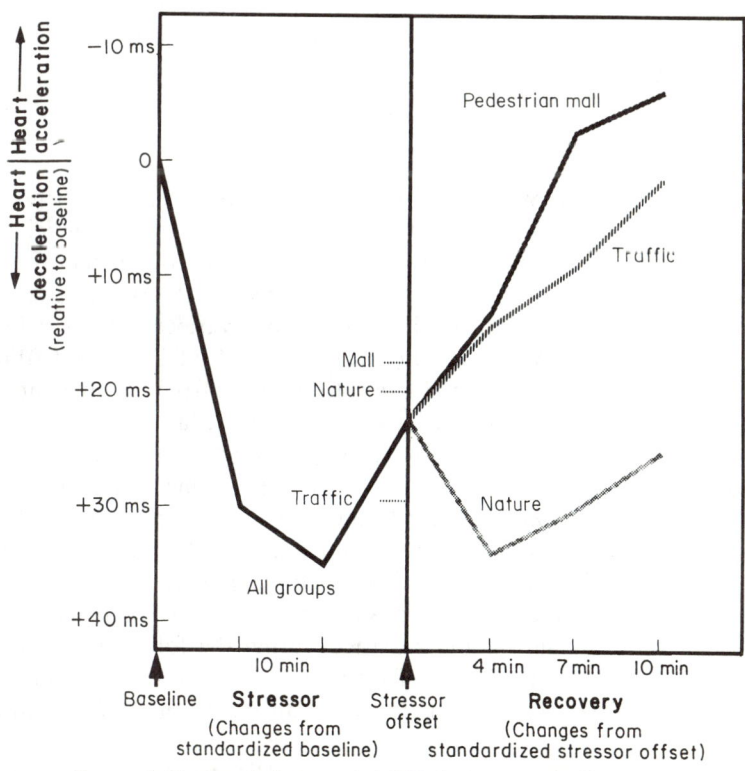

FIGURE 4. Changes in heart period (HP) during stress and recovery.

during the stressor tape, because the ZIPERS assessed internal feelings of attentiveness following offset of the stressor, whereas the heart period measure assessed attention directed to the external stimuli of the videotape.

The correlational analyses revealed several significant relationships among the physiological measures for the baseline-stressor period. As expected, correlations between the two cardiovascular indicators—heart period and pulse transit time—were especially high (e.g. $r = 0.54$, $p = <0.001$, for the last three minutes of the stressor). There were also significant but much lower correlations between skin conductance (SCR) and the cardiovascular measures (e.g. $r = 0.22$, $p = <0.01$, for SCR/HP during the first three minutes of the stressor). These latter relationships are consistent with the fact that SCR, like HP and PTT, reflects activity in the autonomic system. There were no significant correlations between muscle tension (EMG) and any of the autonomic measures, which is in accord with the fact that EMG is not controlled by the autonomic nervous system. In general, the findings support the validity of the physiological measurements because the patterns of relationships are consistent with known connections and lack of connections among different bodily systems.

There were few significant correlations between the ZIPERS self-ratings and physiological results, which is probably due partly to the fact that the affective and physiological data were obtained at different times. The ZIPERS ratings were obtained before and after the stressor, whereas the physiological data were recorded while subjects viewed the stressor tape. The most noteworthy finding was a pattern of positive correlations between pulse transit time and feelings of 'interest' and 'attentiveness' (e.g. $r = 0.27$, $p = <0.01$ for interest/PTT during the second three minutes of the stressor). This suggests that lower blood pressure was associated with higher levels of interest and attention during the stressor phase.

Effects of Environments

Physiological results
As mentioned earlier, PTT, SCR and EMG served as stress measures, whereas HP was considered an indicator of intake/attention. The second mixed-model ANOVA revealed pronounced general differences as a function of environment for all three stress measures. Specifically, significant environment × (linear) recovery period interactions were obtained, indicating that stress recovery trajectories over time varied widely according to category of environment ($p = <0.01$ for PTT; $p = <0.01$ for SCR; $p = <0.05$ for EMG). As Figures 1 to 3 show, the findings from the different measures converge to indicate that recovery from stress was much faster and more complete when subjects were exposed to the natural settings as opposed to either the pedestrian mall or traffic environments. A series of ANOVAs performed for each of the three 3 min recovery periods revealed that significantly greater recovery in terms of SCR had already occurred during the first recovery interval; this therapeutic advantage of nature persisted throughout the other recovery periods ($p = <0.01$ for all periods). The differences in PTT and EMG were significant during the recovery interval of 5–7 min ($p = <0.05$ for both measures), and persisted during the following 8–10 min ($p = <0.05$ for PTT; $p = <0.01$ for EMG). Therefore, greater stress reduction for nature was evident in all three measures, at the latest, during 5–7 min of exposure to the settings.

Despite the conspicuous lack of recovery in PTT for the traffic group, PTT recuperation for the pedestrian mall group was not significantly greater than for traffic (Figure 2). Also, there were no significant differences between the two categories of urban environments with respect to recovery influences expressed in either SCR or EMG.

The heart period recovery data revealed a most interesting pattern of general, directionally different responses to the natural vs urban environments ($p = <0.01$). As the findings in Figure 4 indicate, heart rate following onset of the nature tapes decelerated, despite the pronounced deceleration that had already occurred during the stressor (Figure 4). Compared with baseline (pre-stressor) levels, heart rate levels during the first three minutes of nature exposure were similar to the lowest recorded during the stressor film (Figure 4). By contrast, heart rate during the pedestrian mall and traffic exposures accelerated through the entire recovery period, and by the last recovery interval had increased to pre-stressor or baseline levels. These results suggest that intake/attention was higher for the natural rather than urban settings, and that everyday nature may have sustained as much perceptual intake as the stressor tape which contained scenes of simulated blood and multilation. There were no significant differences in the heart period data for the pedestrian mall and traffic conditions.

The heart period results raise the possibility that during the initial minutes of recovery, responses to the nature but not the urban settings were strongly influenced by the parasympathetic nervous system. Parasympathetically dominated responding is associated with heart rate deceleration, sustained yet non-taxing perceptual intake and sensitivity, and restoration of energy. (In contrast, sympathetic nervous system influences involve energy consuming arousal or mobilization, and are reflected, for instance, in an acceleratory component to heart rate and increased skin conductance.) The heart monitoring methods used here did not make it possible to disentangle precisely the role of parasympathetic and sympathetic influences. In this regard it is conceivable that reduced sympathetic input might have played some role in heart rate responding to nature, perhaps especially during the later minutes of recovery. Running counter to this interpretation, however, is the finding that heart rate during the nature exposures evidenced a slight upward drift in the last two 3 min recovery intervals (Figure 4). Underlying this slight acceleratory trend may have been reduced parasympathetic input associated with some decline in attention/intake during the later minutes of recovery, and possibly the effects on heart rate of homeostatic mechanisms, including metabolic influences.

In any case, the overall pattern of heart rate findings in Figure 4 makes it very unlikely that responses during recovery were confounded or strongly influenced by the recovery or laboratory situation, i.e. by possible arousal reducing effects of sitting in an armchair for several minutes. If the experimental session had played a major role in the outcome, all groups should have evidenced heart deceleration during the final minutes of recovery, not the pattern of acceleration that was actually observed. Also, the possibility of a confounding session effect seems quite remote considering: the directional differences in cardiac responses to the natural vs urban settings during the initial minutes of recovery; the significant differences in heart rate as a function of environment that persisted through the recovery period; the significant differences in SCR, PTT and EMG during recovery as a function of environment; and the absence of differences across groups during the stressor, up to the onset of the environmental videotapes displayed during the recovery phase.

To evaluate the hypothesis derived from arousal theory that recovery influences might vary as a function of high vs low environmental stimulation levels, data for the two high stimulation urban settings (heavy traffic, many pedestrians) were grouped together and compared with the combined data for the two low stimulation urban conditions (light traffic, few pedestrians). When mixed-model analysis of variance was applied to the PTT, SCR and EMG measurements, there were no indications of general differences in recovery influences. A series of ANOVAs performed for each of the 3 min recovery periods revealed no significant variations in PTT and EMG; however, differences emerged in SCR for the second recovery interval (5–7 min, $p = <0.05$) and the third interval (8–10 min, $p = <0.05$). Specifically, the SCR findings suggested that somewhat more recovery occurred during exposure to the higher rather than low stimulation urban settings. These results run counter to the initial expectation that urban environments with relatively low levels of traffic and people would foster greater recuperation.

There were no differences in HP between the high and low stimulation urban environments, which suggests that intake/attention responses during recovery were similar irrespective of urban stimulation levels. Although the natural setting with water may have been higher in stimulation than the forest setting, there was no general variation between the HP recordings for the two nature conditions. Despite indications in the SCR and PTT data that slightly more recuperation might have occurred when individuals experienced nature with water rather than the setting dominated by trees and other vegetation, none of the differences proved significant.

Self-ratings results

Comparisons of the post-stressor ZIPERS ratings with the data obtained after the recovery videotapes indicated that the natural, pedestrian mall, and traffic exposures had markedly different effects on affective states. The ANOVA results revealed significant main effects for type of environment for three ZIPERS factors; together these findings indicate that much more recuperation in the psychological component of stress was produced by the natural environments than by the pedestrian mall or traffic settings (Table 2). Subjects exposed to the natural settings, in contrast to the urban environments, had lower scores for the Anger/Aggression factor ($p = <0.001$), reported lower Fear ($p = <0.05$), and reported far higher levels of Positive affects ($p = <0.001$). Recovery associated with the natural exposures was so pronounced in terms of the Fear, and especially the Anger/Agression and Positive affects factors, that post-recovery affective states were somewhat more positively-toned than those reported during the base-line period. Although the nature groups reported slightly more recovery than the urban groups in terms of the Sadness factor, the difference was not

TABLE 2
Influences of environments on affective states: factor score changes from pre- to post-recovery

ZIPERS factor	Nature	Pedestrian mall	Traffic	F	p
Fear	−1·46	−1·00	−0·77	4·36	0·01
Anger/Aggression	−1·95	+0·18	−0·82	9·97	<0·001
Positive affects	+5·52	+1·18	−0·08	26·33	<0·001
Sadness	−1·51	−1·26	−1·25	0·55	NS
Attentiveness/Interest	−1·02	−1·64	−1·02	1·35	NS

significant. Likewise, there was no significant main effect for the Attentiveness/Interest factor obtained for the post-recovery self-ratings.

A series of pair-wise Newman–Keuls tests of change scores (change from post-stressor to post-environment) were performed to further elucidate differences in feeling states as a function of environment. These *post hoc* tests were warranted for the three ZIPERS factors for which ANOVAs indicated significant general differences. These pair-wise tests confirmed that Positive affects scores increased much more following the natural exposures than after either the pedestrian mall ($p = <0.01$) or traffic ($p = <0.001$) tapes. Likewise, with respect to the Anger/Aggression factor, the natural settings were more restorative than either the mall ($p = <0.01$) or traffic ($p = <0.05$) exposures. Nature produced more recovery in terms of Fear than did the traffic settings ($p = <0.05$); however, there was only a tendency for nature to foster more recovery in Fear compared with the pedestrian mall settings ($p = <0.10$).

Regarding the various urban environments. Newman–Keuls tests indicated that the traffic settings produced more recuperation in Anger/Aggression than did the pedestrian mall exposures ($p = <0.05$). There were no significant differences between the traffic vs mall exposures in terms of the other ZIPERS factors.

Correlations Among Recovery Measures

Aside from indicating recovery influences of the various environments, the multimodal design presented an opportunity for exploring relationships among the physiological measures, and among the verbal and physiological indicators. In view of the absence of research on these issues with respect to everyday physical environments, the major correlation findings are summarized here for the total sample of 120 subjects recovering from stress.

The general pattern of physiological/physiological correlations was similar to findings for the base-line stressor phase; however, nearly all r values were higher during recovery. As before, there were strong relationships among the three autonomic indicators (HP, PTT, SCR), but no significant associations between the somatic indicator (EMG) and the autonomic measures—a pattern that supports the validity of the physiological data. Correlations among the three autonomic indicators were highly significant ($p = <0.001$) for all recovery periods (e.g. $r = 0.44$ for SCR/PTT during the first three minutes of recovery; $r = 0.41$ for SCR/HP during the last three minutes of recovery). There were consistently strong relationships between HP and PTT, the two cardiovascular measures (e.g. $r = 0.68$ for HP/PTT during the first three minutes of the environmental exposures).

Subjects rated their affective states using the ZIPERS before and after exposure to the environments, whereas the physiological recovery data were obtained during the environmental exposures. Because of the temporal non-congruence of the different measurement modes, it seemed likely that correlation analysis could not reveal comparatively short-term or phasic affective/physiological relationships, but would be sensitive to possible associations with respect to longer term or persistent changes in psychophysiological states. The series of correlations indicated that for most ZIPERS items there were no significant relationships with any of the physiological indicators for the three 3 min recovery intervals. However, there was a noteworthy pattern of associations among the autonomic measurements (HP, PTT, SCR) and the data from all four ZIPERS items comprising the Positive affects factor. The ZIPERS items were: 'I feel carefree or playful'; 'feel affectionate or warmhearted'; 'feel elated or pleased'; and 'feel like acting in a friendly or affectionate way'. Thirty-six correlations were performed to assess these Physiological/Positive affects relationships (three autonomic measures × three 3 min recovery periods × four ZIPERS items). Eight of the r values were significant at $p = <0.01$; 18 were significant at $p = <0.05$; and 10 did not reach significance. All three autonomic measures (HP, PTT, and SCR) evidenced some relationships with the Positive Affects items that were significant at the $p = <0.01$ or $p = <0.05$ levels (e.g. $r = 0.30$ for 'carefree or playful'/first 3 min of SCR; $r = 0.23$ for 'elated or pleased'/last 3 min of PTT). Importantly, all 36 correlation values were in the expected directions, i.e. as positively-toned feelings increased during recovery, heart rate declined, blood pressure lowered, and skin conductance fluctuations declined. There were no significant correlations between the somatic indicator—EMG—and any of the ZIPERS items. As a tentative conclusion, it appears that for stress recovery situations involving exposure to everyday outdoor environments, among the strongest affective/physiological associations may be a pattern for positive feelings to increase as autonomic but not somatic arousal declines.

Summary and Discussion

The findings from the physiological and verbal measures converge to indicate that different everyday outdoor environments can have quite different influences on stress recovery. The results strongly support the conclusion that recuperation was faster and more complete when subjects were exposed to the natural settings rather than the various urban environments. Regarding the physiological findings, there was impressive consistency across the stress measures (PTT, SCR, EMG) in indicating greater recovery influences of nature. Also, the heart period data revealed directionally different responses during recovery to the natural vs urban environments; this pattern of variation suggests that intake/attention was significantly higher during the natural exposures, a finding consistent with previous results obtained from verbal measures (Ulrich, 1979, 1981). The four physiological measures, including heart period, reflect activity in different bodily systems that are only weakly coupled or interrelated. The consistency across physiological indicators raises the possibility that differential influences of natural vs urban settings may tend to be widespread in bodily systems. In this regard, a previous study of unstressed subjects found that natural and urban scenes had different influences on activity in the electrocortical system (Ulrich, 1981).

Along with suggesting that nature elicited greater intake/attention, the overall pattern of heart period data raises the possibility that there was a salient parasympathetic component to responses to the natural but not the urban environments, especially during the initial minutes of recovery. (It will be recalled that the autonomic nervous system can be subdivided into the parasympathetic and sympathetic branches.) Because parasympathetic influences have a central role in attention and restoration, whereas sympathetic activation is central in the taxing mobilization involved in responding to stressors, future research in environmental psychology on restoration following stress should attempt to disentangle the influences of these different systems. Distinguishing more clearly between parasympathetic and sympathetic influences will require more complex physiological recordings (Papillo & Shapiro, 1990).

Results from the ZIPERS self-ratings suggested that the natural settings had more restorative influences than the urban environments on three affective dimensions: Positive affects, Anger/Aggression, and Fear. The most salient difference was the comparatively much greater restoration in Positive affects associated with the natural exposures, a finding consistent with results from an earlier study of mildly stressed subjects (Ulrich, 1979). Traditional arousal theory accurately predicts that the surge in Positive affects produced by nature should occur in association with the observed sharp reduction in physiological arousal indicators. As Berlyne (1971) and others have postulated, a lowering of arousal produces an increase in pleasurable feelings if an individual's initial state is stress or excessive arousal. Concerning this issue, a noteworthy finding was the pattern of significant correlations during stress recovery among the autonomic measures and every item comprising the Positive affects factor, indicating that Positive affects increased as autonomic, but not somatic (EMG), arousal lowered. Although only the Positive affects self-ratings correlated significantly with physiological recordings, there was nonetheless broad synchrony between the verbal and physiological findings. In general, individuals exposed to the natural settings both reported improved feeling states and evidenced lower stress levels in physiological indicators. Compared with the nature groups, subjects exposed to the urban environments experienced less recovery as evidenced both by self-ratings and physiological responses. The general pattern of convergence across data from different response modes suggests that the main conclusion regarding differential recovery warrants considerable confidence. The findings indicate that restorative effects of everyday outdoor environments have, at the least, psychological and physiological components. Because stress often has behavioral manifestations, it seems possible that restorative influences of environments may also be expressed in behaviors or enhanced functioning. Future research should investigate, for instance, whether many natural settings might have restorative effects that include increased performance levels on tasks requiring attention and cognitive processing (Hartig *et al.*, 1987; Kaplan & Kaplan, 1989). In view of the finding here that restoration was evident in central nervous system indicators, future research should examine whether such effects are also expressed in the endocrine system as changes in stress hormones, and in indicators of enhanced functioning in the immune system (Kennedy *et al.*, 1990). Additional studies are also needed to reveal the relative contributions of visual and auditory stimulation to restorative influences of everyday outdoor settings.

Apart from differences in levels of recovery, a noteworthy finding obtained from the continuous physiological recordings was the rapidity of recuperation during natural exposures. During the first four minutes of recovery, all groups experienced at least some degree of recuperation, but the nature groups achieved recovery approaching base-line levels in both autonomic and somatic activity. By five to seven minutes, significantly greater recovery for the nature groups, compared with subjects exposed to urban settings, was evident for all three physiological stress indicators (SCR, PTT, EMG). After the 10 min recovery videotapes, self-ratings data for the nature groups evidenced restoration to the point that, broadly speaking, feeling states were slightly more positively-toned than during baseline. The quickness of recovery during the nature conditions raises the possibility that these laboratory findings might be found to apply in many real contexts characterized by short-term contacts with nature. In urbanized countries, the great majority of encounters with nature elements probably are short episodes lasting only several seconds or a few minutes. Common types of nature contacts for urbanities may include, for example, viewing trees through a window in a workplace or residence, lunching in a park, or driving through an urban fringe area where roadsides are undeveloped. The findings of the present study justify the speculation that these and other short duration nature exposures might have an important function for many urbanities in facilitating recovery from such stressors as daily hassles or annoyances. The results cannot be generalized directly to longer term nature exposures that involve active participation such as a wilderness back-packing trip. Nonetheless, the findings may have relevance for research that seeks to understand benefits of wilderness recreation, including why most wilderness users report that reduced tension or stress, or tranquility, are very important benefits of their experiences (e.g. Driver, 1976).

Implications for theory
Some aspects of the findings are consistent with the conceptual speculations of Olmsted, Kaplan and Kaplan and others, in the sense that strong intake/attention was a concomitant of restorative influences of the nature settings. However, the overall pattern of findings indicates that a theoretical perspective emphasizing attention or 'fascination' is inadequate for explaining restorative influences of nature. In this regard, the present findings showed that the stressor film also elicited strong 'involuntary' or automatic attention. The stressor film depicted simulated blood and mutilation, stimuli which arguably should elicit involuntary attention or fascination because of their survival relevance during evolution (Hare *et al.*, 1970). This combination of findings is consistent with Ulrich's theoretical position (1983) that attention holding properties of nature work both ways; that is, involuntary attention can be a salient component of non-restorative and even stressful reactions to certain natural stimuli, and can also be a prominent component of restorative responses to unthreatening natural settings. Put differently, the findings concerning attention indicate that stress reducing or restorative responses to nature must involve more than involuntary attention or fascination. In this regard, the present physiological and verbal findings are consistent with the predictions of Ulrich's psycho-evolutionary theory (1983) that, following a stressor, the restorative influences of exposure to nature involve, among other responses, a broad shift in feelings towards a more positively-toned emotional state, positive changes in activity levels in different physiological systems, and that these changes are accompanied by moderately high levels of sustained attention. As was emphasized in an earlier conceptual section, there are theoretical grounds for suggesting that a critical element in restorative effects of natural scenes is a quick-onset positive affective reaction which may have a central role in shaping the positive character of changes in psychological and physiological states, and functioning or behavior (Ulrich, 1983). This theoretical position is consistent with growing scientific evidence that the initial levels of responding to natural stimuli involve quick-onset affective responses that appear to be closely linked with attention and subsequent conscious processing (e.g. Öhman *et al.*, 1989; Dimberg, 1990). With respect to stress recovery or restoration, a positive initial affective response, comprised of liking and moderate to high interest, should motivate and sustain prolonged attention/intake, should produce higher levels of positive feelings, reduce negatively-toned or stress related feelings such as fear and anger, and suppress stressful or extraneous thoughts (Ulrich, 1981, 1983). This combination of positive influences should be associated with reductions in taxing physiological mobilization, and perhaps with involvement of the parasympathetic nervous system that would function to restore energy. However, if the initial affective response is negative (e.g. dislike, fear), as many studies have shown

occurs for such natural stimuli or configurations as snakes and heights, the ensuing emotional/cognitive/physiological responding probably will be non-restorative and possibly even stressful, regardless of whether the response involves involuntary attention or 'fascination' (Ulrich, 1983).

How does arousal theory fare in accounting for the findings regarding both intake/attention and recovery? Whereas arousal theory predicts the observed surge in positive feelings that accompanied sharp declines in physiological arousal indicators during recovery, the main findings are at odds with arousal-based perspectives. Central to the arousal perspective in environmental psychology is the notion that various arousal-increasing properties (e.g. movement, quantities of stimuli) strongly influence attention, affective responses, and activity levels in physiological systems (e.g. Berlyne, 1971; Mehrabian & Russell, 1974). According to arousal theory, the urban settings with their movement, quantities of visual stimuli and comparatively variable, intense sounds, should have elicited far more intake/attention than the natural environments, yet they elicited much less as indicated by heart rate responses. The findings did not support our hypothesis based on arousal theory that attention/intake responses to the high stimulation urban conditions (heavy traffic, many pedestrians) would be greater than to the low stimulation urban conditions (light traffic, few pedestrians). Most fundamentally, contrary to the prediction of arousal theory, there was no general relationship between quantities of stimulation and recovery influences. Findings from most of the recovery measures suggested that similarly low levels of restoration occurred during exposures to the high vs low stimulation urban settings. An exception to this pattern was the SCR finding suggesting somewhat more recovery during the high rather than low stimulation urban exposures, a result that runs directly counter to the prediction of arousal theory.

In general, the findings strongly suggest that content differences in terms of natural vs human-made properties, rather than variations in stimulation levels, were decisive in accounting for the differences in recovery and intake/attention. To explain this outcome, it might be argued from a culture-based point of view that American society conditions positive response dispositions to nature and negative dispositions to urban environments. However, a cultural perspective could also lead to a very different interpretation. For instance, it is certainly the case that each of the subjects in this study had previously been exposed by television and other media to thousands of advertizements touting the positive characteristics of automobiles; accordingly, the individuals arguably should have evidenced strong intake and positively toned emotional responses to the urban settings with traffic.

On the basis of the heart rate findings, it does not appear that the nature settings produced restoration because they elicited an elaborated, active process of cognition entailing positive associations or memories. Such mental activity is often associated with an acceleratory component to the cardiac response; the overall deceleration that actually occurred during the natural exposures is perhaps associated with parasympathetic influences involving reduced baroreceptor feedback, and increases in perceptual activity and sensitivity to external stimuli (Lacey & Lacey, 1974). To the extent that cognition may have played a role in the restorative effects of nature, conceivably the forest and water settings might have elicited effortless, well-formed affective/cognitive structures.

Regarding the less positive influences of the urban environments, a learning-based speculation is that the settings with traffic and pedestrians might have elicited cognitive appraisals that included slight risk or tension. Such appraisals would tend to be associated with mild sympathetic mobilization that could contribute an acceleratory component to heart rate and somewhat inhibit recovery. In physiological terms, perhaps a slight defense reaction (i.e. heart acceleration, higher SCR) can be a component of responsiveness to many urban settings. But this perspective also implies the possibility, for instance, that the natural setting with fast-moving water could elicit mild defense reactions that would hinder recovery.

Alternatively, it seems reasonable to propose that evolutionary influences, along with learning, may underlie the differential intake and recovery responses to the natural vs urban environments. In an earlier theoretical section it was proposed that the rewards associated with natural settings during human evolution have been sufficiently critical to favor individuals who quickly and easily learned, and persistently retained, two related types of adaptive positive responding to nature: restoration following stress or taxing activities; and, in the absence of stress, positive emotional/attentional/ approach responses to nature contents and configurations, especially those that favored well-being or survival because of such advantages as high food potential and low risk. From these arguments it follows that biologically prepared learning may be evident in positive responses to many unthreatening natural settings, but that biological preparedness should not be manifested in responses to urban or built stimuli. An evolutionary perspective implies that adaptive responses to unthreatening natural settings should include quick-onset positive affects and sustained intake and perceptual sensitivity; in physiological terms this would often be a parasympathetically dominated response that included heart deceleration—similar to the observed response to the natural settings in the present study. Arguably, it would have been exceedingly maladaptive for early humans to easily and quickly learn, and over time not forget, to respond with perceptual rejection and sympathetic mobilization to unthreatening ambient environmental content. Sympathetic and other physiological mobilization would have been fatiguing, and over a prolonged period would be linked with chronic cardiovascular and endocrine responses that adversely affected health. Further, perceptual rejection or low attention would have been maladaptive from the standpoint of the need to exploit food, water or other survival related advantages of a natural setting. By contrast, an adaptive, parasympathetically dominated response would be associated with sustained yet non-taking intake and perceptual sensitivity, and maintenance or restoration of energy. Perhaps this biologically prepared constellation of responses would not only foster psychophysiological restoration following, for instance, encounters with threatening objects or situations, but would also function to maintain an appropriate 'base-line' state of environmental intake/ sensitivity which would leave the individual primed to very quickly mobilize and respond effectively to a sudden threat. Following a prolonged episode of fatiguing mobilization, it is not too great a speculation to suggest that some unthreatening natural settings, such as the water and forest settings in the study, might elicit a parasympathetically dominated response similar to a mild, eyes-open form of 'relaxation response' or wakeful, meditation-like state (e.g. Benson et al., 1974). Likewise, Katcher et al. (1984) have suggested that meditation-like relaxation can be induced by visual contemplation of a different configuration of natural content, an aquarium with fish.

The roles of culture, learning and possibly biological preparedness in differential response to natural vs urban settings represent fundamental issues that should be addressed in future research. Further studies are also needed to investigate psychophysiological influences of natural and urban content across varied situations including, for instance, contexts where individuals initially are unstressed, or are bored or chronically understimulated. Also, research should examine person-based variables (e.g. perceived control) that may influence the extent of recovery during encounters with natural and urban settings. The results of the present study clearly imply the need for a broader agenda regarding environmental stress research that goes beyond a focus on stressors to include concern for settings that tend to facilitate recovery. The findings strongly suggest that environments of importance to well-being and stress are not confined to settings having extreme or unusual properties, such as loud noise or extreme temperatures, but also include very common environments that most urbanites in developed nations encounter daily.

Note

(1) This research was supported by National Science Foundation grant SES-8317803. Portions of the physiological findings were presented at the 17th Annual Conference of the Environmental Design Research Association, Atlanta, Georgia, April, 1986 (Ulrich & Simons, 1986). The authors thank psychophysiologists Ulf Dimberg and Louis Tassinary for their comments regarding interpretation of the heart period findings, and also thank Russ Parsons and Bruce Hull for their helpful comments on an earlier draft.

References

Aiello, J. R., Epstein, Y. M. & Karlin, R. A. (1975). Effects of crowding on electrodermal activity. *Sociological Symposium*, **14**, 43–57.
Anderson, L. M., Mulligan, B. E., Goodman, L. S. & Regen, H. Z. (1983). Effects of sounds on preferences for outdoor settings. *Environment and Behavior*, **15**, 539–566.
Appleton, J. (1975). *The Experience of Landscape*. London, U.K.: Wiley.
Baum, A., Fleming, R. & Singer, J. E. (1985). Understanding environmental stress: strategies for conceptual and methodological integration. In A. Baum & J. E. Singer, Eds., *Advances in Environmental Psychology*. Hillsdale, NJ: Lawrence Erlbaum Associates, Vol. 5, *Methods and Environmental Psychology*, 185–205.
Benson, H., Beary, J. F. & Carol, M. P. (1974). The relaxation response. *Psychiatry*, **37**, 37–46.
Berlyne, D. E. (1971). *Aesthetics and Psychobiology*. New York: Appleton-Century-Crofts.
Berlyne, D. E. & Lewis, J. L. (1963). Effects of heightened arousal on human exploratory behavior. *Canadian Journal of Psychology*, **17**, 398–411.
Bernaldez, F. G. & Parra, F. (1979). Dimensions of landscape preferences from pairwise comparisons. In *Proceedings of Our National Landscape: A Conference on Applied Techniques for Analysis and Management of the Visual Resource*. USDA Forest Service General Technical Report PSB-35. Berkeley: USDA Forest Service, pp 256–262.
Cermak, G. W. & Cornillon, P. C. (1976). Multidimensional analyses of judgments about traffic noise. *Journal of the Acoustical Society of America*, **59**, 1412–1420.
Cohen, S. (1978). Environmental load and the allocation of attention. In A. Baum, J. E. Singer & S. Valins, Eds., *Advances in Environmental Psychology*, Vol. 1. Hillsdale, NJ: Lawrence Erlbaum Associates.
Cohen, S., Evans, G. W., Stokols, D. & Krantz, D. S. (1986). *Behavior, Health, and Environmental Stress*. New York: Plenum Press.
Dimberg, U. (1986). Facial reactions to fear-relevant and fear-irrelevant stimuli. *Biological Psychology*, **23**, 153–161.
Dimberg, U. (1990). Facial electromyography and emotional reactions. (Distinguished Contribution Award Address). *Psychophysiology*, **27**, 481–494.
Dimberg, U. & Thell, S. (1988). Facial electromyography, fear relevance, and the experience of stimuli. *Journal of Psychophysiology*, **2**, 213–219.

Driver, B. L. (1976). Quantification of outdoor recreationists' preferences. In B. Smissen & J. Myers, Eds., *Research: Camping and Environmental Education, HPEP Series No. 11.* University Park, PA: Pennsylvania State University, pp 165–187.

Driver, B. L. & Greene, P. (1977). Man's nature: innate determinants of response to natural environments. In *Children, Nature, and the Urban Environment,* USDA Forest Service Report NE-30. Upper Darby, Pennsylvania: Northeastern Forest Experiment Station, pp 63–70.

Driver, B. L. & Knopf, R. C. (1975). Temporary escape: one product of sport fisheries management. *Fisheries,* **1**, 24–29.

Evans, G. W. & Cohen, S. (1987). Environmental stress. In D. Stokols & I. Altman, Eds., *Handbook of Environmental Psychology* (2 Vols) New York: John Wiley, pp 571–610.

Evans, G. W., Cohen, S. & Brennan, P. (1986). Stress and properties of the physical environment. In J. Wineman, R. Barnes & C. Zimring, Eds., *Proceedings of the Seventeenth Annual Conference of the Environmental Design Research Association.* Washington, DC: EDRA, pp 91–98.

Frankenhaeuser, M. (1980). Psychoneuroendocrine approaches to the study of stressful person-environment transactions. In H. Selye, Ed., *Selye's Guide to Stress Research.* New York: Van Nostrand Reinhold, Vol. 1, 46–70.

Glacken, C. J. (1967). *Traces on the Rhodian Shore: Nature and Culture in Western Thought From Ancient Times to the End of the Eighteenth Century.* Berkeley: University of California Press.

Glass, D. C. & Singer, J. E. (1972). *Urban Stress: Experiments On Noise and Social Stressors.* New York: Academic Press.

Hartig, T., Mang, M. & Evans, G. W. (1987). Perspectives on wilderness: testing the theory of restorative environments. Paper presented at the *Fourth World Wilderness Congress,* Estes Park, Colorado, September, 1987.

Hare, R. D., Wood, K., Britain, S. & Shadman, J. (1970). Autonomic responses to affective visual stimulation. *Psychophysiology,* **7**, 408–417.

Heerwagen, J. H. (1990). Psychological aspects of windows and window design. In R. I. Selby, K. H. Anthony, J. Choi & B. Orland, Eds., *Proceedings of the 21st Annual Conference of the Environmental Design Research Association.* Oklahoma City: EDRA, pp 269–280.

Hockey, R. (Ed.) (1983). *Stress and Fatigue in Human Performance.* New York: John Wiley.

Holding, D. H. (1983) Fatigue. In R. Hockey, Ed., *Stress and Fatigue in Human Performance.* New York: John Wiley, pp 145–167.

Honeyman, M. (1990). Vegetation and stress: a comparison study of varying amounts of vegetation in countryside and urban scenes. Paper presented at the *National Symposium on the Role of Horticulture in Human Well-being and Social Developments,* Washington D.C., April, 1990.

Hull, R. B. (1990). Mood as a product of leisure: causes and consequences. *Journal of Leisure Research,* **22**, 99–111.

Kaplan, R. & Kaplan, S. (1989). *The Experience of Nature.* New York: Cambridge University Press.

Kaplan, S. & Talbot, J. F. (1983). Psychological benefits of a wilderness experience. In I. Altman & J. F. Wohlwill, Eds., *Human Behavior and Environment.* New York: Plenum Press, Vol. 6, *Behavior and the Natural Environment,* 163–203.

Kaplan, S., Kaplan, R. & Wendt, J. S. (1972). Rated preference and complexity for natural and urban visual material. *Perception and Psychophysics,* **12**, 354–356.

Katcher, A. H., Friedman, E., Beck, A. M. & Lynch, T. (1983). Looking, talking, and blood pressure: the physiological consequences of interaction with the living environment. In A. H. Katcher & A. M. Beck, Eds., *New Perspectives on Our Lives with Comparison Animals.* Philadelphia: University of Pennsylvania Press, pp 351–359.

Katcher, A., Segal, H. & Beck, A. (1984). Comparison of contemplation and hypnosis for the reduction of anxiety and discomfort during dental surgery. *American Journal of Clinical Hypnosis,* **27**, 14–21.

Kennedy, S., Glaser, R. & Kiecolt-Glaser, J. (1990). Psychoneuroimmunology. In J. T. Cacioppo & L. G. Tassinary, Eds., *Principles of Psychophysiology: Physical, Social, and Inferential Elements.* New York: Cambridge University Press, pp 177–190.

Klorman, R. & Ryan, R. M. (1980). Heart rate, continguent negative variation, and evoked potentials during anticipation of affective stimulation. *Psychophysiology,* **17**, 513–523.

Knopf, R. C. (1987). Human behavior, cognition and affect in the natural environment. In D. Stokols & I. Altman, Eds., *Handbook of Environmental Psychology* (2 Vols). New York: John Wiley, pp 783–825.

Lacey, J. I. & Lacey, B. C. (1970). Some autonomic-central nervous system interrelationships. In P. Black, Ed., *Physiological Correlates of Emotion*. New York: Academic Press, pp 205–227.

Lacey, B. C. & Lacey, J. I. (1974). Studies of heart rate and other bodily processes in sensorimotor behavior. In P. A. Obrist, A. H. Black, J. Brener & L. V. DiCara, Eds., *Cardiovascular Psychophysiology*. Chicago: Aldine, pp 538–564.

Lazarus, R. S., Opton, E. M., Norrikos, M. S. & Rankin, N. O. (1965). The principle of short-circuiting of threat: further evidence. *Journal of Personality*, **33**, 622–635.

Libby, W. L. Jr., Lacey, B. C. & Lacey, J. (1973). Pupillary and cardiac activity during visual attention. *Psychophysiology*, **10**, 270–294.

Lundberg, U., Melin, B., Holmberg, L. & Evans, G. (1990). Psychobiological stress responses during and after VDT work: repetitive data entry versus stimulating learning. Paper presented at the *First International Congress of Behavioral Medicine*, Uppsala, Sweden, June, 1990.

Marie, G. V., Lo, C. R., Van Jones, J. & Johnston, D. W. (1984). The relationship between arterial blood pressure and pulse transit time during dynamic and static exercise. *Psychophysiology*, **21**, 521–527.

Mehrabian, A. & Russell, J. A. (1974). *An Approach to Environmental Psychology*. Cambridge, MA: MIT Press.

Moore, E. O. (1982). A prison environment's effect on health care service demands. *Journal of Environmental Systems*, **11**, 17–34.

Obrist, P. A., Light, K. C., McCubbin, J. A., Hutcheson, J. S. & Hoffer, J. L. (1979). Pulse transit time: relationship to blood pressure and myocardial performance. *Psychophysiology*, **13**, 292–301.

Öhman, A. (1986). Face the beast and fear the face: animal and social fears as prototypes for evolutionary analyses of emotion (Presidential Address). *Psychophysiology*, **23**, 123–145.

Öhman, A., Dimberg, U. & Esteves, F. (1989). Preattentive activation of aversive emotions. In T. Archer & L-G. Nilsson, Eds., *Aversion, Avoidance, and Anxiety*. Hillsdale, NJ: Lawrence Erlbaum Associates, pp 169–193.

Olmsted, F. L. (1865). The value and care of parks. Report to the Congress of the State of California. [Reprinted in R. Nash, Ed., (1976). *The American Environment*. Reading, MA: Addison-Wesley, pp 18–24.]

O'Leary, K. S. (1965). Preference for variability of stimuli as a function of experimentally induced anxiety. *Psychological Reports*, **16**, 1202.

Orians, G. H. (1986). An ecological and evolutionary approach to landscape aesthetics. In E. C. Penning-Rowsell & D. Lowenthal Eds., *Meanings and Values in Landscape*. London: Allen & Unwin, pp 3–25.

Orians, G. H. & Heerwagen, J. H. (in press). Evolved responses to landscapes. In J. Barkow, L. Cosmides & J. Tooby, Eds., *The Adapted Mind: Evolutionary Psychology and the Generation of Culture*. Oxford, U.K.: Oxford University Press.

Papillo, J. F. & Shapiro, D. (1990). The cardiovascular system. In J. T. Cacioppo & L. G. Tassinary, Eds., *Principles of Psychophysiology: Physical, Social, and Inferential Elements*. New York: Cambridge University Press, pp 456–512.

Rylander, R., Sorenson, S. & Kajland, A. (1976). Traffic noise exposure and annoyance reactions. *Journal of Sound and Vibration*, **47**, 237–242.

Schriffin, R. M. & Schneider, W. (1977). Controlled and automatic human information processing: perceptual learning, automatic attending, and a general theory. *Psychological Review*, **84**, 127–190.

Schroeder, H. W. (1989). Environment, behavior, and design research on urban forests. In E. H. Zube & G. T. Moore, Eds., *Advances in Environment, Behavior, and Design*, New York: Plenum, Vol. 2, 87–117.

Schroeder, H. W. & Anderson, L. M. (1984). Perception of personal safety in urban recreation sites. *Journal of Leisure Research*, **16**, 177–194.

Seligman, M. E. P. (1971). Phobias and prepardness. *Behavior Therapy*, **2**, 307–321.

Shuttleworth, S. (1980). The use of photographs as an environment presentation medium in landscape studies. *Journal of Environmental Management*, **11**, 61–76.

Stainbrook, E. (1968). Human needs and the natural environment. In *Man and Nature in the City*. Proceedings of a symposium sponsored by the Bureau of Sport Fisheries and Wildlife. Washington, DC: U.S. Department of the Interior, pp 1–9.

Tuan, Y. F. (1974). *Topophilia: A Study of Environmental Perception, Attitudes, and Values*. Englewood Cliffs, NJ: Prentice Hall.

Ulrich, R. S. (1979). Visual landscapes and psychological well-being. *Landscape Research*, **4**, 17–23.

Ulrich, R. S. (1981). Natural versus urban scenes: some psychophysiological effects. *Environment and Behavior*, **13**, 523–556.

Ulrich, R. S. (1983). Aesthetic and affective response to natural environment. In I. Altman & J. F. Wohlwill, Eds., *Human Behavior and Environment*. New York: Plenum Press, Vol. 6, *Behavior and the Natural Environment*, 85–125.

Ulrich, R. S. (1984). View through a window may influence recovery from surgery. *Science*, **224**, 420–421.

Ulrich, R. S. & Parsons, R. (1990). Influences of passive experiences with plants on individual well-being and health. Paper presented at the *National Symposium on the Role of Horticulture in Human Well-Being and Social Development*, Washington, D.C., April, 1990.

Ulrich, R. S. & Simons, R. F. (1986). Recovery from stress during exposure to everyday outdoor environments. In J. Wineman, R. Barnes & C. Zimring, Eds., *Proceedings of the Seventeenth Annual Conference of the Environmental Design Research Association*. Washington, D.C.: EDRA, pp 115–122.

Verderber, S. (1986). Dimensions of person-window transactions in the hospital environment. *Environment and Behavior*, **18**, 450–466.

Ward, L. M. & Russell, J. A. (1981). Cognitive set and the perception of place. *Environment and Behavior*, **13**, 610–632.

West, M. J. (1985). *Landscape virsus and stress response in the prison environment*. M.L.A. thesis. Department of Landscape Architecture, University of Washington, Seattle, WA.

Wohlwill, J. F. (1976). Environmental aesthetics: the environment as a source of affect. In I. Altman & J. F. Wohlwill, Eds., *Human Behavior and Environment*. New York: Plenum, Vol. 1, 37–86.

Wohlwill, J. F. (1983). The concept of nature: a psychologist's view. In I. Altman & J. F. Wohlwill, Eds., *Human Behavior and Environment*, New York: Plenum Press, Vol. 6, *Behavior and the Natural Environment*, 5–37.

Zajonc, R. B. (1980). Feeling and thinking: preferences need no influences. *American Psychologist*, **35**, 151–175.

Zube, E. H., Vining, J., Law, C. S. & Bechtel, R. B. (1985). Perceived urban residential quality: a cross-cultural bimodal study. *Environment and Behavior*, **17**, 327–350.

Zuckerman, M. (1977). Development of a situation-specific trait-state test for the prediction and measurement of affective responses. *Journal of Consulting and Clinicial Psychology*, **45**, 513–523.

A LIFESPAN DEVELOPMENTAL STUDY OF LANDSCAPE ASSESSMENT

ERVIN H. ZUBE*, DAVID G. PITT** AND GARY W. EVANS‡
*School of Renewable Natural Resources, University of Arizona, Tucson
**Department of Horticulture, University of Maryland, College Park
‡Program in Social Ecology, University of California, Irvine

Abstract

This study compares scenic quality ratings across age groups. Previous landscape perception research has tended to limit participants to young adult and middle aged persons. The 294 subjects in this study range in age from six years to over 70 years. Subjects sorted each of 56 colored photographs on scenic quality. For each photograph, four dimensions were derived (perceived naturalism, land use compatability and relative relief) and used in testing hypotheses about the relationship of age with specific attributes of the landscape. Findings from the study indicate that young children do rate landscapes differently from adults and that the ratings of the older adults differ slightly from those of young and middle-aged adults. Relationships of the four descriptive dimensions with scenic quality judgments varied by age group.

Introduction

A recent review of the research literature on landscape perception and assessment identified over 160 studies published during the period from 1965 through 1980 (Zube, Sell and Taylor, 1982). Within this body of research there is a generally accepted premise that values associated with scenic landscape quality are broadly shared and variability in perceptions is minimal. As a test of this premise, a number of studies have investigated the extent of agreement among various sub-groups of the study population. Sub-groups representing several professional or special interests in the landscapes being studied generally show high intergroup agreement in scenic quality assessments (Craik, 1972; Daniel and Boster, 1976; Shafer and Meitz, 1969; Zube, Pitt and Anderson, 1975). In other studies, subjects have been drawn from college student pools or have consisted of opportunity samples (see Zube et al., 1982 for a review). Regardless of the procedure followed for selecting subjects, the majority have been drawn from a restricted age span, ranging from young adult to middle-aged

One aim of the present study is to compare scenic quality ratings across a wider age span than has been previously measured. The development of a body of knowledge on landscape assessment limited to young and middle-aged adult samples entails potentially important conceptual and practical limitations. From a policy standpoint, demographic research indicates an increasingly large proportion of the U.S. population falls out of the middle-age range. Furthermore, the use of natural recreation areas by the elderly continues at a high rate and is predicted to increase (U.S. Department of the Interior, 1979).

The authors acknowledge the assistance of Javier Bonapont, Pamela Hathaway and Richard Morton in data collection for this study.

A fairly consistent finding in landscape perception research to date has been the preference for natural scenes over human-made landscapes (Fines, 1968; Kaplan and Kaplan, 1982; Ulrich, 1981; Zube et al., 1975). A cross-cultural study by Zube and Pitt (1981), however, found that West Indians did not share Americans' perceptions that natural landscapes have greater scenic quality than landscapes containing structures such as houses and hotels. This suggested that this difference may be attributable to differences in education and environmental experiences.

In a study of child (eight to 11-year-olds) and adult (age unspecified) perceptions of natural landscapes, Miller and Rutz (1980) found children were less discriminating than adults and exhibited higher variability in response to photographs of rural landscapes of the western United States of America. The authors suggest that children may not have fully acquired, through education and experience, the cultural values associated with adult American perceptions of landscape beauty.

Balling and Falk (1982) investigated the developmental course of landscape preferences for five different natural biomes: tropical rain forest, desert, savanna, temperate deciduous forest and coniferous forest. Their subjects ($n = 548$) were divided among eight, 11 and 15-year-olds, college students, adults and senior citizens. They found that third and fifth graders' preferences for savanna landscapes were significantly higher than for either coniferous or deciduous forest landscapes, while preferences for these three biomes were statistically indistinguishable by mid-adolescence and thereafter. They suggest that there may be an innate preference for savanna landscapes that is modified through experience over time.

A second objective of our study is to develop some theoretical concepts that may assist our understanding of landscape perception across the life span. Children have a limited home range that gradually expands with increasing experience throughout adolescence (Stea, 1970). Increasing geographic experience is among the most important variables that infuence a child's ability to understand spatial relationships in the large-scale environment (Evans, 1980; Hart, 1979). On the other hand, old age is a time when the individual may be confronted with problems of sensory limitations, motor impairment and frailty resulting in a more restricted home range. Lawton (1980) points to a considerable body of data indicating that older persons are more prone than others to express satisfaction or preference for what they have. This tendency may be an adaptational response to a more restricted home range, increased dependency on the immediate environment, and reduced opportunities for diverse environmental experiences. Thus the elderly may be less likely than young adults to devalue scenes with human-made influences.

Piaget discusses three types of intellectual tendency for child thought: realism, animism and artificialism (Piaget, 1929). Of particular interest here are animism and artificialism. Animism is the tendency to animate physical objects and events, to give them life, and artificialism is the belief that all objects and events are made by humans to serve human purposes. Young children who are at the preoperational stage of thought (less than eight years old) are less able to distinguish between animate and inanimate objects. This notion has been adapted to landscape perception by Holcomb (1977) who argues that the distinction between natural and human-made environments is unimportant to young children. Holcomb suggests that adults impose their tastes and preferences on children, claiming they need trees, grass and flowers when it is the adults who want them.

Furthermore, we would also expect young children to be less cognizant of the connotative meaning of landscape scenes. For example, a mix of variable, incompatible land uses may depress adult judgments of scenic quality (Wohlwill, 1978). Young children, however, may not have learned the meaning of land use or appreciate the negative aspects of incompatible uses.

One additional implication of young childrens' relative insensitivity on social and cultural meanings in landscape may be their greater responsiveness to the diversity or complexity of the physical form itself. Whereas adults' judgments of scenic quality are affected by both the form and meaning of the elements in a landscape, young children will respond primarily to physical form.

Our primary objectives in this study are: (1) to explore potential differences related to age in the perception of landscape scenic quality; and (2) to provide some preliminary, theoretical explanations for these ontogenetic differences. The study builds upon a data base from earlier research (Zube et al., 1975; Zube, 1976) and expands the subject pool used in that research (high school to 65 years of age) to encompass a range of ages from six-year-olds to over 70-year-olds. Specifically, this study addresses the following hypotheses.

H_1 There will be high agreement among adolescents, young adults and middle-aged adults in scenic value perceptions. Very young children and older adults will have distinct scenic value perceptions.

H_2 Except for the very young and the older adults, a positive relationship exists between scenic value and naturalism in the landscape.

H_3 Except for the very young and the older adults, a positive relationship exists between scenic value and land use compatibility in the landscape.

H_4 Young children are affected more than adults by the diversity and complexity created by landform.

Method

Subjects

Two hundred and ninety-four subjects participated in this study. All were drawn from opportunity samples in four regions of the country: New England, Mid-Atlantic, Central Mid-West and Southwest. Subjects were broken down into six age groups: six to eight years old, nine to 11 years old, 12 to 18 years old, 19 to 35 years old, 36 to 65 years old and over 65 years old. All subjects were middle and upper class volunteers. Forty-nine persons were randomly selected from the larger subject pools to match the smallest age sample size obtained (over 65 years old).

Age category breakdown for children is based on the Piagetian theorty of development. First and second graders (ages six to eight years old) are hypothesized to differ from fifth and sixth graders (ages nine to 11 years old because the latter age group is less subject to the concept of artificialism according to Piagetian theory (Piaget, 1929).

Setting

A set of 56 mounted color photographs measuring five by seven inches was used to represent the range of landscapes found within the southern Connecticut River Valley, exclusive of major urban areas. The landscapes included town centers, suburban areas, rural industrial settings, agricultural areas, forested lands and surface water in the form of lakes, rivers, rapid flowing creeks and wet lands [Figures 1(a) through 1(h)].

FIGURE 1. Representative views from set of 56 landscape photographs indicating percentile ranking on the perceived naturalism dimension and for the six to eight, 19 to 35 and over 65 year old subjects. (a) Percentile ranking: naturalism 45%; six to eight, 20%; 19 to 35, 64%; over 65, 66%. (b) Percentile ranking: naturalism 32%; six to eight, 93%; 19 to 35, 21%; over 65, 82%.

(c) Percentile ranking: naturalism 84%; six to eight, 71%; 19 to 35, 91%; over 65, 93%. (d) Percentile ranking: naturalism 66%; six to eight, 75%; 19 to 35, 36%; over 65, 23%.

(e) Percentile ranking: naturalism 100%; six to eight, 96%; 19 to 35, 98%; over 65, 98%. (f) Percentile ranking naturalism 5%; six to eight, 95%; 19 to 35, 45%; over 65, 88%.

(g) Percentile ranking: naturalism 4%; six to eight, 2%; 19 to 35, 1%; over 65, 4%. (h) Percentile ranking: naturalism, 16%; six to eight, 25%; 19 to 35, 11%; over 65, 29%.

Procedure

The Q-Sort method (Kerlinger, 1973; Pitt and Zube, 1979) was used for eliciting responses of perceived scenic quality for the 56 landscapes depicted in the color photographs. Subjects were instructed to sort the photographs into seven piles: first selecting the three highest scenic quality, then the three lowest scenic quality for piles one and seven, respectively; then selecting the next seven highest and seven lowest scenes into piles two and six, respectively; followed by selections of the next eleven highest and eleven lowest into piles three and five, respectively; leaving the remaining fourteen at the mid-range of scenic quality in pile four. Each photograph is assigned a scenic value of one to seven according to the pile into which it is sorted.

For each of these 56 landscapes a set of physical and perceptual dimensions had been derived in earlier research (Zube *et al.*, 1975) and was used here in testing the several hypotheses of the present study. The dimensions are as follows.

(1) Perceived naturalism: the degree of naturalism indicated by land use as perceived by a panel of 10 judges.
(2) Land use compatibility: an indication of the visual congruence of adjacent land uses as perceived by a panel of 10 judges.
(3) Relative relief: the range of vertical elevations within the view area.
(4) Percent water: the amount of surface water per unit area.

Findings

Table 1 presents Pearson product-moment correlation coefficients for between-age group relationships in the mean scenic value ratings for all 56 photographs. Noticeable patterns emerge from visual inspection of these data. The six to eight-year-old subjects' scenic value ratings are consistent with those of the nine to eleven-year-old age group ($r = $ A and B in Table 1) are only moderately associated with the remaining age groups. Among the scenic value ratings of the remaining four groups, higher levels of agreement are indicated by correlation coefficients from 0·78 to 0·96.

Two and possibly three sub-sets of age groups emerge from this analysis. The two youngest groups agree on scenic value ratings, but their ratings deviate considerably from those of the remaining four age groups. Within the remaining age groups, very high relationships ($r = 0.90$ to 0.96) exist among the ratings of the 12 to 18-year-olds,

TABLE 1

Pearson product moment correlation coefficients among mean scenic value ratings of six age groups for 56 photographs

Age group		A	B	C	D	E	F
6–8 years	(A)	—	0·86	0·53	0·53	0·66	0·55
9–11 years	(B)		—	0·69	0·66	0·72	0·54
12–18 years	(C)			—	0·96	0·90	0·78
19–35 years	(D)				—	0·94	0·79
36–65 years	(E)					—	0·87
Over 65 years	(F)						—

Coefficients above 0·341 are significant at $P < 0.01$.

19 to 35-year-olds and 36 to 65-year-olds; and lower relationships ($r = 0.78$ to 0.87) exist between the ratings of these three age groups and those of the subjects over 65-years-old.

A further examination of the divergence of young peoples' ratings from those of adults of various ages was conducted using the Student's t-test for the difference between two correlation coefficients that share a variable.[1] The research hypotheses for this study suggest that the landscape perceptions of the 19 to 35-year-old and the 36 to 65-year-old age groups are most likely to reflect normative values and that the six to eight-year-old and the over 65-year-old group are least likely to subscribe to normatively valued perceptions. The correlation of the six to eight-year-olds with the 19 to 35-year-olds ($r = 0.53$) is significantly different ($P < 0.01$) than the correlation of the 19 to 35-year-olds with the 36 to 65-year-olds ($r = 0.94$). Furthermore, the correlation of the six to eight-year-olds with the nine to 11-year-olds ($r = 0.86$) is significantly different ($P < 0.05$) than the correlation of the youngest group with the oldest group ($r = 0.55$). Similarly, the correlation of the over 65-year-old group with the 19 to 35-year-old group ($r = 0.79$) is not significantly different than the correlation of the 19 to 35-year-old group with the 36 to 65-year-old group ($r = 0.94$). Thus, the response patterns of the very youngest age group were significantly different than the ratings of either the normative age group (19 to 35-years-old) or the over 65 year age group; and the response patterns of the elderly also varied significantly from those of the normative group.

The correlations between each age group's scenic value ratings and selected landscape dimensions for all 56 photographs are presented in Table 2. Perceived naturalism in Table 2 relates specifically to hypothesis two: age as a moderator of the relationship between scenic value and naturalism. Significant relationships are obtained for perceived naturalism only when this dimension is correlated with the scenic value ratings of the 12 to 18-year-old group and the 19 to 35-year-old group. Furthermore, Table 3 illustrates that the correlation coefficients describing the relationship between scenic value ratings and perceived naturalism are significantly different when either the six to eight-year-old group or the over 65-year-old group is compared with the 19 to 35-year-old group. However, the correlation of percent naturalism with ratings of the youngest age group is not significantly different from the correlation of naturalism with the elderly age group.[2]

Similar patterns exist in Table 2 and Table 3 when each age group's scenic value

TABLE 2
Pearson product moment correlation coefficients between each age group's mean scenic value ratings and selected landscape dimensions for 56 photographs

Landscape dimension	Age group (years)					
	6–8	9–11	12–18	19–35	36–65	Over 65
Perceived naturalism	−0.02	0.09	0.38**	0.37**	0.20	0.02
Land use compatibility	0.31*	0.32*	0.52**	0.47**	0.41**	0.20
Relative relief	0.01	0.19	0.43**	0.38**	0.26	0.30*
Percent water	0.45**	0.22	0.08	0.10	0.20	0.19

* = $P < 0.05$; ** = $P < 0.01$.
Intercorrelations of the landscape dimensions are: perceived naturalism (PN) with land use compatibility (LUC), $r = 0.59$; PN with relative relief (RR), $r = 0.44$; PN with percent water (PW), $r = -0.09$; LUC with RR, $r = 0.22$; LUC with PW, $r = -0.20$; and RR with PW, $r = -0.27$.

TABLE 3

Significance of t values calculated to test difference in correlation coefficients between selected age groups' mean scenic value ratings and various landscape dimensions for 56 photographs

Landscape dimension	Age group comparison (years)		
	6–8 vs. 19–35[1]	19–35 vs. 65+[1]	6–8 vs. 65+[2]
Perceived naturalism	−3·28***	4·74***	−0·30
Land use compatibility	−1·37*	3·60***	0·89
Relative relief	−3·08***	0·96	−2·37

* = $P < 0.10$; ** = $P < 0.05$; *** = $P < 0.01$.

[1] One-tailed probabilities are depicted since alternative hypothesis specifies expected direction of relationship.

[2] Two-tailed probabilities are depicted since alternative hypothesis does not specify expected direction.

ratings are correlated with land use compatibility. While significant relationships exist between land use compatibility and five of the six age groups scenic value ratings, these relationships are strongest for the 12 to 18-year-old, 19 to 35-year-old and 36 to 65-year-old groups. The correlation coefficient describing the relationship of the youngest age group's ratings with land use compatibility is not significantly different from the coefficient describing the same relationship for the elderly, however, both of these coefficients are different from that for the 19 to 35-year-old group.

Contrary to what would be expected from the fourth research hypothesis, strongest relationships between scenic value and the physical dimension of relative relief are observed in the 12 to 18 and 19 to 35-year-old age groups.

An interesting finding somewhat incidental to the main research hypotheses is presented in Table 2 under the column heading, percent water. The scenic value ratings of the six to eight-year-old age group are significantly and quite strongly correlated ($r = 0.45$) with the percent of water present in the photographs. For none of the remaining five age groups is this relationship significant.

Discussion

This study was initiated to test several hypotheses that fall within two basic objectives: (1) to examine possible life span development differences in landscape assessment; and (2) to develop some preliminary, theoretical explanations of those differences centering on Piagetian theory and life experiences with the landscape.

Analyses of age differences in scenic quality assessment, as depicted in Tables 1 and 2, reveals three distinct, age-related clusters of scenic quality assessment. Young children's judgments of scenic quality are similar to one another (comparing the six to eight-year-olds with the nine to 11-year-olds) but different from the young adults typically used in landscape perception research. This finding is consistent with Balling and Falk's (1982) recent study suggesting that third and fifth graders exhibited different preferences for natural biomes that young adults did. The elderly sample is both less consistent with the three young and middle-aged adult samples' scenic assessments (Table 1) and significantly different in their scenic quality judgments from the judgments of young and middle aged adults. The elderly also differ significantly from the young children. This finding contradicts one theoretical, developmental perspective in gerontology that aging is a regressive process wherein cognitive functioning passes through Piagetian-like stages in reverse order (Lawton, 1980).

This set of findings on age differences lends credence to the importance of more careful sampling of different age groups in landscape assessment research. As recent reviews of the landscape assessment literature acknowledge (cf. Zube et al., 1982), nearly all empirical studies have used highly restricted age samples of young adults. Young children and the elderly have distinctly different scenic quality assessments of natural landscapes. It may not be prudent policy to suggest landscape management strategies for the public based only on the responses of young adult samples. Furthermore as recent cross-cultural, landscape perception research indicates (Zube and Pitt, 1981), we must be cautious in generalizing landscape assessment principles to non-European cultures.

The second objective of this study was to develop some preliminary theoretical concepts for explaining life-span differences in landscape assessment. Inspection of Tables 2 and 3 reveals some interesting facts that any integrative theory of landscape perception will have to encompass. First, as hypothesized, young children are less affected by the presence of human influences in the natural landscape, whereas young and middle-aged adults deflate scenic quality judgments as naturalism decreases. One reasonable explanation of this finding is that young children are cognitively unable to distinguish animate and inanimate objects (Piaget, 1929). Elderly adults' scenic assessments are also not significantly influenced by the degree of naturalism found in landscape scenes. As noted above, greater dependence upon the immediate, physical environment coupled with reduced environmental exploration may impair the elderly's ability to make and/or care about distinctions in the physical landscape. Another possible explanation is there may be cohort effects attributable to the group having been socialized prior to the environmental movement of the 1960s and 1970s.

Second, children's judgments of scenic value tend not to be influenced as strongly as adult's judgments are by land use compatibility. This finding probably reflects children's inexperience or inability to distinguish between various land uses. Further research could test this hypothesis by measuring children's ability to perceptually distinguish and classify land uses (e.g. Palmer, 1979; Palmer and Zube, 1976). Then one could examine the relationship between this ability and how well the child's scenic quality judgments match the adults'. The elderly are affected by land use compatibility but less strongly than young adults (e.g. Hendrix and Fabos, 1975; Wohlwill, 1978). This may reflect the elderly's less critical evaluation of existing settings (Lawton, 1980).

Third, contrary to our hypothesis, young and middle-aged adults are more sensitive than children to physical indices of complexity in the landform. Higher relative relief strongly enhances scenic quality for young adults, has a moderate positive effect for the elderly, but is irrelevant for young children. One tentative explanation of this finding maybe Wohlwill's (1974; 1976) research suggesting that moderate levels of complexity in the landscape are preferable because of their optimal, arousal-inducing properties. Developmental work suggests that optimal arousal levels in children in comparison to adults are elicited by less physically complex stimuli (Wohlwill, 1974; 1976).

To test for the existence of a curvilinear relationship between complexity (as manifest through landform) and perceived scenic value, the contribution of the quadratic form of relative relief toward explaining scenic value variance was examined for each age group. The addition of the quadratic relative relief term to the linear functions described in Table 2 did not significantly increase the amount of explained variance for any of the six age groups. The failure of these findings to substantiate the optimal level of complexity hypothesis must, however, be qualified on two accounts: (1) the range of landform complexity depicted in the 56 photographs may have been insufficient for the emergence of a curvilinear relationship; and (2) landform diversity (at least as measured by relative topographic relief) may not be a dimension of complexity and curvilinear relationship with scenic value perceptions would therefore not be expected. Both of these caveats could be further examined by comparing perceptions of scenic value and complexity with several dimensions of landform diversity (e.g. topographic texture, angle of slope—see Zube et al., 1975 for other examples) over a much broader range of topographic variability.

One final result worth noting is the apparent, strong attachment of children to water. Only the youngest group of six to eight-year-olds were significantly influenced by the amount of water in visual scenes. Appleton (1975) suggests that human landscape responses are in part inborne and derive from basic biological requirements for survival. Balling and Falk (1982) have hypothesized that such innate preferences are modified over time by environmental experience. Kaplan and Kaplan's research, which is founded on a functional, evolutionary based framework, maintains that physical elements that enhance meaningful, cognitive clarity or that afford important survival functions both contribute to higher landscape value (Kaplan and Kaplan, 1982) and enhanced personal growth. Perhaps as Balling and Falk suggest, some hierarchy of functional importance exists wherein young children are maximally sensitive to the most basic, elementary functional aspects of landscape. With cognitive development, other more complex, information-based principles of coherence, complexity and mystery emerge. Clearly, more research is necessary to adequately account for the differential value of water in scenic assessments by young children.

Recent reviews of landscape assessment research have noted the marked paucity of theory coupled with an overemphasis in empirical endeavors on either human components (e.g. personality, culture) or on landscape variables (e.g. physical elements, compositional features) (Porteous, 1982; Wohlwill, 1976; Zube et al., 1982). Our research demonstrates that a more integrative approach to aesthetic quality may reveal important facts about the functional relationships between landscape elements and scenic evaluation.

To summarize the major findings of this study we can draw up the following statements.

(1) Young children in comparison to adults have distinct preferences for scenic quality in natural landscapes.

(2) The elderly in comparison to young and middle-aged adults have different landscape preferences.

(3) High naturalism is an important component of scenic value for young and middle aged adults but is relatively unimportant to young children and the elderly.

(4) Greater compatibility in land use increases scenic value for all age groups but is more influential for young and middle-aged adults.

(5) Physical complexity of landform is an important feature in landscape assessment for young and elderly adults but not children.

(6) Water significantly enhances scenic values for young children but is of minor importance to adults.

Notes

[1] When two correlation coefficients share a variable, the variance and covariance imposed by the sharing must be factored out in testing for differences between the two coefficients. Thus, $H_o: r_{ab} = r_{cb}$ is tested using the formula (Blalock, 1979):

$$t = \frac{(r_{ab} - r_{bc})\sqrt{(N-3)(1+r_{ac})}}{\sqrt{2(1 - r_{ab}^2 - r_{bc}^2 - r_{ac}^2 + 2r_{ab}r_{bc}r_{ac})}}.$$

[2] An objectively determined measure of naturalism, percent tree cover, was used as a reliability check on the perceptually based perceived naturalism dimension. When correlated with each age group's scenic value ratings, the two naturalism dimensions yielded nearly identical patterns.

References

Appleton, J. (1975). *The Experience of Landscape*. London: John Wiley & Sons.
Balling, J. D. and Falk, J. H. (1982). Development of preference for natural environments. *Environment and Behavior*, **14**, 5–28.
Blalock, H. M. Jr (1979). *Social Statistics*. New York: McGraw Hill.
Craik, K. H. (1972). Appraising the objectivity of landscape dimensions. In J. V. Krutilla (ed.), *Natural Environments*. Baltimore: Johns Hopkins University Press, pp. 292–346.
Daniel, T. C. and Boster, R. S. (1976). *Measuring Scenic Beauty: The Scenic Beauty Estimation Method*. USDA Forest Service Research Paper, RM–167. Fort Collins, CO.: Rocky Mountain Forest and Range Experiment Station.
Evans, G. W. (1980). Environmental cognition. *Psychological Bulletin*, **88**, 259–87.
Fines, K. D. (1968). Landscape evaluation—a research project in East Sussex. *Regional Studies*, **2**, 40–55.
Hart, R. A. (1979). *Children's Experience of Place*. New York: Irvington.
Hendrix, W. G. and Fabos, J. G. (1975). Visual land use compatibility as a significant contributor to visual resource quality. *International Journal of Environmental Studies*, **8**, 21–8.
Holcomb, B. (1977). The perception of natural vs. built environments by young children. *Children, Nature and the Environment*. USDA Forest Service General Technical Report NE–30. Upper Darby, PA.: Northeastern Forest Experiment Station.
Kaplan, S. and Kaplan, R. (1982). *Cognition and Environment*. New York: Praeger.
Kerlinger, F. N. (1973). *Foundations of Behavioral Science*. New York: Holt, Rinehart and Winston, Inc.
Lawton, M. P. (1980). *Environment and Aging*. Monterey, CA: Brooks/Cole Publishing Co.
Miller, P. A. and Rutz, M. E. (1980). *A Comparison of Scenic Preference Dimensions for Children and Adults*. Paper presented at Council of Educators in Landscape Architecture Meeting, Madison, WI.
Palmer, J. F. (1979). The conceptual typing of trail environments: a tool for recreation research and management. In T. C. Daniel, E. H. Zube and B. L. Driver (eds), *Assessing Amenity Resource Values*. GTR RM68, USDA Forest Service, Fort Collins, CO.: Rocky Mountain Forest and Range Experiment Station, pp. 14–21.
Palmer, J. F. and Zube, E. H. (1976). Numerical and perceptual classification. In E. H. Zube (ed.), *Studies in Landscape Perception*. Institute for Man and Environment, University of Massachusetts, Amherst, pp. 70–142.
Piaget, J. (1929). *The Child's Conception of the World*. New York: Harcourt and Brace.
Pitt, D. G. and Zube, E. H. (1979). The Q-Sort method: use in landscape assessment research and landscape planning. In G. H. Elsner and R. C. Smardon (eds), *Our National Landscape*. GTR PSW–35 USDA Forest Service, Berkeley, CA.: Pacific Southwest Forest and Range Experiment Station, pp. 227–34.
Porteous, D. (1982). Approaches to environmental aesthetics. *Environmental Psychology*, **2**, 53–66.
Shafer, E. L. and Meitz, J. (1969). It seems possible to quantify scenic beauty in photographs.

USDA Forest Service Research Paper NE-162. Upper Darby, PA.: Northeastern Forest Experiment Station.

Stea, D. (1970). Home range and space. In L. A. Pastalan and D. H. Carson (eds), *Spatial Behaviour and Older People*. Ann Arbor: University of Michigan, pp. 138–47.

Ulrich, R. S. (1981). Natural versus urban scenes, some psychophysiological effects. *Environment and Behavior*, **13**, 523–56.

United States Department of the Interior. (1979). *The Third Nationwide Outdoor Recreation Plan* (The assessment). Washington D.C.: U.S. Government Printing Office.

Wohlwill, J. F. (1974). Human response to levels of environmental stimulation. *Human Ecology*, **2**, 127–47.

Wohlwill, J. F. (1976). Environmental aesthetics: the environment as a source of affect. In I. Altman and J. F. Wohlwill (eds), *Human Behavior and the Environment: Advances in Theory and Research*. New York: Plenum.

Wohlwill, J. F. (1978). What belongs where: research on fittingness of man-made structures in natural settings. *Landscape Research*, **3**, 3–5.

Zube, E. H. (1976). Perception of landscape and land use. In I. Altman and J. F. Wohlwill (eds), *Human Behavior and Environment, Vol. 1*. New York: Plenum Press, pp. 87–122.

Zube, E. H. and Pitt, D. G. (1981). Cross-cultural perceptions of scenic and heritage landscapes, *Landscape Planning*, **8**, 69–87.

Zube, E. H., Pitt, D. G. and Anderson, T. W. (1975). Perception and prediction of scenic resource values of the Northeast. In E. H. Zube, R. O. Brush and J. Gy. Fabos (eds), *Landscape Assessment*. Stroudsburg, PA.: Dowden, Hutchinson and Ross, pp. 151–67.

Zube, E. H., Sell, J. L. and Taylor, J. E. (1982). Landscape perception: research, application and theory. *Landscape Planning*, **9**, 1–33.

INDEX

Absolute scale, for scenic beauty perception 30–3
  and Scenic Beauty Estimation method 33–5
Access, and scenic beauty 90
Aesthetic quality. *See* Scenic beauty
Affordance 48, 66
  locomotion 48
  prospect 48
  safety 48
Age 67, 69, 141, 179–92
  and landscape preference 11–18
Aggressive scenes 11–18
Arboretum landscapes 119–36
  see also Forests
Arboretum management recommendations 133–5
Animism 180
Arizona 21, 26
Arousal theories 153, 157–8
Artificialism 180
'At-homeness' concept 39
Attention, and stress recovery 154–15
Authentic–inauthentic dichotomy 38–9
Autotelic experiences 146
Avoidance. *See* Stress recovery

Background vegetation. *See* Vegetation, distant, and scenic beauty
Bali 83–97
Bland, smooth texture scenes 11–18
Building. *See* Urban nature

Camping. *See* Wilderness experience
Campuan River Valley (Bali) 91
Canary Islands 11–18
Categorization 70–9
Children 179–92
  landscape preferences of 11–18
  see also Age
Cognitive analysis 47–63, 65–81
Coherence 47–63
  definition 51, 68
Color slides. *See* Photography
Complexity 47–63
  definition of 68
Composition, and scenic beauty prediction 99–118

Concealed foregrounds. *See* Urban nature
Contemporary buildings. *See* Urban nature
Content categorization 47–8, 58–62
Content, and scenic beauty prediction 99–118
Context, and scenic beauty 19–20
Correspondence analysis 12
Cross-culture scenic beauty evaluation 83–97
Culture
  and scenic beauty evaluation 3–97
  and stress 153

Decision-making, and recreation place 37–46
Detrended correspondence analysis 12
Distance, vegetation location and 99–118

Ecological view, of environment Psychology 9
Electrocardiography 160–2, 166–71
Electromyography (EMG) 162, 164, 166–71
Environment
  recreational 37–46
  stress recovery 149–78
Environmental categories. *See* Categorization
Environmental enhanced perceptions 142–5
Environmental psychology 1–10
  ecological view of 9
  evolutionary view of 3–4
  idealist (Romantic) 6–7
  transcendentalist view of 7–9
  utilitarian view 4–5
Environmental quality assessment 19–36
  see also Scenic Beauty Estimation method
Environmental stress. *See* Stress; Stress recovery
Evolution, and stress recovery 153–4
  psycho- 155–7
Evolutionary view, of environmental psychology 3–4
Experiences, of the environment 128–30
Experimental approach 47–8
External validity 20

Familiarity 49, 67, 95–6
Fascination, and stress recovery 154–5
Fear. *See* Stress recovery
Feeling subject 38–9
Flow experiences 146

Foliage 67
    see also Forests; Vegetation
Forced-choice procedures 29
Foreground vegetation. See Vegetation, distant, and scenic beauty; Forests; Arboretum landscapes
Forest scenes 19–36
Forests 19–36
    see also Arboretum landscapes; Vegetation, distant, and scenic beauty

Gran Canaria 11–18
Guttman–Lingoes Smallest Space Analysis III 51–2, 69, 70

Harvesting, forest 19–36
Heart period 160–2, 164, 166–71
Human–environment interaction 37–8, 120, 138

Idealism 6–7
Identifiability 47–63
    definition of 50–1
Illinois State Park 39
Illuminated scenes 11–18
Indigenous populations, vs. tourists, scene beauty and 91–3, 95–6
Information processing 84
Informational approach 65–7
Insideness–outsideness dichotomy 39
Inter-observer preferences. See Preferences
Involvement 48–9

Journal-keeping. See Wilderness experiences
Judgement criterion scales, for scenic beauty 29

Landscape assessment, and lifespan development 179–92
Landscape clusters 126
Landscape content. See Content
Landscape diversity 11–18
Landscape evaluation 85–6
    inter-observer agreement 86
    purpose and 86
    selection of landscapes 85–6
    valid construct for 85
Landscape perception 47–8
    See also Perception
Landscape preference, of children 11–18
    See also Preference
Landscape quality rating 19–36
    by children 11–18
Landscapes, and recreation-place decisions 37–46
    See also Scenic beauty and also specific landscape forms
Land use compatibility 179–92
Lifespan 179–92
Life–world perception 37–46
    definition of 38

Legibility 16
    definition of 68

Mental fatigue. See Stress recovery
Michigan Upper Peninsula 138
Middleground vegetation. See Vegetation, distant, and scenic beauty; Forests; Arboretum landscapes
Mountain waterscapes 47–63
Morton Arboretum (Chicago) 119–36
Muscle tension 162
Mystery 16, 51, 68

Novelty, and scenic beauty 90

'Oneness', and the wilderness 144–5
Old buildings. See Urban nature
Outdoor Challenge Program. See Wilderness experiences
Outward Bound. See Wilderness experiences
Overload 153

Paired-comparison 29
Pearson correlation coefficient 24
Perceived naturalism 179–92
Perception enhancement, and wilderness experiences 142–4
Perception theory 85
Perceptual processes 29
Person–place relationship 37–46
Personal constructs theory 85
Personality, and wilderness experiences 137–48
Phenomenological approach 47–8
Phenomenology, definition of 38
Photography, landscape 11–18, 101–2, 179–92
    arboretum landscapes 119–36
    in Bali 87, 88, 91
    scenic beauty perception 19–36
    urban nature 68
    waterscapes 47–63
Piaget theory 180
Picture-pairing. See Photography, landscape
Pine forest 19–36
'Place' 37–46
Preference
    arboretum landscapes 119–36
    children, landscapes and 11–18
    for environmental quality 19–36
    recreational places 37–46
    urban nature 65–81
    waterscapes 47–63
Primary landscape qualities 66
Process-tracing methodology 37–46
Prospect-refuge theory 83–4
Protection, and recreation 37–46
Psycho-evolutionary theory 155–7
Psychology. See Environmental psychology
Pulse transit time 160–1, 164, 166–71
Purpose, and landscape evaluation 86, 95

Index

Qualitative–quantitative research   119–36

Rating, of scenic beauty   19–36
   and Scenic Beauty Estimation method   33–5
Realism   180
Recreation Opportunity Spectrum   38
Recreation places   37–46
Recreation-site decisions   37–46
Refuge   66, 83–4
   definition of   68
Relative scale, for scenic beauty perception   30–3
   and Scenic Beauty Estimation method   33–5
Research, quantitative vs. qualitative   120–1, 130–2
Restoration. *See* Stress recovery
Romanticism   6–7
Rough, harsh scenes   11–18
Rural landscapes, in Bali   83–97

Scene composition. *See* Composition
Scene feature analyss   102–3
Scenic beauty   19–36
   and age   179–92
   children's preferences for   11–18
   evaluation   83–97; *See also* Scenic Beauty Estimation method
   novelty and   90
   prediction of   99–118
   public access and   90
   scaling   102
   tradition and   90
Scenic Beauty Estimation method   33–4, 102–3, 110–11, 115
Self-fulfilment, and outdoors. *See* Wilderness experiences
Sense, making   48–9
Shadowed dimensions   11–18
Skin conductance time   160–2, 164, 166–71
Slides. *See* Photography
Spaciousness   47–63, 66–7
   definition   51, 68
Spearman–Brown formula   51–3
Stress, nature of   149–51
Stress recovery   149–78
   environments and   159–60, 166–9
      physiology and   166–8
      self-rating and   168–9
   measurement of   160–2, 169–70
   statistical analysis for   162–3
   theory of   152–8, 172–5
      arousal and   153
      attention and   154–5
      culture and   153
      evolution and   153–4

      fascination and   154–5
      overload and   153
      psycho-evolutionary   155–7
Stressors   158
   effects of   163–6
Swampy areas   47–63

Tenerife   11–18
Texture   47–63
   definition of   51
'Thought-aloud' methodology   37–46
Tourists, to Bali   83–97
Tradition, and scenic beauty   90
Traffic, and stress   158–9
Transcendentalism   7–9
Trees. *See* Arboretum landscapes; Forests; Vegetation, distant, and scenic beauty
Typicality, definition of   68–9

Ubud (Bali)   87–8
Ulrich's psycho-evolutionary theory   155–7, 172–3
Urban nature   65–81
Utilitarianism   4–5

Vegetation, distant, and scenic beauty   99–118
   see also Arboretum landscape; Forests
Viewing time   49–50, 67–8, 74–7
   experimental results on   53, 55, 57–8, 61
Vision perception, and age   11–18

Water area   186, 188–90
Waterscapes   47–63
Western scenic beauty, perceptions, in Bali   83–97
Wilderness experiences   137–48
   and age   41
   environmental perception enhancement   142–4
   gender and   141
   immediate assessment of   139–41
   individual   141–2
   negative   140
   and 'oneness'   145
   positive   139–40
   responses to   139–45
Wildlife   127–8
   trips, assessment   140

Zuckerman Inventory of Personal Reactions (ZIPERS)   161, 163, 166, 168–9